Comprehensive Orton-Gillingham Plus Teacher Guide

Comprehensive OG Plus Scope & Sequence
Phonics Lessons for Early Elementary and Intervention

Kindergarten (Student Book A)

IMSE's Comprehensive Orton-Gillingham Plus Teacher Guide

Phonics Lessons for Early Elementary and Intervention

Acknowledgments

Teachers, we listened, researched, and delivered. IMSE will continue to provide you with the best instruction and up-to-date research so you can concentrate on what you do best: teach!

I would like to express special thanks and gratitude to Janice Kohler who worked tirelessly to write and provide IMSE and teachers around the world with effective teacher guides to implement IMSE's structured literacy program.

In addition Kimberley Collins, our inside editor, we couldn't have done it without you. Your dedication and keen vision of the edits and content has been undeniably excellent.

I would also like to extend my thanks to Amy Gulley for her support and contributions to the teacher guides as well as all the various Instructors of IMSE who provided feedback, experience, and knowledge to provide state-of-the-art instruction in literacy.

Michael A. Satina, thank you for your design and partnership in the production of IMSE Impact.

Jeanne M. Jeup
IMSE Co-founder

The Institute for Multi-Sensory Education
24800 Denso Dr., Suite 202
Southfield, MI 48033
Phone 800-646-9788
Fax 248-735-2927
E-mail: info@imse.com
www.imse.com

To learn more about implementing the content in this book with fidelity, register to take IMSE's Comprehensive Orton-Gillingham Plus Training by visiting the website www.imse.com. IMSE is committed to providing quality professional development training in accredited structured literacy programs. Our instructors must meet the highest of standards and complete rigorous training to acquire qualifying credentials. Additional training and certification in IMSE's methodology, not included in this Teacher Guide, are required to become an IMSE Instructor. If you are interested in training fellow teachers in your district, please contact IMSE at 800-646-9788 for more information on how to become a district trainer.

COMPREHENSIVE SCOPE AND SEQUENCE

Concept #	Concept	Red Words		Card Pack #	Decodable Reader #
		Spell & Read	Read Only		
1	Mm /m/ (marshmallow)	the		1	
2	Aa /ă/ (apple)	was		2	
3	Ll /l/ (log)	is		3	
4	Oo /ŏ/ (octopus)	a		4	
5	Hh /h/ (hammer)	on		5	
6	Gg /g/ (goat)	and		6	
7	Cc /k/ (cat)	to		7	
8	Dd /d/ (dog)	for		8	
9	Tt /t/ (turtle)	go	orange, white	9	1
10	Ii /ĭ/ (igloo)	I, like	brown, stop	10	2
11	Jj /j/ (jam)	of, will	said	11	3
12	Kk /k/ (kite)	get, no	red, see	12	4
13	Pp /p/ (pig)	want, with	yellow	13	5
14	Uu /ŭ/ (umbrella)	said, you		14	6
15	Bb /b/ (bat)	in, put	bus	15	7
16	Rr /r/ (raccoon)	see, stop	blue, eek	16	8
17	Ff /f/ (fish)	from, off	sun	17	9
18	Nn /n/ (nose)	he, has	ouch	18	10
19	Ee /ĕ/ (edge)	have, me	pink	19	11
20	Ss /s/ (sun)	his, as	green	20	12
21	Ww /w/ (wagon)	my, into		21	13
22	Yy /y/ (yo-yo)	now, new		22	14
23	Vv /v/ (violin)	give	black	23	15
24	Xx /ks/ (box)	or, by	look	24	16
25	Zz /z/ (zebra)	went		25	17
26	qu /kw/ (queen)	do, are	good	26	18
27	Long vowels: /ā/, /ē/, /ī/, /ō/, /yōō/ (me, no, hi, mu/sic, ra/ven)	they, any	fish	2, 4, 10, 14, 19	19
28	Digraph: ch /ch/ (chin)	½ color list	help	27	20

Concept #	Concept	Red Words		Card Pack #	Decodable Reader #
		Spell & Read	Read Only		
29	Digraph: sh /sh/ (shoe)	½ color list		28	21
30	Digraph: th /TH/ (voiced) (feather)	one, two (could teach the whole number list)	three, four, five, seven, eight, nine	29	22
31	Digraph: th /th/ (unvoiced) (thumb)	come	her	29	23
32	Digraph: wh /w/ or /hw/ (whistle)	who, what, where, why		30	24
Optional: Two-Syllable Closed/Open Decodable Reader			play, ball		25

First Grade

Concept #	Concept	Red Words		Card Pack #	Decodable Reader #
		Spell & Read	Read Only		
33	ss, ll, ff, zz (Sammy Loves Friendly Zebras) 1-1-1 Rule (kiss, bell, huff, jazz)	were, does	our	31	26
34	Compound Words (sunset)	some, good		None	27
35	Closed/Open Syllables with VC/CV and V/CV (ra/ven, Ve/nus, si/lo, hel/lo, mu/sic)	there, done	help (review)	2, 4, 10, 14, 19	28
36	Two-Consonant Beginning R Blends (truck)	her, here		32	29
37	Two-Consonant Beginning L Blends (sled)	under, down		33	30
38	Two-Consonant Beginning S Blends (snail)	onto, people	oven	34	31
39	Two-Consonant Beginning W Blends (swing)	saw, both	park	35	32

Concept #	Concept	Red Words		Card Pack #	Decodable Reader #
		Spell & Read	Read Only		
40	Ending T Blends (left)	should, could, would, over		36	33
41	Ending L Blends (milk)	love, live, out		37	34
42	Remaining Ending Blends (jump) and syllabication of 3 or more syllables (hob/gob/lin)	day, too, eye		38	35
43	y as a vowel /ī/ (cry)	all, again		39	36
44	-ng/-nk /ŋ/ (sang, sink)	boy, girl, sign	play	40	37
45	-ck /k/ (rock) 1-1-1 Rule	your, which, look	way	41	38
46	-tch /ch/ (match) 1-1-1 Rule	also, use		42	39
47	-dge /j/ (fudge) 1-1-1 Rule	today, yesterday	chair	43	40
48	3rd Syllable Type and 3rd Syllable Pattern: Magic E and VC/V (bike, fixate)	first, around, going		44	41
49	y as a vowel /ē/ (baby)	walk		39	42
50	Soft c /s/ and g /j/ (city, giraffe)	say, their	center	6 and 7 Plus 45	43
51	-ed /id/, /d/, /t/ (folded, soared, crashed)	how, once		46	44
52	-s /s/ or /z/, -es /iz/ (cats, dogs, dishes)	another		47	45
53	4th Syllable Type: Vowel Team: ea/ee /ē/ (treat, bee)	pull, wash		48	46
54	Vowel Team: ai/ay /ā/ (sail, clay)	every, everyone	school, tractor	49	47
55	Vowel Team: oa/oe /ō/ (boat, toe)	know, knew		50	48
56	-ing (walking)	friend		51	49
57	Contractions with am, is, are, has, not (I'm, he's, we're, isn't)	been, our, other		None	50

Second Grade

Concept #	Concept	Red Words		Card Pack #	Decodable Reader #
		Spell & Read	Read Only		
58	Three-Consonant Blends and Blends with Digraphs (scr, shr, spl, spr, squ, str, thr) (scream, shrimp, splash, spring, squid, street, thread)	away, after		52	51
59	Schwa (bacon)	few, many		None	52
60	5th Syllable Type: Bossy R: er (fern)	call, room, ball	swollen	53	53
61	Bossy R: ir (birth)	water, watch		54	54
62	Bossy R: ur (fur)	far, goes	pizza	55	55
63	Diphthongs: oi, oy (oil, boy) and 4th Syllable Pattern: V/V (poem, employee)	because, very		56	56
64	Diphthongs: ou, ow (out, brown)	door, car		57	57
65	igh (light)	great, though		58	58
66	3 Great Rules: Doubling (zapped)	don't, little		None	59
67	3 Great Rules: Drop (liked)	through		None	60
68	3 Great Rules: Change (cried)	always, hour		None	61
69	6th Syllable Type: Consonant-le (saddle)	sure, buy		59	62
70	Kind Old Words (kind, old, wild, colt, post)			None	63
71	Bossy R: ar (farm)	only		60	64
72	Bossy R: or (torn)	these, those, took		61	65
73	/aw/ spelled au and aw (August, fawn)	work, word, world		62	66

Concept #	Concept	Red Words		Card Pack #	Decodable Reader #
		Spell & Read	Read Only		
74	Contractions with have, would, will (they've, she'd, we'll)	touch	house	None	67
75	Other uses for silent e (house, love, face, huge, nose)			None	68
76	y as a vowel /ĭ/ (gym)	hall		39	69
77	ph /f/, gh /f/ (phone, cough)	enough, laugh, read		63 and 64	70
78	ch /k/ and /sh/ (echo, chef)	often		27	71
79	/o͞o/ spelled oo and ew (scoop, stew)	heard, thought		65 and 66	72
80	/o͞o/ spelled oo and u (took, put)	together		65 and 14	73
81	Other Bossy R Combinations: /air/ ar, ear, er (bear) /ar/ ear (heart) /er/ or, ar, ear, our (earth) /or/ ar, our (ward)	different		None	74
82	Silent Letters (Could also discuss Greek unusual spellings) (ghost, gnat, knife, lamb, scent, write, castle)	move		None	75
83	Homophones (to, two, too, there, their, they're)			None	76

Notes:

_____

_____

_____

_____

_____

_____

_____

_____

_____

_____

_____

_____

_____

_____

_____

_____

_____

_____

_____

_____

About IMSE

The Institute for Multi-Sensory Education (IMSE) was founded in 1996 by educators Jeanne Jeup and Bronwyn Hain and is headquartered in Southeast Michigan. Just as many educators have experienced frustration in not feeling adequately prepared to teach reading after teacher preparatory programs, Jeanne and Bronwyn felt the same. In an effort to increase literacy proficiency, they made it their life's work to prepare educators to teach all students to read using a structured approach.

Based on the Orton-Gillingham approach, IMSE's explicit, sequential, systematic, multi-sensory instruction is imperative to student success. IMSE's IDA Accredited Structured Literacy courses include a literacy trifecta. *IMSE's Phonological Awareness Course* focuses on the importance of orthographic mapping, phonological awareness, and phonemic awareness. It is designed for teachers who teach all ages. *IMSE's Comprehensive Orton-Gillingham Plus Course* focuses on phonics and orthography. It is geared toward general education grades K-2 and teachers whose students require intervention in phonics and orthography. *IMSE's Morphology Plus Course* focuses on morphology, fluency, vocabulary, comprehension, and written expression. It is geared toward general education grades 3-5 and teachers whose students require intervention in those areas.

What is Structured Literacy™ and the Science of Reading?

Structured Literacy is supported by research (known as the Science of Reading) and is explicit, systematic, and cumulative. It also integrates listening, speaking, reading, and writing. Structured Literacy emphasizes the structure of language across all components, including phonology, orthography, syntax, morphology, semantics, and discourse. The key features of any Structured Literacy program include explicit, systematic, sequential instruction; cumulative practice and ongoing review; a high level of student-teacher interaction; use of examples and non-examples; decodable text; and prompt, corrective feedback (Spear-Swerling, 2018). Educators should also optimize academic learning time (ALT) by being prepared and on time, using a routine, decreasing transition times, avoiding digressions, utilizing small groups, increasing time spent in critical content, and making sure the materials are not too difficult or too easy (Archer & Hughes, 2011). To read more on the elements of Structured Literacy, visit IDA at https://dyslexiaida.org/effective-reading-instruction/.

The term Science of Reading is often misinterpreted as a specific teaching program. Therefore, to help eliminate confusion, a team of top literacy experts came together to define the Science of Reading. This definition was released on February 3, 2021, at The Reading League's Winter Symposium. The definition reads:

> The Science of Reading is a vast, interdisciplinary body of scientifically-based research about reading and issues related to reading and writing. This research has been conducted over the last five decades across the world, and it is derived from thousands of studies conducted in multiple languages. The science of reading has culminated in a preponderance of evidence to inform how proficient reading and writing develop;

why some have difficulty; and how we can most effectively assess and teach and, therefore, improve student outcomes through prevention of and intervention for reading difficulties. The Science of Reading is derived from researchers from multiple fields, including cognitive psychology, communication sciences, developmental psychology, education, implementation science, linguistics, neuroscience, and school psychology.

To join the Science of Reading movement and to learn more, visit https://www.whatisthescienceofreading.org/.

IMSE and the Science of Reading

The basis of IMSE's foundational approach to teaching reading can be tied to Jeanne Chall's *Learning to Read: The Great Debate* (1967). During Chall's three years of observing classrooms, studying textbooks, and analyzing research studies on how children learn to read, the determination was made that instruction to beginning or emergent readers supported the skill of decoding. The study found that early decoding produced better word recognition and spelling and made it easier for the child to read with understanding. The study also found that the knowledge of symbols (letters) and sounds had more of an influence on a child's reading achievement than that child's IQ, or mental ability.

IMSE's trainings provide educators with the skills needed to integrate research-based, explicit, systematic, and multi-sensory instruction into their current curriculum. The Theoretical Models of Reading (Gough and Tunmer's Simple View of Reading; Hollis Scarborough's The Reading Rope; Linnea Ehri's The Four Phases of Word Reading; and Seidenberg and McClelland's The Four-Part Processing Model for Word Recognition) are the backbone of IMSE's training programs. In addition, IMSE follows and abides by *The Knowledge and Practice Standards for Teachers of Reading* (International Dyslexia Association [IDA], 2018). The Science of Reading research supports the approach IMSE uses in their training courses.

The multi-sensory approach to teaching reading is supported by studies conducted on reading. In one such study, Joshi et al. (2002) concluded:

> The results of this study showed that first-grade children taught with the multisensory teaching approach based on Orton-Gillingham principles performed better on tests of phonological awareness, decoding and reading comprehension than the control groups. It may, therefore, be concluded that the higher scores for children from the treatment groups may be attributed to the multisensory approach used in this study. (pp. 237-238)

To learn more about the Science of Reading and the research indicated, consider taking an IMSE course.

About This Teacher Guide

IMSE's Comprehensive Orton-Gillingham Plus Teacher Guide was written as the scope and sequence that correlates with the 30-hour *IMSE Comprehensive Orton-Gillingham Plus Course.* There is no common, standard scope and sequence utilized throughout the field of reading. Grade-level skills are approximated and will vary based on student achievement. IMSE's systematic scope and sequence was selected based on a number of factors. These factors include the frequency of the concept, the type of sound, and the similarities in the written features of the grapheme. The concepts gradually go from simple to more complex. The scope and sequence also includes two vowels within the first four lessons so that words can be read and spelled. Sentences can be read and written after the first nine concepts are taught.

Routines are provided for the concepts taught in *IMSE's Comprehensive Orton-Gillingham Plus Course,* including the Three-Part Drill, Teaching a New Concept with the Application of the New Concept, Red Words, and Syllabication. General education classroom teachers in grades K-2 can begin with the appropriate grade level. Teachers who wish to use this scope and sequence as an intervention should give IMSE's Level 1 Initial Assessment to determine where to begin instruction. This assessment is taught in *IMSE's Comprehensive Orton-Gillingham Plus* 30-hour course.

Instruction in phonological awareness is also imperative in grades K-2 (and beyond for struggling readers). Consider taking the *IMSE Phonological Awareness Course* to learn more about assessment and skills in this area. Assess students using the PAST to determine a starting point for instruction in phonological awareness. IMSE recommends *Equipped for Reading Success,* by Dr. David Kilpatrick, and/or *Interventions for All: Phonological Awareness* by Yvette Zgonc. Teachers should implement these strategies into daily lesson plans.

Instruction in fluency, vocabulary, and comprehension is also imperative for all students. Incorporate fluency into your literacy lessons daily/weekly (minimum 30 minutes per week) by using Rapid Word Charts, *IMSE Decodable Readers,* words and sentences, Acadience Reading K-6 or DIBELS 8th Edition, repeated reading, and other activities.

Incorporate vocabulary into your literacy lessons daily/weekly (minimum 50 minutes per week) by choosing 3-5 appropriate tier two words (can pull from rich literature or decodable readers). Teach the words through explicit, direct instruction using student-friendly definitions, word webs, vocabulary charts, illustrations, and other activities.

In grades K-2, the focus for comprehension should be on language comprehension. Incorporate oral language comprehension into your literacy lessons daily/weekly (approximately 100 minutes per week). Comprehension instruction should be explicit, direct instruction that includes teacher modeling, guided practice, and independent practice. Plan ahead to build on students' background knowledge, language structures, verbal reasoning, and literacy knowledge.

Building a shared-knowledge classroom and school opens the ability to communicate with one another and share a common language. Building background knowledge for all students is essential in helping disadvantaged students "catch up." According to Hirsch (2020):

> There is only one kind of school that accomplishes that double goal of quality and equality. It is the shared-knowledge school. Such a school transforms each classroom into a speech community. . . . because all genuine learning requires the possession of shared, unspoken knowledge that enables accurate comprehension. (pp. 58-59)

Core Knowledge provides a free literacy curriculum for preschool through eighth grade. This can be used as the language comprehension piece of your literacy block. This curriculum provides read-aloud books on topics that spread both horizontally (across different classrooms within the same grade) and vertically (across grade levels). This curriculum includes a teacher's guide to help lead discussions on the topics and is highly recommended by IMSE. You can find the free downloads at https://www.coreknowledge.org/curriculum/download-curriculum/.

To learn more about morphology, fluency, vocabulary, and comprehension, consider taking *IMSE's Morphology Plus Course*. Participants in the course also receive the *IMSE Writing and Grammar* video course.

EL Considerations for Teaching a New Concept

Alliteration & New Card: Briefly discuss the differences and similarities between the English sound for a new concept and the native languages represented in your classroom, if applicable. Highlight what your articulators are doing to produce proper pronunciation of the new concept. If the new concept is a sound that does not exist in an EL's native language, this explicit instruction on how to form the new sound will be needed.

Object & Brainstorm: If necessary, provide a guided brainstorm activity for your ELs to help them contribute to the brainstorming list. Teacher-directed brainstorming can be done by providing images of words with the target initial sound and a quick translation into the ELs' native language to help build meaning and vocabulary.

Letter Formation: Teachers must be aware of whether a student's native language uses alphabetic print. Even if ELs have no instruction in the native language, environmental exposure to a different writing system can affect how they recognize and reproduce written letters in the English alphabet. Provide students with an explanation of how letters in the English alphabet are formed with straight lines, circles, and curved lines. Repeat the letter formation practice regularly as needed.

Word & Sentence Dictation: Dictate known words and phrases for ELs. In addition to using the word in a sentence to create meaning, provide a translation of the word and sentence when possible to help students make connections to background knowledge with the target word or phrase and make connections to their native language.

Decodable Reader: If you are using the booklet version of the decodable reader, engage in a quick picture walk to provide a context for the story. Provide students with native language translation of unknown content words to help build an understanding of the story before reading.

Kindergarten Teacher Guide

SCOPE AND SEQUENCE

It is recommended that *general education* teachers assess students prior to instruction. The PAST assessment and IMSE's Beginning Reading Skills Assessment can help guide instruction and provide a baseline for students. Kindergarten teachers can readminister the assessments at midyear. Kindergarten teachers should give the IMSE Level 1 Initial Assessment at the end of the year.

Teachers using the guide for *intervention* should assess to determine a starting point. The PAST assessment, IMSE's Beginning Reading Skills Assessment, and IMSE's Level 1 Initial are recommended. Provide intervention for missed concepts, reassess to ensure mastery, and then continue assessing at the next level. Repeat the same pattern (teach missed concepts, assess for mastery, move forward and assess at the next level).

Teachers who have completed *IMSE's Comprehensive Orton-Gillingham Plus* 30-hour course should follow the Blue Flip Chart and refer to the *IMSE Comprehensive Orton-Gillingham Plus Teacher Training Manual* for the *why* and *how* of instruction.

Student workbooks for word and sentence dictation practice are available from IMSE's website. The workbooks have prepared visual cues aligned with the words and sentences included in this guide. Five phonetic words for dictation are included within each lesson for Days 1-3. Dictation for some concepts may include pseudowords or review words from previous lessons. A practice spelling test is recommended for Day 4, and a regular spelling test is recommended for Day 5. For these assessments, students are not provided visual cues. Words for Days 4 and 5 may be selected from Days 1-3, any additional words that may be listed with Days 4-5, or words from previous lessons.

The dictation sentences included in this guide are aligned with the student workbooks as follows: Sentences #1 and #2 are for Day 1; sentences #3 and #4 are for Day 2; and sentences #5 and #6 are for Day 3. The remaining sentences may be used for additional practice or for the assessment on Days 4 and 5.

Please note that children need repeated reading opportunities to apply learned phonics skills. In addition to dictation practice, the words and sentences in this guide can be used for reading practice. Those words, along with *IMSE Decodable Readers*, provide valuable opportunities to develop decoding skills through controlled text.

The following lessons are meant to be completed on a weekly basis but can be individualized for students as needed.

See the sample weekly lesson plans on the following pages: Sample Weekly Lesson and B Lesson.

Guidelines for Lessons (m-wh)

Below are guidelines for implementing IMSE's approach for 90 minutes or 30 minutes, depending on whether it is being used as the curriculum or as a supplement to a current curriculum. If used as supplemental, it is important to regularly incorporate the Three-Part Drill (review), decodable readers, and practice with spelling phonetic and irregular words. In addition, it is imperative to include phonological awareness each day in grades K-2 and beyond if necessary.

When implementing this approach as an intervention, the time spent in each area will depend on the student's individual goals, Individualized Education Program (IEP), or area of weakness.

Sample Weekly Lesson (m-wh) for a minimum of 90 min. of literacy instruction (Some literacy blocks are up to 120 minutes.)

Component	Monday	Tuesday	Wednesday	Thursday	Friday
Three-Part Drill	Three-Part Drill (10)	Optional: Three-Part Drill (10)	Three-Part Drill (10)	Optional: Three-Part Drill (10)	Three-Part Drill (10)
Phonological Awareness	PA Direct Instruction (10) • Activity in Zgonc's PA book • One-Minute Activity in Kilpatrick's Equipped (Incorporate additional One-Minute Activities 5-10x/day in various time periods.)	Kilpatrick's One-Minute PA Activity (1-10) (Incorporate additional One-Minute Activities 5-10x/day in various time periods.)	PA Direct Instruction (10) • Activity in Zgonc's PA book • One-Minute Activity in Kilpatrick's Equipped (Incorporate additional One-Minute Activities 5-10x/day in various time periods.)	Kilpatrick's One-Minute PA Activity (1-10) (Incorporate additional One-Minute Activities 5-10x/day in various time periods.)	Kilpatrick's One-Minute PA Activity and/or Direct Instruction (1-10) • One-Minute Activity in Kilpatrick's Equipped (Incorporate additional One-Minute Activities 5-10x/day in various time periods.)
Teaching a New Concept (phonics, spelling rules, etc.)	Multi-Sensory Experience (25) • card • object • literature	Optional Centers: • Practice capital and lowercase letters on house paper.	Optional Centers: • Practice letter formation using house paper.	Optional Centers: • Review new concept, continue with letter formation practice (e.g., capital letters, cursive).	Optional Centers: • Practice letter formation using house paper.
Word and Sentence Dictation	Application of Words and Sentences (10) • Select words and sentences for dictation from *IMSE's Comprehensive OG Plus Teacher Guide.*	Application of Words and Sentences (10) • Select words and sentences for dictation from *IMSE's Comprehensive OG Plus Teacher Guide.*	Application of Words and Sentences (10) • Select words and sentences for dictation from *IMSE's Comprehensive OG Plus Teacher Guide.*	Concept and Red Word Practice Test (20) • Select concept words and sentences as well as Red Words from *IMSE's Comprehensive OG Plus Teacher Guide.*	Concept and Red Word Test (20) • Select concept words and sentences as well as Red Words from *IMSE's Comprehensive OG Plus Teacher Guide.*
Red Words	Optional: Review from last week's words	Teach 1-5 New Red Words (25+)	Review (15)	Review (15)	Assess (see above)
Decodable Reader	IMSE Book (15) • Highlight concept words in green and read. • Underline Red Words in red and read.	IMSE Book (15) • Read pages. Students should read without errors. If there is an error, correct and have them reread the sentence.	IMSE Book (15) • Read pages. Students should read without errors. If there is an error, correct and have them reread the sentence.	IMSE Book (15) • Read pages. Students should read without errors. If there is an error, correct and have them reread the sentence.	IMSE Book (15) • Use a clean copy without pictures for students to read. Can combine this with fluency. • Comprehension questions

Component	Monday	Tuesday	Wednesday	Thursday	Friday
Fluency (CBM, decodable reader, words/sentences, Rapid Word Chart)	Optional: • Cold read decodable for repeated reading throughout the week. • Rapid Word Chart	Rapid Word Charts (10)	Optional: • Rapid Word Charts • IMSE Practice Book • Can assign either of these for homework	• Rapid Word Charts (10) • IMSE Practice Book	Progress Monitor & Practice (10) • Read clean copy of decodable reader. • Progress Monitor with CBM.
Language Comprehension (background knowledge, language structures, verbal reasoning, vocabulary, literacy knowledge)	Total Time: (20) Read rich literature to students. • Identify concept words. Vocabulary (3-5, Tier 2 words from decodable readers or rich literature) Comprehension • Discussion questions	Total Time: (20) Vocabulary (3-5, Tier 2 words from decodable readers or rich literature) Comprehension • Discussion questions	Total Time: (30) Vocabulary (3-5, Tier 2 words from decodable readers or rich literature) Comprehension • Discussion questions	Total Time: (20) Vocabulary (3-5, Tier 2 words from decodable readers or rich literature) Comprehension • Discussion questions	Total Time: (30) Vocabulary (3-5, Tier 2 words from decodable readers or rich literature) • Assess Comprehension • Reread the story for deeper understanding.
Written Expression	Optional: • Daily journal writing or other skills (sentence writing, paragraph writing, etc.)	Activity (10) • Select one of the oral language comprehension questions and have students write a written response in their journals.	Optional: • Daily journal writing or other skills (sentence writing, paragraph writing, etc.)	Activity (10) • Incorporate writing activity that correlates with the decodable reader.	Optional: • Daily journal writing or other skills (sentence writing, paragraph writing, etc.)
Homework Options	Rapid Word Chart, Decodable Reader, Study Weekly Red Words	Rapid Word Chart, Decodable Reader, Study Weekly Red Words	Rapid Word Chart, Decodable Reader, Study Weekly Red Words	Rapid Word Chart, Decodable Reader, Study Weekly Red Words	Rapid Word Chart, Decodable Reader, Study Weekly Red Words

Sample Weekly Lesson (advanced) for a minimum of 30 min. of supplemental literacy instruction

Component	Monday	Tuesday	Wednesday	Thursday	Friday
Three-Part Drill	Three-Part Drill (10)		Three-Part Drill (10)		Three-Part Drill (10)
Phonological Awareness		Kilpatrick's One-Minute PA Activity (1)	Kilpatrick's One-Minute PA Activity (1)	Kilpatrick's One-Minute PA Activity (1)	Kilpatrick's One-Minute PA Activity (1)
Teaching a New Concept (phonics, spelling rules, etc.)	Multi-Sensory Experience (15)				
Word and Sentence Dictation	Application of Words and Sentences (5)	Application of Words and Sentences (10)	Application of Words and Sentences (5)	Concept and Red Word Review and Pretest (e.g., activities, sentence dictation) (20)	Concept and Red Word Test (10)
Red Words		Teach 1-5 New Red Words (10)	Review New Red Words (5)		
Decodable Reader		IMSE Book (10)	IMSE Book (10)	IMSE Book (10)	IMSE Book (10)
Homework Options	Rapid Word Chart, Decodable Reader, Study Weekly Red Words	Rapid Word Chart, Decodable Reader, Study Weekly Red Words	Rapid Word Chart, Decodable Reader, Study Weekly Red Words	Rapid Word Chart, Decodable Reader, Study Weekly Red Words	Rapid Word Chart, Decodable Reader, Study Weekly Red Words

Bb /b/ Weekly Lesson

Sample Weekly Lesson (b) for a minimum of 90 min. of literacy instruction (Some literacy blocks are up to 120 minutes.)

Component	Monday	Tuesday	Wednesday	Thursday	Friday
Three-Part Drill	Three-Part Drill (10) • m–u	Optional: Three-Part Drill (10)	Three-Part Drill (10) • m–b	Optional: Three-Part Drill (10)	Three-Part Drill (10) • m–b
Phonological Awareness	PA Direct Instruction (10) • P. 88 "Sticky Power, Activate" in Zgonc's PA book • D1.1 in Kilpatrick's *Equipped* (Incorporate additional One-Minute Activities 5-10x/day in various time periods.)	Kilpatrick's One-Minute PA Activity (1-10) • D1.2 in Kilpatrick's *Equipped* (Incorporate additional One-Minute Activities 5-10x/day in various time periods.)	PA Direct Instruction (10) • P. 90 "Hideaway Syllables" in Zgonc's PA book • D1.3 in Kilpatrick's *Equipped* (Incorporate additional One-Minute Activities 5-10x/day in various time periods.)	Kilpatrick's One-Minute PA Activity (1-10) • D1.4 in Kilpatrick's *Equipped* (Incorporate additional One-Minute Activities 5-10x/day in various time periods.)	Kilpatrick's One-Minute PA Activity and/or Direct Instruction (1-10) • D1.5 in Kilpatrick's *Equipped* (Incorporate additional One-Minute Activities 5-10x/day in various time periods.)
Teaching a New Concept (phonics, spelling rules, etc.)	Multi-Sensory Experience (25) • Bb /b/ card #15 • buttons • *Buzzy the Bumblebee*	Optional Centers: • Practice capital B and lowercase b on house paper.	Optional Centers: • Practice letter formation using house paper.	Optional Centers: • Review new concept, continue with letter formation practice (e.g., capital letters, cursive)	Optional Centers: • Practice letter formation using house paper.
Word and Sentence Dictation	Application of Words and Sentences (10) • pp. 110-111 in *IMSE's Comprehensive OG Plus Teacher Guide* • bad, bug, dab, lob, bit 1. Jim and Kim had a big tub. 2. The bad bug bit Bob.	Application of Words and Sentences (10) • pp. 110-111 in *IMSE's Comprehensive OG Plus Teacher Guide* • bid, tub, lab, bog, cob 1. Did the cub tug on the bag? 2. Bob had a job to get the cub.	Application of Words and Sentences (10) • pp. 110-111 in *IMSE's Comprehensive OG Plus Teacher Guide* • bag, hub, bop, tab, big 1. Tom got a cab with Tad. 2. Did the kid put the bug on the mat?	Concept and Red Word Practice Test (20) • Red Words: in, put, said, you, want • Concept Words pp. 110-111 in *IMSE's Comprehensive OG Plus Teacher Guide* • dab, dub, bit, hub, jab, bop, bad, job, cub, big 1. Jim had to lug the pug to the tub. 2. Did Bob want the bag? Read: bus	Concept and Red Word Test (20) • Red Words: in, put, said, you, want • Concept Words pp. 110-111 in *IMSE's Comprehensive OG Plus Teacher Guide* • bat, bid, lob, pub, tab, bud, gab, bob, cab, but 1. Kim lit the big log. 2. Tab got in the cab. Read: bus
Red Words	Optional: Review from last week's words	Teach 1-5 New Red Words (25+) • in, put • Read-only: bus	Review: (15) • in, put • Read-only: bus	Review: (15) • in, put • Read-only: bus	Assess (see above)

Component	Monday	Tuesday	Wednesday	Thursday	Friday
Decodable Reader	IMSE Book #7 (15) • Highlight concept words in green and read. • Underline Red Words in red and read.	IMSE Book #7 (15) • Read pages. Students should read without errors. If there is an error, correct and have them reread the sentence.	IMSE Book #7 (15) • Read pages. Students should read without errors. If there is an error, correct and have them reread the sentence.	IMSE Book #7 (15) • Read pages. Students should read without errors. If there is an error, correct and have them reread the sentence.	IMSE Book #7 (15) • Use a clean copy without pictures for students to read. Can combine this with fluency. • Comprehension questions
Fluency (CBM, decodable reader, words/sentences, Rapid Word Chart)	Optional: • Cold read decodable for repeated reading throughout the week. • Rapid Word Chart	Rapid Word Charts: (10) • lab, hub, job, tab, bid • said, put, in, bus, you	Optional: • Rapid Word Charts • IMSE Practice Book • Can assign either of these for homework	• Rapid Word Charts (10) • IMSE Practice Book	Progress Monitor & Practice (10) • Read clean copy of decodable reader. • Progress Monitor with CBM.
Language Comprehension (background knowledge, language structures, verbal reasoning, vocabulary, literacy knowledge)	Total Time: (20) Read rich literature to students. • *Buzzy the Bumblebee* by Denise Brennan-Nelson • Identify concept words. Vocabulary (3-5, Tier 2 words from decodable readers or rich literature) • startled, envious, tentatively, relief, believe Comprehension • Background knowledge of bumblebees • Clarify: Why did Buzzy think he couldn't fly? • Predict: How will Buzzy get home? Do you think he will fly again?	Total Time: (20) Vocabulary (3-5, Tier 2 words from decodable readers or rich literature) • startled, envious, tentatively, relief, believe • synonyms: scared, jealous, carefully, thankful, I "can" Comprehension • How might you feel if you were told you couldn't do something? • Have you ever been told that? What happened? • Discuss narrative elements.	Total Time: (30) Vocabulary (3-5, Tier 2 words from decodable readers or rich literature) • startled, envious, tentatively, relief, believe • Word Web Comprehension Clarification: • "heavy-hearted" • "filled with relief" • "danced with the flowers and swayed with the breeze" • "peering through the thick green grass" • "He heard a voice...looked up to see where it came from."	Total Time: (20) Vocabulary (3-5, Tier 2 words from decodable readers or rich literature) • startled, envious, tentatively, relief, believe • Act out the words. Comprehension • What is a limitation? • How can "fear" block our way? • Why should we believe in ourselves?	Total Time: (30) Vocabulary (3-5, Tier 2 words from decodable readers or rich literature) Assess • startled, envious, tentatively, relief, believe • Use the words in sentences (orally). Comprehension • Reread the story for deeper understanding.
Written Expression	Optional: • Daily journal writing or other skills (sentence writing, paragraph writing, etc.)	Activity (10) • Select one of the oral language comprehension questions and have students write a written response in their journals.	Optional: • Daily journal writing or other skills (sentence writing, paragraph writing, etc.)	Activity (10) • Write about a time when you rode a bus. (correlates with the decodable reader)	Optional: • Daily journal writing or other skills (sentence writing, paragraph writing, etc.)

Table of Contents
Kindergarten

Concept #	Concept	Red Words		Card Pack #	Decodable Reader #	Page #
		Spell & Read	Read Only			
1	Mm /m/ (marshmallow)	the		1		9
2	Aa /ă/ (apple)	was		2		15
3	Ll /l/ (log)	is		3		21
4	Oo /ŏ/ (octopus)	a		4		27
5	Hh /h/ (hammer)	on		5		35
6	Gg /g/ (goat)	and		6		41
7	Cc /k/ (cat)	to		7		47
8	Dd /d/ (dog)	for		8		53
9	Tt /t/ (turtle)	go	orange, white	9	1	59
	Review for Concepts m–t					67
10	Ii /ĭ/ (igloo)	I, like	brown, stop	10	2	69
11	Jj /j/ (jam)	of, will	said	11	3	77
12	Kk /k/ (kite)	get, no	red, see	12	4	85
13	Pp /p/ (pig)	want, with	yellow	13	5	93
14	Uu /ŭ/ (umbrella)	said, you		14	6	101
15	Bb /b/ (bat)	in, put	bus	15	7	109
16	Rr /r/ (raccoon)	see, stop	blue, eek	16	8	117
17	Ff /f/ (fish)	from, off	sun	17	9	125
18	Nn /n/ (nose)	he, has	ouch	18	10	133
	Review for Concepts m–n					141
19	Ee /ĕ/ (edge)	have, me	pink	19	11	143
20	Ss /s/ (sun)	his, as	green	20	12	151
21	Ww /w/ (wagon)	my, into		21	13	159
22	Yy /y/ (yo-yo)	now, new		22	14	167
23	Vv /v/ (violin)	give	black	23	15	175
24	Xx /ks/ (box)	or, by	look	24	16	183
25	Zz /z/ (zebra)	went		25	17	191
26	qu /kw/ (queen)	do, are	good	26	18	199

Concept #	Concept	Red Words		Card Pack #	Decodable Reader #	Page #
		Spell & Read	**Read Only**			
27	Long vowels: /ā/, /ē/, /ī/, /ō/, /yo͞o/ (me, no, hi, mu/sic, ra/ven)	they, any	fish	2, 4, 10, 14, 19	19	207
Review for Concepts m–long vowels						215
28	Digraph: ch /ch/ (chin)	½ color list	help	27	20	217
29	Digraph: sh /sh/ (shoe)	½ color list		28	21	225
30	Digraph: th /TH/ (voiced) (feather)	one, two (could teach the whole number list)	three, four, five, seven, eight, nine	29	22	233
31	Digraph: th /th/ (unvoiced) (thumb)	come	her	29	23	241
32*	Digraph: wh /w/ or /hw/ (whistle)	who, what, where, why		30	24	249
Review for Concepts m–wh						257
Optional: Two-Syllable Closed/Open Decodable Reader		play, ball			25	

*The Level 1 Initial assessment, which includes concepts m–wh, can be administered after this lesson.

Mm as in marshmallow

Card Pack #1	
Object Ideas:	**Literature Ideas:**
moon, money, marble, marshmallow, muffin, mouse, mask, milkshake, music, macaroni, mitten, magazine	▪ *If You Give A Mouse a Cookie* by Laura Numeroff ▪ *If You Give a Moose a Muffin* by Laura Numeroff ▪ *Mouse Count* by Ellen Walsh ▪ *Madeline* by Ludwig Bemelmans ▪ *The Math Curse* by Jon Scieszka and Lane Smith ▪ *Muggie Maggie* by Beverly Cleary ▪ *Hugh Manatee for President* by Carla Siravo ▪ *Mixed Me* by Taye Diggs ▪ *Martin's Big Words: The Life of Dr. Martin Luther King, Jr.* by Doreen Rappaport ▪ *"More More More," Said the Baby* by Vera Williams ▪ *Matilda* by Roald Dahl ▪ *M Is for Melanin: A Celebration of the Black Child* by Tiffany Rose ▪ *In My Mosque* by M.O. Yuksel

Notes

- Use the Comprehensive Flip Chart for the steps on how to teach each part of IMSE's Lesson Plan.
    - Use the (m-wh) Lesson Plan for these lessons.
- Mm /m/ is a voiced, continuant consonant formed by pressing the lips together. This is a nasal sound where the air is pushed out of the nose.

Phonological Awareness:

Materials Needed:
tokens, sound boxes, one-minute activities, or Zgonc PA book

Use the PAST assessment to determine a starting point for instruction. Incorporate daily phonological awareness activities by using Zgonc's tiered activities and/or Kilpatrick's One-Minute Activities in *Equipped for Reading Success*.

Phonemic awareness warm-up: Use tokens (or letter tiles once concepts have been taught) and sound boxes to do a quick phonemic awareness activity that ties in with the new concept, if appropriate.

Three-Part Drill

Materials Needed:
review cards, sand, blending board, vowel tents or sticks

(After teaching Oo /ŏ/)

Teaching a New Concept

Materials Needed:
concept card, screen, green crayon, object, sand, decodable readers (beginning with the "t" lesson), literature, P/G chart

Introduce on Monday, and practice daily.

1. (T) Reads alliteration sentences. (S) Identify the target sound.
    a. Mom made muffins.
    b. Mona Mouse met many marvelous mice.
2. (T) Shows the new concept card.
    a. (T) Tells students the letter name and sound. Have (S) repeat, 3 times (m says /m/).
    b. (T) Tells students that "m" is a consonant.
    c. (T) Tells students it is a voiced sound.
    d. (T) Asks students where they find "m" in the alphabet.
    e. (T) Uses mirrors to discuss the mouth, tongue, and teeth placement.
3. (T) Shows an object.
    a. (T) Allows students to manipulate the object and discuss prior knowledge. Reminds (S) that the object has the target sound spelled with the target letter.
4. (S) Brainstorm.
    a. Brainstorm words that have the target sound. (Accept all answers, but place incorrect answers in a "thought bubble" to discuss.) The brainstorming can be a teacher-directed activity if students need extra support.
5. (T) Teaches Letter Formation. Use house paper to teach lowercase letters.
    a. (T) models with the solid letter. The letter "m" starts at the ceiling and moves to the floor of the house. Then come back up to the ceiling, curve around, and go down. Go back up to the ceiling, curve around one more time, and go back down to the floor.
    b. Using the screen and green crayon, (T&S) trace the solid while saying, "m says /m/" (3x).
    c. (T&S) use their finger to trace the solid while saying, "m says /m/" (3x).
    d. (S) trace the dotted letter and complete the remainder of the row independently.
    e. (S) move to smaller house and repeat process if needed.

f. Teach capital letters throughout the week using the same process. Capital letters go outside the house.

6. (T) Dictates target sound. (S) Practice in the sand or other medium.

   a. Practice writing the letter using a different medium, such as sand, shaving cream, finger paint, gel board, iPad app, air writing, etc.

   b. Do this while stating: m says /m/, 3 times.

7. (T) Connects with literature.

   a. Have students signal when they hear the /m/ sound for the first page or two.

   b. Read again for language comprehension.

   c. Continue to work on language comprehension with rich literature throughout the week.

8. Use decodable readers beginning with the "t" lesson.

9. (T&S) Mark the Phoneme/Grapheme (P/G) chart by highlighting the target sound.

Word Dictation

Materials Needed:
fingertapping hand, dictation paper, pencil

(After teaching Oo /ŏ/)

Sentence Dictation

(After teaching Tt /t/)

Weekly Red Words

Materials Needed:
screen, red crayon, red word paper

Introduce on Tuesday, and practice daily. Use the Flip Chart for steps on how to teach a Red Word.

New:	Review:	New Read-Only:	Review Read-Only:
the			

Steps for Teaching a New Red Word:

1. (T) States the word. (*the*)

2. (T&S) Use tokens to determine how many sounds are in the word. (/TH/ /ŭ/; 2)

3. (T&S) Discuss how we would expect to spell each sound as the teacher writes the grapheme(s) correctly. Identify what is unexpected or irregular about the spelling of the word. It could also be expected, but the concept hasn't been taught yet.

4. (T&S) Discuss the etymology of the word, if appropriate (lexical words). Visit www. etymonline.com for more information on the word.

5. (T) Defines the word, and writes a sentence using the word.

6. (T) Writes the word on Red Word paper with the screen underneath, using red crayon.

7. (S) Write the word on Red Word paper with the screen underneath, using red crayon. (S) Show the word to the teacher.
   (**NOTE:** The teacher should have students chunk the word if it has more than four letters.)

8. (T&S) Stand up, holding the Red Word in the nondominant hand. Armtap word while naming each letter. Then "underline" the word by sweeping left to right while stating the word, 3x. (**NOTE:** Left-handed students will place their left hand on their right wrist. They tap to their right shoulder. Underline from wrist to shoulder. Right-handed students place their right hand on their left shoulder. They tap to their left wrist. Underline shoulder to wrist.)

9. (T&S) Trace crayon bumps with the pointer finger while naming the letters, 3x.

10. (T&S) Place the screen over the paper and trace the word with the pointer finger while naming the letters, 3x.

11. (S) Turn paper over. With red crayon, write the word without the screen one time, and hold up the word for the teacher to check. (S) Write the word two more times.

12. (S) Write an original sentence in pencil and underline the Red Word with a red crayon. (**NOTE:** The sentence can also be dictated by the teacher while the student writes or dictated by the student while the teacher writes it.)

Review Ideas for Red Words:

- Sculpt the word using red Play-Doh or clay. Have students spell the word as they smash each letter.
- Print flashcards from IOG, and practice reading.
- Armtap the word to review.
- Cross-clap the word to review.
- Do Spelling Aerobics.

Fluency, Vocabulary, and Comprehension

- Incorporate fluency into your literacy lessons daily/weekly (minimum 30 min/week) by using Rapid Word Charts, IMSE Decodable Readers, words and sentences, Acadience Reading K-6 or DIBELS 8th Edition, repeated reading, and other activities.
- Incorporate vocabulary into your literacy lessons daily/weekly (minimum 50 min/week) by choosing 3-5 appropriate tier two words (can pull from rich literature or decodable readers). Teach the words through explicit, direct instruction using student-friendly definitions, word webs, vocabulary charts, illustrations, and other activities.
- Incorporate oral language comprehension into your literacy lessons daily/weekly (approximately 100 min/week). Comprehension instruction should be explicit, direct instruction that includes teacher modeling, guided practice, and independent practice. Plan ahead to build on students' background knowledge, language structures, verbal reasoning, and literacy knowledge.

Extension Activity Ideas

- Start a multi-sensory ABC book. Have students glue macaroni (or another object) in the shape of the target letter.
- Have students compare and contrast milk and milkshakes using a Venn Diagram.
- Make a paper mouse. Have students glue pictures of words that begin with the /m/ sound on the mouse.
- Divide students into teams of 3 and have them lie on the ground to form the target letter. Take pictures to hang around the classroom.
- Create the target letter out of green Play-Doh or clay.
- Have students use a bingo dauber to find the target letter on a page filled with various letters.
- Have students go on a "sound hunt" around the room or outside to find objects that begin with the target sound.
- Visit IMSE's Orton-Gillingham's Pinterest page for more ideas.

Weekly Lesson Reminders

- Any of the above extension activities
- Daily practice writing the target letter (capital and lowercase) using a screen, green crayon, and house paper
- Practice writing the target letter using another medium (sand, paint, shaving cream, pudding, iPad app, etc.).
- Practice writing the target letter with age-appropriate paper and pencil.
- Daily practice writing the weekly Red Word(s)
- Kilpatrick's "One-Minute Activities" for daily phonological awareness practice
- Zgonc's phonological awareness activities
- Listen to rich literature to work on oral language comprehension.
- Target letter practice sheets from IMSE's practice books (after o) and handwriting books

Notes:

_____

_____

_____

_____

_____

_____

_____

_____

_____

_____

_____

_____

_____

_____

_____

_____

_____

_____

_____

_____

Aa as in apple

Card Pack #2	
Object Ideas:	**Literature Ideas:**
Initial position: apple, alligator, ant, apple pie, applesauce **Medial position:** hat, cap, can, pan, mad, jam	▪ *Zack's Alligator* by Shirley Mozelle ▪ *Ten Apples up on Top* by Dr. Seuss ▪ *Johnny Appleseed* ▪ *The Cat in the Hat* by Dr. Seuss ▪ *Caps for Sale* by Esphyr Slobodkina ▪ *Alexander and the Terrible, Horrible, No Good, Very Bad Day* by Judith Viorst ▪ *I Am Enough* by Grace Byers ▪ *The Alphabet War: A Story about Dyslexia* by Diane Burton Robb ▪ *Alma and How She Got Her Name* by Juana Martinez-Neal

 ## Notes

- Use the Comprehensive Flip Chart for the steps on how to teach each part of IMSE's Lesson Plan.
- Aa /ă/ is a voiced, continuant vowel. To produce vowel sounds, articulators hold a shape but do not obstruct air. Refer to the Vowel Valley on sound production.
- Create a vowel tent or stick for the Vowel Intensive Drill.
- Teach the visual cue: hand under the chin.

 ## Phonological Awareness:

Materials Needed:
tokens, sound boxes, one-minute activities, or Zgonc PA book

Use the PAST assessment to determine a starting point for instruction. Incorporate daily phonological awareness activities by using Zgonc's tiered activities and/or Kilpatrick's One-Minute Activities in *Equipped for Reading Success.*

Phonemic awareness warm-up: Use tokens (or letter tiles once concepts have been taught) and sound boxes to do a quick phonemic awareness activity that ties in with the new concept, if appropriate.

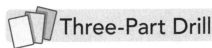

Three-Part Drill

Materials Needed:
review cards, sand, blending board, vowel tents or sticks

(After teaching Oo /ŏ/)

Teaching a New Concept

Materials Needed:
concept card, screen, green crayon, object, sand, decodable readers (beginning with the "t" lesson), literature, P/G chart

Introduce on Monday, and practice daily.

1. (T) Reads alliteration sentence. (S) Identify the target sound.

   a. Alex admired Abby's apples.

   (T) Reads the following sentence in which /ă/ is in the medial position. (S) Identify the target sound.

   b. Pam had cats.

2. (T) Shows the new concept card.

   a. (T) Tells students the letter name and sound. Have (S) repeat, 3 times (a says /ă/).

   b. (T) Tells students that "a" is a vowel.

   c. (T) Tells students it is a voiced sound.

   d. (T) Asks students where they find "a" in the alphabet.

   e. (T) Uses mirrors to discuss the mouth, tongue, and teeth placement.

3. (T) Shows an object.

   a. (T) Allows students to manipulate the object and discuss prior knowledge. Reminds (S) that the object has the target sound spelled with the target letter.

4. (S) Brainstorm.

   a. Brainstorm words that have the target sound. (Accept all answers, but place incorrect answers in a "thought bubble" to discuss.) The brainstorming can be a teacher-directed activity if students need extra support. (**NOTE:** For short vowels, students can brainstorm word families or rhyming words containing the vowel sound.)

5. (T) Teaches Letter Formation. Use house paper to teach lowercase letters.

   a. (T) models with the solid letter. The letter "a" starts just below the ceiling. Then bump the ceiling, and curve around to the floor. Then come back up to the ceiling and straight down to the floor.

   b. Using the screen and green crayon, (T&S) trace the solid while saying, "a says /ă/" (3x).

   c. (T&S) use their finger to trace the solid while saying, "a says /ă/" (3x).

   d. (S) trace the dotted letter and complete the remainder of the row independently.

   e. (S) move to smaller house and repeat process if needed.

   f. Teach capital letters throughout the week using the same process. Capital letters go outside the house.

6. (T) Dictates target sound. (S) Practice in the sand or other medium.
   a. Practice writing the letter using a different medium, such as sand, shaving cream, finger paint, gel board, iPad app, air writing, etc.
   b. Do this while stating: a says /ă/, 3 times.
7. (T) Connects with literature.
   a. Have students signal when they hear the /ă/ sound for the first page or two.
   b. Read again for language comprehension.
   c. Continue to work on language comprehension with rich literature throughout the week.
8. Use decodable readers beginning with the "t" lesson.
9. (T&S) Mark the Phoneme/Grapheme (P/G) chart by highlighting the target sound.

Word Dictation

Materials Needed:
fingertapping hand, dictation paper, pencil

(After teaching Oo /ŏ/)

Sentence Dictation

(After teaching Tt /t/)

Weekly Red Words

Materials Needed:
screen, red crayon, red word paper

Introduce on Tuesday, and practice daily. Use the Flip Chart for steps.

New:	Review:	New Read-Only:	Review Read-Only:
was	the		

Steps for Teaching a New Red Word:

1. (T) States the word. (*was*)
2. (T&S) Use tokens to determine how many sounds are in the word. (/w/ /ŭ/ /z/; 3)
3. (T&S) Discuss how we would expect to spell each sound as the teacher writes the grapheme(s) correctly. Identify what is unexpected or irregular about the spelling of the word. It could also be expected, but the concept hasn't been taught yet.
4. (T&S) Discuss the etymology of the word, if appropriate (lexical words). Visit www.etymonline.com for more information on the word.
5. (T) Defines the word, and writes a sentence using the word.
6. (T) Writes the word on Red Word paper with the screen underneath, using red crayon.

7. (S) Write the word on Red Word paper with the screen underneath, using red crayon. (S) Show the word to the teacher.
(**NOTE:** The teacher should have students chunk the word if it has more than four letters.)

8. (T&S) Stand up, holding the Red Word in the nondominant hand. Armtap word while naming each letter. Then "underline" the word by sweeping left to right while stating the word, 3x. (**NOTE:** Left-handed students will place their left hand on their right wrist. They tap to their right shoulder. Underline from wrist to shoulder. Right-handed students place their right hand on their left shoulder. They tap to their left wrist. Underline shoulder to wrist.)

9. (T&S) Trace crayon bumps with the pointer finger while naming the letters, 3x.

10. (T&S) Place the screen over the paper and trace the word with the pointer finger while naming the letters, 3x.

11. (S) Turn paper over. With red crayon, write the word without the screen one time, and hold up the word for the teacher to check. (S) Write the word two more times.

12. (S) Write an original sentence in pencil and underline the Red Word with a red crayon. (**NOTE:** The sentence can also be dictated by the teacher while the student writes or dictated by the student while the teacher writes it.)

Review Ideas for Red Words:

- Sculpt the word using red Play-Doh or clay. Have students spell the word as they smash each letter.
- Print flashcards from IOG, and practice reading.
- Armtap the word to review.
- Cross-clap the word to review.
- Do Spelling Aerobics.

Fluency, Vocabulary, and Comprehension

- Incorporate fluency into your literacy lessons daily/weekly (minimum 30 min/week) by using Rapid Word Charts, IMSE Decodable Readers, words and sentences, Acadience Reading K-6 or DIBELS 8th Edition, repeated reading, and other activities.

- Incorporate vocabulary into your literacy lessons daily/weekly (minimum 50 min/week) by choosing 3-5 appropriate tier two words (can pull from rich literature or decodable readers). Teach the words through explicit, direct instruction using student-friendly definitions, word webs, vocabulary charts, illustrations, and other activities.

- Incorporate oral language comprehension into your literacy lessons daily/weekly (approximately 100 min/week). Comprehension instruction should be explicit, direct instruction that includes teacher modeling, guided practice, and independent practice. Plan ahead to build on students' background knowledge, language structures, verbal reasoning, and literacy knowledge.

Extension Activity Ideas

- Continue the multi-sensory ABC book. Have students glue apples (or another object) in the shape of the target letter.
- Have students compare and contrast apples and applesauce using a Venn Diagram.
- Make a paper apple pie. Have students glue pictures of words that have the target sound on the apple pie.
- Follow a recipe to make an apple pie.
- Divide students into teams of 3 and have them lie on the ground to form the target letter. Take pictures to hang around the classroom.
- Create the target letter out of green Play-Doh or clay.
- Using the grid, screen, and green crayon, have students practice writing and/or tracing the letters they know as the teacher dictates each sound. Example: (T) Spell /ă/. Repeat. (S) /ă/, a says /ă/ (while writing [or tracing] the correct letter on the grid).
- Have students use a bingo dauber to find the target letter on a page with various letters.
- Have students go on a "sound hunt" around the room or outside to find objects that begin with the target sound.
- Visit IMSE's Orton-Gillingham's Pinterest page for more ideas.

Weekly Lesson Reminders

- Any of the above extension activities
- Daily practice writing the target letter (capital and lowercase) using a screen, green crayon, and house paper
- Practice writing the target letter using another medium (sand, paint, shaving cream, pudding, iPad app, etc.).
- Practice writing the target letter using age-appropriate paper and pencil.
- Daily practice writing the weekly Red Word(s)
- Kilpatrick's "One-Minute Activities" for daily phonological awareness practice
- Zgonc's phonological awareness activities
- Listen to rich literature to work on oral language comprehension.
- Target letter practice sheets from IMSE's practice books (after o) and handwriting books
- Practice test on Thursday and test on Friday

Notes:

Ll as in log

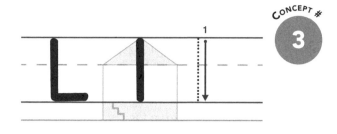

Card Pack #3	
Object Ideas:	**Literature Ideas:**
log, laugh, licorice, lollipop, LEGO, ladybug, leaf, lion, lemon/lime, ladder, line, leap	• *Is Your Mama a Llama?* by Deborah Guarino • *The Little Prince* by Antoine de Saint-Exupéry • *Lilly's Purple Plastic Purse* by Kevin Henkes • *The Grouchy Ladybug* by Eric Carle • *The Teacher From the Black Lagoon* by Mike Thaler • *Llama Llama Misses Mama* by Anna Dewdney • *Honey, I Love* by Eloise Greenfield • *Lola at the Library* by Anna McQuinn • *A Letter to Amy* by Ezra Jack Keats • *Louie* by Ezra Jack Keats

Notes

- Use the Comprehensive Flip Chart for the steps on how to teach each part of IMSE's Lesson Plan.
- Ll /l/ is a voiced, continuant consonant created with the tip of the tongue on the ridge behind the front teeth and with the lips parted. This is a liquid sound that can be challenging for students to produce.
- Keep "l" in the initial position at first. If /l/ is at the end of a one-syllable word with one short vowel, it is spelled "-ll." After open and closed syllables have been taught, "l" can be moved to the final position to support syllables such as "hel" in "helmet."

Phonological Awareness:

Materials Needed:
tokens, sound boxes, one-minute activities, or Zgonc PA book

Use the PAST assessment to determine a starting point for instruction. Incorporate daily phonological awareness activities by using Zgonc's tiered activities and/or Kilpatrick's One-Minute Activities in *Equipped for Reading Success*.

Phonemic awareness warm-up: Use tokens (or letter tiles once concepts have been taught) and sound boxes to do a quick phonemic awareness activity that ties in with the new concept, if appropriate.

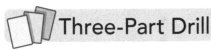

Three-Part Drill

Materials Needed:
review cards, sand, blending board, vowel tents or sticks

(After teaching Oo /ŏ/)

Teaching a New Concept

Materials Needed:
concept card, screen, green crayon, object, sand, decodable readers (beginning with the "t" lesson), literature, P/G chart

Introduce on Monday, and practice daily.

1. (T) Reads alliteration sentences. (S) Identify the target sound.
   a. Luckily, Llama laughed loudly.
   b. Lulu likes to lick lemon-lime lollipops.
2. (T) Shows the new concept card.
   a. (T) Tells students the letter name and sound. Have (S) repeat, 3 times (l says /l/).
   b. (T) Tells students that "l" is a consonant.
   c. (T) Tells students it is a voiced sound.
   d. (T) Asks students where they find "l" in the alphabet.
   e. (T) Uses mirrors to discuss the mouth, tongue, and teeth placement.
3. (T) Shows an object.
   a. (T) Allows students to manipulate the object and discuss prior knowledge. Reminds (S) that the object has the target sound spelled with the target letter.
4. (S) Brainstorm.
   a. Brainstorm words that have the target sound. (Accept all answers, but place incorrect answers in a "thought bubble" to discuss.) The brainstorming can be a teacher-directed activity if students need extra support.
5. (T) Teaches Letter Formation. Use house paper to teach lowercase letters.
   a. (T) models with the solid letter. The letter "l" starts at the ceiling and goes to the floor.
   b. Using the screen and green crayon, (T&S) trace the solid while saying, "l says /l/" (3x).
   c. (T&S) use their finger to trace the solid while saying, "l says /l/" (3x).
   d. (S) trace the dotted letter and complete the remainder of the row independently.
   e. (S) move to smaller house and repeat process if needed.
   f. Teach capital letters throughout the week using the same process. Capital letters go outside the house.
6. (T) Dictates target sound. (S) Practice in the sand or other medium.
   a. Practice writing the letter using a different medium, such as sand, shaving cream, finger paint, gel board, iPad app, air writing, etc.
   b. Do this while stating: l says /l/, 3 times.

7. (T) Connects with literature.
    a. Have students signal when they hear the /l/ sound for the first page or two.
    b. Read again for language comprehension.
    c. Continue to work on language comprehension with rich literature throughout the week.
8. Use decodable readers beginning with the "t" lesson.
9. (T&S) Mark the Phoneme/Grapheme (P/G) chart by highlighting the target sound.

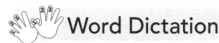 Word Dictation

Materials Needed:
fingertapping hand, dictation paper, pencil

(After teaching Oo /ŏ/)

Sentence Dictation

(After teaching Tt /t/)

Weekly Red Words

Materials Needed:
screen, red crayon, red word paper

Introduce on Tuesday, and practice daily. Use the Flip Chart for steps on how to teach a Red Word.

New:	Review:	New Read-Only:	Review Read-Only:
is	the, was		

Steps for Teaching a New Red Word:

1. (T) States the word. (*is*)
2. (T&S) Use tokens to determine how many sounds are in the word. (/ĭ/ /z/; 2)
3. (T&S) Discuss how we would expect to spell each sound as the teacher writes the grapheme(s) correctly. Identify what is unexpected or irregular about the spelling of the word. It could also be expected, but the concept hasn't been taught yet.
4. (T&S) Discuss the etymology of the word, if appropriate (lexical words). Visit www.etymonline.com for more information on the word.
5. (T) Defines the word, and writes a sentence using the word.
6. (T) Writes the word on Red Word paper with the screen underneath, using red crayon.
7. (S) Write the word on Red Word paper with the screen underneath, using red crayon. (S) Show the word to the teacher.
    (**NOTE:** The teacher should have students chunk the word if it has more than four letters.)

8. (T&S) Stand up, holding the Red Word in the nondominant hand. Armtap word while naming each letter. Then "underline" the word by sweeping left to right while stating the word, 3x. (**NOTE:** Left-handed students will place their left hand on their right wrist. They tap to their right shoulder. Underline from wrist to shoulder. Right-handed students place their right hand on their left shoulder. They tap to their left wrist. Underline shoulder to wrist.)

9. (T&S) Trace crayon bumps with the pointer finger while naming the letters, 3x.

10. (T&S) Place the screen over the paper and trace the word with the pointer finger while naming the letters, 3x.

11. (S) Turn paper over. With red crayon, write the word without the screen one time, and hold up the word for the teacher to check. (S) Write the word two more times.

12. (S) Write an original sentence in pencil and underline the Red Word with a red crayon. (**NOTE:** The sentence can also be dictated by the teacher while the student writes or dictated by the student while the teacher writes it.)

Review Ideas for Red Words:

- Sculpt the word using red Play-Doh or clay. Have students spell the word as they smash each letter.
- Print flashcards from IOG, and practice reading.
- Armtap the word to review.
- Cross-clap the word to review.
- Do Spelling Aerobics.

Fluency, Vocabulary, and Comprehension

- Incorporate fluency into your literacy lessons daily/weekly (minimum 30 min/week) by using Rapid Word Charts, IMSE Decodable Readers, words and sentences, Acadience Reading K-6 or DIBELS 8th Edition, repeated reading, and other activities.
- Incorporate vocabulary into your literacy lessons daily/weekly (minimum 50 min/week) by choosing 3-5 appropriate tier two words (can pull from rich literature or decodable readers). Teach the words through explicit, direct instruction using student-friendly definitions, word webs, vocabulary charts, illustrations, and other activities.
- Incorporate oral language comprehension into your literacy lessons daily/weekly (approximately 100 min/week). Comprehension instruction should be explicit, direct instruction that includes teacher modeling, guided practice, and independent practice. Plan ahead to build on students' background knowledge, language structures, verbal reasoning, and literacy knowledge.

Extension Activity Ideas

- Continue to add to the multi-sensory ABC book. Have students glue leaves (or another object) in the shape of the target letter.
- Have students compare and contrast lemons and limes using a Venn Diagram.
- Make a paper lollipop. Have students glue pictures of words that begin with the /l/ sound on the lollipop.
- Divide students into teams of 3 and have them lie on the ground to form the target letter. Take pictures to hang around the classroom.
- Create the target letter out of green Play-Doh or clay.
- Using the grid, screen, and green crayon, have students practice writing and/or tracing the letters they know as the teacher dictates each sound. Example: (T) Spell /l/. Repeat. (S) /l/, l says /l/ (while writing [or tracing] the correct letter on the grid).
- Have students use a bingo dauber to find the target letter on a page with various letters.
- Have students go on a "sound hunt" around the room or outside to find objects that begin with the target sound.
- Visit IMSE's Orton-Gillingham's Pinterest page for more ideas.

Weekly Lesson Reminders

- Any of the above extension activities
- Daily practice writing the target letter (capital and lowercase) using a screen, green crayon, and house paper
- Practice writing the target letter using another medium (sand, paint, shaving cream, pudding, iPad app, etc.).
- Practice writing the target letter using age-appropriate paper and pencil.
- Daily practice with writing the weekly Red Word(s)
- Kilpatrick's "One-Minute Activities" for daily phonological awareness practice
- Zgonc's phonological awareness activities
- Listen to rich literature to work on oral language comprehension.
- Target letter practice sheets from IMSE's practice books (after o) and handwriting books
- Practice test on Thursday and test on Friday

Notes:

_____

_____

_____

_____

_____

_____

_____

_____

_____

_____

_____

_____

_____

_____

_____

_____

_____

_____

_____

_____

Oo as in octopus

Card Pack #4	
Object Ideas:	**Literature Ideas:**
Initial position: olive, octopus, octagon, ox, otter **Medial position:** hop, pop, cop, stop, pot, shop, fox	▪ *Olive, the Other Reindeer* by J. Otto Seibold ▪ *Hop on Pop* by Dr. Seuss ▪ *Paul Bunyan and Babe the Blue Ox: The Great Pancake Adventure* by Matt Luckhurst ▪ *Last Stop on Market Street* by Matt de la Peña

 Notes

- Use the Comprehensive Flip Chart for the steps on how to teach each part of IMSE's Lesson Plan.
- Oo /ŏ/ is a voiced, continuant vowel. To produce vowel sounds, articulators hold a shape but do not obstruct air. Refer to the Vowel Valley on sound production.
- Create a vowel tent or stick for the Vowel Intensive Drill.
- Teach the visual cue: circle mouth with your finger.
- Teach Oo /ŏ/ as the New Concept on Monday.
- Do the Three-Part Drill and Vowel Intensive on Tuesday.
- Do Word Dictation on Tuesday (make fingertapping hands or blending strips).
- Right-handed students fingertap with the left hand:

- Left-handed students fingertap with the right hand:

After Teaching "O"

Begin Teaching:

Three-Part Drill (Review)

1. **Visual:** Show cards in random order
2. **Auditory/Kinesthetic:** Use p/g chart, dotted letter grid, screen, green crayon
3. **Blending:** VC and CVC cards on blending board

*Vowel Intensive: use tents or sticks

Dictation/Application of Words

1. (T) States the word: *mom*.
   (T) Uses the word in a sentence.
   (T) States the word while pounding *(mom)*, models fingertapping (if appropriate), then pounds the word.
2. (S) State the word while pounding *(mom)*.
   (S) Fingertap the word with off hand *(/m/ /ŏ/ /m/)*, and pound the word *(mom)*.
   (S) Write the word on appropriate paper.
3. (S) Check word and rewrite.
4. (S) Read all words to practice fluency.

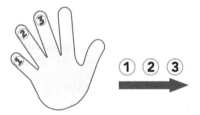

 ## Phonological Awareness:

Materials Needed:
tokens, sound boxes, one-minute activities, or Zgonc PA book

Use the PAST assessment to determine a starting point for instruction. Incorporate daily phonological awareness activities by using Zgonc's tiered activities and/or Kilpatrick's One-Minute Activities in *Equipped for Reading Success.*

Phonemic awareness warm-up: Use tokens (or letter tiles once concepts have been taught) and sound boxes to do a quick phonemic awareness activity that ties in with the new concept, if appropriate.

Three-Part Drill

Materials Needed:
review cards, sand, blending board, vowel tents or sticks

Do this at least 3x per week. Use the Flip Chart for steps. Wait to incorporate the drill until the Day 1 lesson for "o" has been taught.

- This will be the first drill for kindergarten students. Use the steps on the Comprehensive Flip Chart. Incorporate only the letters taught thus far (i.e., "m," "a," "l," and "o"). (The card pack contains an extra "m" so it can be used in both the initial and final position on the blending board.)

- Remember to use the grid, green crayon, and screen for the Auditory/Kinesthetic part of the drill instead of sand until students have the letter formation skills needed for writing in the sand.

- Include the Vowel Intensive with "a" and "o" after "o" has been taught. Use the Flip Chart for directions.

V	VC	CVC
a	ag, ap, ab	lat, cad, zan
e	et, en, eb	zeg, ren, med
i	ig, ib, im	lin, hib, fid
o	ob, ot, oz	rom, hob, cog
u	un, ud, ub	sup, pum, dut

- Below is a sample script. Remember to use all of the review concepts.

1. **Visual:**
   (T) Tell me the sounds you know for these letters.
   (S) /m/, /l/, etc.
   Alternative: (T) Tell me the names and sounds you know for these letters.
   (S) m says /m/, l says /l/, etc.

2. **Auditory/Kinesthetic:**
   (T) Eyes on me. Spell /m/. Repeat.
   (S) /m/ m says m.

3. **Blending:**
   (T) Tell me the sound for each letter as I point. Then blend the sounds together to read the word or syllable. Give me a thumbs up if it is a real word.
   (S) /mmm/ /ŏŏŏ/ /mmm/ *mom* (thumbs up)
   Alternative:
   (T) Watch me first. /mmm/ /ŏŏŏ/ /mmm/ *mom*
   (T) Do it with me. (T&S) /mmm/ /ŏŏŏ/ /mmm/ *mom*
   (T) Your turn. (S) /mmm/ /ŏŏŏ/ /mmm/ *mom* (thumbs up)

   *Vowel Intensive: Model the visual cue while calling out the sound. Students will do the visual cue as they repeat the sound. Students will then hold up the vowel tent while stating the letter name and sound.

   - (T): Eyes on me. The sound is /ă/. Repeat.

   - (S): /ă/ a says /ă/

Teaching a New Concept

Materials Needed:
concept card, screen, green crayon, object, sand, decodable readers (beginning with the "t" lesson), literature, P/G chart

Introduce on Monday, and practice daily.

1. (T) Reads alliteration sentence. (S) Identify the target sound.

   a. Ozzy octopus offers olives.

   (T) Reads the following sentence in which /ŏ/ is in the medial position. (S) Identify the target sound.

   b. Hop on top of Pop.

2. (T) Shows the new concept card.

   a. (T) Tells students the letter name and sound. Have (S) repeat, 3 times (o says /ŏ/).

   b. (T) Tells students that "o" is a vowel.

   c. (T) Tells students it is a voiced sound.

   d. (T) Asks students where they find "o" in the alphabet.

   e. (T) Uses mirrors to discuss the mouth, tongue, and teeth placement.

3. (T) Shows an object.

   a. (T) Allows students to manipulate the object and discuss prior knowledge. Reminds (S) that the object has the target sound spelled with the target letter.

4. (S) Brainstorm.

   a. Brainstorm words that have the target sound. (Accept all answers, but place incorrect answers in a "thought bubble" to discuss.) The brainstorming can be a teacher-directed activity if students need extra support. (**NOTE:** For short vowels, students can brainstorm word families or rhyming words containing the vowel sound.)

5. (T) Teaches Letter Formation. Use house paper to teach lowercase letters.

   a. (T) models with the solid letter. The letter "o" starts near the ceiling, curves around, touches the floor, and then curves back up towards the ceiling.

   b. Using the screen and green crayon, (T&S) trace the solid while saying, "o says /ŏ/" (3x).

   c. (T&S) use their finger to trace the solid while saying, "o says /ŏ/" (3x).

   d. (S) trace the dotted letter and complete the remainder of the row independently.

   e. (S) move to smaller house and repeat process if needed.

   f. Teach capital letters throughout the week using the same process. Capital letters go outside the house.

6. (T) Dictates target sound. (S) Practice in the sand or other medium.

   a. Practice writing the letter using a different medium, such as sand, shaving cream, finger paint, gel board, iPad app, air writing, etc.

   b. Do this while stating: o says /ŏ/, 3 times.

7. (T) Connects with literature.

   a. Have students signal when they hear the /ŏ/ sound for the first page or two.

b. Read again for language comprehension.

c. Continue to work on language comprehension with rich literature throughout the week.

8. Use decodable readers beginning with the "t" lesson.

9. (T&S) Mark the Phoneme/Grapheme (P/G) chart by highlighting the target sound.

Word Dictation

Materials Needed:
fingertapping hand, dictation paper, pencil

Create any syllables using the new concept and previously taught concepts. Practice daily. Use the Flip Chart to follow the steps for word dictation.

Day 1:	1. Al	2. am	3. lam	4. mam	5. mom
Day 2:	1. mom	2. lam	3. Al	4. am	5. mam
Day 3:	1. lam	2. am	3. mam	4. mom	5. Al
Days 4-5:	Review prior words.				

Below is a sample script:

1. (T) States word: *mom*. Uses it in a sentence: My *mom* is a wonderful lady. (Pounds) *mom*. (T) Models fingertapping if needed: /m/ /ŏ/ /m/. (Pounds) *mom*.

2. (S) State while pounding: *mom*. (Fingertap) /m/ /ŏ/ /m/. (Pound) *mom*. Write the letters known for the sounds.

3. (T) When yours looks like mine, rewrite the word.

4. (S) Rewrite.

5. Repeat the process for each word.

6. (S) Read the list of words multiple times to build automaticity.

Sentence Dictation

(After teaching Tt /t/)

Weekly Red Words

Materials Needed:
screen, red crayon, red word paper

Introduce on Tuesday, and practice daily. Use the Flip Chart for steps.

New:	Review:	New Read-Only:	Review Read-Only:
a	the, was, is		

Steps for Teaching a New Red Word:

1. (T) States the word. (a pronounced /ŭ/)
2. (T&S) Use tokens to determine how many sounds are in the word. (/ŭ/; 1)
3. (T&S) Discuss how we would expect to spell each sound as the teacher writes the grapheme(s) correctly. Identify what is unexpected or irregular about the spelling of the word. It could also be expected, but the concept hasn't been taught yet.
4. (T&S) Discuss the etymology of the word, if appropriate (lexical words). Visit www.etymonline.com for more information on the word.
5. (T) Defines the word, and writes a sentence using the word.
6. (T) Writes the word on Red Word paper with the screen underneath, using red crayon.
7. (S) Write the word on Red Word paper with the screen underneath, using red crayon. (S) Show the word to the teacher.
   (**NOTE:** The teacher should have students chunk the word if it has more than four letters.)
8. (T&S) Stand up, holding the Red Word in the nondominant hand. Armtap word while naming each letter. Then "underline" the word by sweeping left to right while stating the word, 3x. (**NOTE:** Left-handed students will place their left hand on their right wrist. They tap to their right shoulder. Underline from wrist to shoulder. Right-handed students place their right hand on their left shoulder. They tap to their left wrist. Underline shoulder to wrist.)
9. (T&S) Trace crayon bumps with the pointer finger while naming the letters, 3x.
10. (T&S) Place the screen over the paper and trace the word with the pointer finger while naming the letters, 3x.
11. (S) Turn paper over. With red crayon, write the word without the screen one time, and hold up the word for the teacher to check. (S) Write the word two more times.
12. (S) Write an original sentence in pencil and underline the Red Word with a red crayon. (**NOTE:** The sentence can also be dictated by the teacher while the student writes or dictated by the student while the teacher writes it.)

Review Ideas for Red Words:

▪ Sculpt the word using red Play-Doh or clay. Have students spell the word as they smash each letter.
▪ Print flashcards from IOG, and practice reading.
▪ Armtap the word to review.
▪ Cross-clap the word to review.
▪ Do Spelling Aerobics.

Fluency, Vocabulary, and Comprehension

- Incorporate fluency into your literacy lessons daily/weekly (minimum 30 min/week) by using Rapid Word Charts, IMSE Decodable Readers, words and sentences, Acadience Reading K-6 or DIBELS 8th Edition, repeated reading, and other activities.

- Incorporate vocabulary into your literacy lessons daily/weekly (minimum 50 min/week) by choosing 3-5 appropriate tier two words (can pull from rich literature or decodable readers). Teach the words through explicit, direct instruction using student-friendly definitions, word webs, vocabulary charts, illustrations, and other activities.

- Incorporate oral language comprehension into your literacy lessons daily/weekly (approximately 100 min/week). Comprehension instruction should be explicit, direct instruction that includes teacher modeling, guided practice, and independent practice. Plan ahead to build on students' background knowledge, language structures, verbal reasoning, and literacy knowledge.

Extension Activity Ideas

- Continue the multi-sensory ABC book. Have students glue octagons (or another object) in the shape of the target letter.
- Have students compare and contrast a fox and an ox using a Venn Diagram.
- Make an octopus. Have students glue pictures of words that have the /ŏ/ sound on the octopus.
- Divide students into teams of 3 and have them lie on the ground to form the target letter. Take pictures to hang around the classroom.
- Create the target letter out of green Play-Doh or clay.
- Have students use a bingo dauber to find the target letter on a page with various letters.
- Have students go on a "sound hunt" around the room or outside to find objects that begin with the target sound.
- Coding activity: Have students underline and label the letters in words or syllables with a "v" for vowels and a "c" for consonants. For example, when using the word *mom*, each letter should be underlined with the labels "cvc" underneath the word. This activity will help prepare students for decoding multisyllabic words later in the sequence.
- Visit IMSE's Orton-Gillingham's Pinterest page for more ideas.

Weekly Lesson Reminders

- Any of the above extension activities
- Daily practice writing the target letter (capital and lowercase) using a screen, green crayon, and house paper
- Practice writing the target letter using another medium (sand, paint, shaving cream, pudding, iPad app, etc.).
- Practice writing the target letter using age-appropriate paper and pencil.
- Daily practice with writing the weekly Red Word(s)
- Kilpatrick's "One-Minute Activities" for daily phonological awareness practice
- Zgonc's phonological awareness activities
- Listen to rich literature to work on oral language comprehension.
- Target letter practice sheets from IMSE's practice books and handwriting books
- Practice test on Thursday and test on Friday

Hh as in hammer

Card Pack #5	
Object Ideas:	**Literature Ideas:**
hat, helicopter, hand, hammer, horse, house, heart, hippo, hopscotch, hot potato, hurricane, hula-hoop, Hershey's Kiss, hiss, howl	<ul><li>*The Cat in the Hat* by Dr. Seuss</li><li>*A House for Hermit Crab* by Eric Carle</li><li>*Harold and the Purple Crayon* by Crockett Johnson</li><li>*A Picture Book of Harriet Tubman* by David A. Adler</li><li>*Harry the Dirty Dog* by Gene Zion</li><li>Henry and Mudge series by Cynthia Rylant</li><li>*Horton Hears a Who!* by Dr. Seuss</li><li>*The Hiccupotamus* by Aaron Zenz</li><li>*Honey, I Love* by Eloise Greenfield</li><li>*Say Hello!* by Rachel Isadora</li><li>*Harvesting Hope: The Story of Cesar Chavez* by Kathleen Krull</li><li>Harry Potter series by J.K. Rowling</li><li>*My Heart Fills With Happiness* by Monique Gray Smith</li></ul>

Notes

- Use the Comprehensive Flip Chart for the steps on how to teach each part of IMSE's Lesson Plan.
- Hh /h/ is an unvoiced consonant created with the throat open and a push of air. This is a glottal fricative sound.
- For now, keep "h" in the initial position. If "h" is at the end of a one-syllable word, it will mix with a vowel or consonant to make a new sound.

Phonological Awareness:

Materials Needed:
tokens, sound boxes, one-minute activities, or Zgonc PA book

Use the PAST assessment to determine a starting point for instruction. Incorporate daily phonological awareness activities by using Zgonc's tiered activities and/or Kilpatrick's One-Minute Activities in *Equipped for Reading Success.*

Phonemic awareness warm-up: Use tokens (or letter tiles once concepts have been taught) and sound boxes to do a quick phonemic awareness activity that ties in with the new concept, if appropriate.

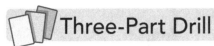 # Three-Part Drill

> **Materials Needed:**
> review cards, sand, blending board, vowel tents or sticks

Do this at least 3x per week. Use the Flip Chart for steps. Include the new concept after Day 1.

- Remember to use the grid, green crayon, and screen for the Auditory/Kinesthetic part of the drill instead of sand until students have the letter formation skills needed for writing in the sand.
- Include the Vowel Intensive with "a" and "o."

V	VC	CVC
a	ag, ap, ab	lat, cad, zan
e	et, en, eb	zeg, ren, med
i	ig, ib, im	lin, hib, fid
o	ob, ot, oz	rom, hob, cog
u	un, ud, ub	sup, pum, dut

- Below is a sample script. Remember to use all of the review concepts.

---

1. **Visual:**
   (T) Tell me the sounds you know for these letters.
   (S) /m/, /l/, etc.
   Alternative:
   (T) Tell me the names and sounds you know for these letters.
   (S) m says /m/, l says /l/, etc.

2. **Auditory/Kinesthetic:**
   (T) Eyes on me. Spell /m/. Repeat.
   (S) /m/ m says m.

3. **Blending:**
   (T) Tell me the sound for each letter as I point. Then blend the sounds together to read the word or syllable. Give me a thumbs up if it is a real word.
   (S) /mmm/ /ŏŏŏ/ /mmm/ *mom* (thumbs up)
   Alternative:
   (T) Watch me first. /mmm/ /ŏŏŏ/ /mmm/ *mom*
   (T) Do it with me. (T&S) /mmm/ /ŏŏŏ/ /mmm/ *mom*
   (T) Your turn. (S) /mmm/ /ŏŏŏ/ /mmm/ *mom* (thumbs up)

   *Vowel Intensive: Model the visual cue while calling out the sound. Students will do the visual cue as they repeat the sound. Students will then hold up the vowel tent while stating the letter name and sound.
   - (T): Eyes on me. The sound is /ă/. Repeat.
   - (S): /ă/ a says /ă/

🧠 Teaching a New Concept

Materials Needed:
concept card, screen, green crayon, object, sand, decodable readers (beginning with the "t" lesson), literature, P/G chart

Introduce on Monday, and practice daily.

1. (T) Reads alliteration sentences. (S) Identify the target sound.
    a. Harry has hilarious horses.
    b. Happy Hal hikes high.
2. (T) Shows the new concept card.
    a. (T) Tells students the letter name and sound. Have (S) repeat, 3 times (h says /h/).
    b. (T) Tells students that "h" is a consonant.
    c. (T) Tells students it is an unvoiced sound.
    d. (T) Asks students where they find "h" in the alphabet.
    e. (T) Uses mirrors to discuss the mouth, tongue, and teeth placement.
3. (T) Shows an object.
    a. (T) Allows students to manipulate the object and discuss prior knowledge. Reminds (S) that the object has the target sound spelled with the target letter.
4. (S) Brainstorm.
    a. Brainstorm words that have the target sound. (Accept all answers, but place incorrect answers in a "thought bubble" to discuss.) The brainstorming can be a teacher-directed activity if students need extra support.
5. (T) Teaches Letter Formation. Use house paper to teach lowercase letters.
    a. Use the steps for teaching letter formation on the Flip Chart. The letter "h" starts at the ceiling and goes to the floor. Then come back up, curve around in the middle of the house, and come back down to the floor.
    b. Using the screen and green crayon, (T&S) trace the solid while saying, "h says /h/" (3x).
    c. (T&S) use their finger to trace the solid while saying, "h says /h/" (3x).
    d. (S) trace the dotted letter and complete the remainder of the row independently.
    e. (S) move to smaller house and repeat process if needed.
    f. Teach capital letters throughout the week using the same process. Capital letters go outside the house.
6. (T) Dictates target sound. (S) Practice in the sand or other medium.
    a. Practice writing the letter using a different medium, such as sand, shaving cream, finger paint, gel board, iPad app, air writing, etc.
    b. Do this while stating: h says /h/, 3 times.
7. (T) Connects with literature.
    a. Have students signal when they hear the /h/ sound for the first page or two.
    b. Read again for language comprehension.
    c. Continue to work on language comprehension with rich literature throughout the week.
8. Use decodable readers beginning with the "t" lesson.
9. (T&S) Mark the Phoneme/Grapheme (P/G) chart by highlighting the target sound.

Word Dictation

Materials Needed:
fingertapping hand, dictation paper, pencil

Create any syllables using the new concept and previously taught concepts. Practice daily. Use the Flip Chart to follow the steps for word dictation.

Day 1:	1. Al	2. ham	3. mom	4. am	5. Hal
Day 2:	1. Hal	2. ham	3. Al	4. mom	5. am
Day 3:	1. ham	2. Al	3. mom	4. Hal	5. am
Days 4-5:	Review prior words.				

Below is a sample script:

1. (T) States word: *mom*. Uses it in a sentence: My *mom* is a wonderful lady. (Pounds) *mom*. (T) Models fingertapping if needed: /m/ /ŏ/ /m/. (Pounds) *mom*.
2. (S) State while pounding: *mom*. (Fingertap) /m/ /ŏ/ /m/. (Pound) *mom*. Write the letters known for the sounds.
3. (T) When yours looks like mine, rewrite the word.
4. (S) Rewrite.
5. Repeat the process for each word.
6. (S) Read the list of words multiple times to build automaticity.

Sentence Dictation

(After teaching Tt /t/)

Weekly Red Words

Materials Needed:
screen, red crayon, red word paper

Introduce on Tuesday, and practice daily. Use the Flip Chart for steps.

New:	**Review:**	**New Read-Only:**	**Review Read-Only:**
on	the, was, is, a		

Steps for Teaching a New Red Word:

1. (T) States the word. (*on*)
2. (T&S) Use tokens to determine how many sounds are in the word. (/ŏ/ /n/; 2)
3. (T&S) Discuss how we would expect to spell each sound as the teacher writes the grapheme(s) correctly. Identify what is unexpected or irregular about the spelling of the word. It could also be expected, but the concept hasn't been taught yet.

4. (T&S) Discuss the etymology of the word, if appropriate (lexical words). Visit www.etymonline.com for more information on the word.

5. (T) Defines the word, and writes a sentence using the word.

6. (T) Writes the word on Red Word paper with the screen underneath, using red crayon.

7. (S) Write the word on Red Word paper with the screen underneath, using red crayon. (S) Show the word to the teacher.
(**NOTE:** The teacher should have students chunk the word if it has more than four letters.)

8. (T&S) Stand up, holding the Red Word in the nondominant hand. Armtap word while naming each letter. Then "underline" the word by sweeping left to right while stating the word, 3x. (**NOTE:** Left-handed students will place their left hand on their right wrist. They tap to their right shoulder. Underline from wrist to shoulder. Right-handed students place their right hand on their left shoulder. They tap to their left wrist. Underline shoulder to wrist.)

9. (T&S) Trace crayon bumps with the pointer finger while naming the letters, 3x.

10. (T&S) Place the screen over the paper and trace the word with the pointer finger while naming the letters, 3x.

11. (S) Turn paper over. With red crayon, write the word without the screen one time, and hold up the word for the teacher to check. (S) Write the word two more times.

12. (S) Write an original sentence in pencil and underline the Red Word with a red crayon. (**NOTE:** The sentence can also be dictated by the teacher while the student writes or dictated by the student while the teacher writes it.)

Review Ideas for Red Words:

- Sculpt the word using red Play-Doh or clay. Have students spell the word as they smash each letter.
- Print flashcards from IOG, and practice reading.
- Armtap the word to review.
- Cross-clap the word to review.
- Do Spelling Aerobics.

Fluency, Vocabulary, and Comprehension

- Incorporate fluency into your literacy lessons daily/weekly (minimum 30 min/week) by using Rapid Word Charts, IMSE Decodable Readers, words and sentences, Acadience Reading K-6 or DIBELS 8th Edition, repeated reading, and other activities.
- Incorporate vocabulary into your literacy lessons daily/weekly (minimum 50 min/week) by choosing 3-5 appropriate tier two words (can pull from rich literature or decodable readers). Teach the words through explicit, direct instruction using student-friendly definitions, word webs, vocabulary charts, illustrations, and other activities.
- Incorporate oral language comprehension into your literacy lessons daily/weekly (approximately 100 min/week). Comprehension instruction should be explicit, direct instruction that includes teacher modeling, guided practice, and independent practice. Plan ahead to build on students' background knowledge, language structures, verbal reasoning, and literacy knowledge.

Extension Activity Ideas

- Continue to add to the multi-sensory ABC book. Have students glue hearts (or another object) in the shape of the target letter.
- Have students compare and contrast hopscotch and hula-hoops using a Venn Diagram.
- Make a paper hat. Have students glue pictures of words that begin with the /h/ sound on the hat.
- Divide students into teams of 3 and have them lie on the ground to form the target letter. Take pictures to hang around the classroom.
- Create the target letter out of green Play-Doh or clay.
- Have students use a bingo dauber to find the target letter on a page with various letters.
- Have students go on a "sound hunt" around the room or outside to find objects that begin with the target sound.
- Coding activity: Have students underline and label the letters in words or syllables with a "v" for vowels and a "c" for consonants. For example, when using the word *mom*, each letter should be underlined with the labels "cvc" underneath the word. This activity will help prepare students for decoding multisyllabic words later in the sequence.
- Visit IMSE's Orton-Gillingham's Pinterest page for more ideas.

Weekly Lesson Reminders

- Any of the above extension activities
- Daily practice writing the target letter (capital and lowercase) using a screen, green crayon, and house paper
- Practice writing the target letter using another medium (sand, paint, shaving cream, pudding, iPad app, etc.).
- Practice writing the target letter using age-appropriate paper and pencil.
- Daily practice with writing the weekly Red Word(s)
- Kilpatrick's "One-Minute Activities" for daily phonological awareness practice
- Zgonc's phonological awareness activities
- Listen to rich literature to work on oral language comprehension.
- Target letter practice sheets from IMSE's practice books and handwriting books
- Practice test on Thursday and test on Friday

Gg as in goat

Card Pack #6	
Object Ideas:	**Literature Ideas:**
game, gum, goat, garden, guitar, gummy bear, gumdrop, glue, glitter	▪ *Gordon Parks: How the Photographer Captured Black and White America* by Carole Boston Weatherford ▪ *Goggles!* by Ezra Jack Keats ▪ *Go, Dog. Go!* by P. D. Eastman ▪ *Gregory, the Terrible Eater* by Mitchell Sharmat ▪ *The Goat in the Rug* by Charles L. Blood and Martin Link ▪ *Goldilocks and the Three Bears* ▪ *Good Night, Gorilla* by Peggy Rathman ▪ *Goodnight Moon* by Margaret Wise Brown ▪ *The Giving Tree* by Shel Silverstein ▪ *We Are Grateful: Otsaliheliga* by Traci Sorrell ▪ *A Hat for Mrs. Goldman: A Story About Knitting and Love* by Michelle Edwards

Notes

- Use the Comprehensive Flip Chart for the steps on how to teach each part of IMSE's Lesson Plan.
- Gg /g/ is a voiced, stopped consonant created with the lips parted and the back of the tongue on the back roof of the mouth.
- Keep "g" in the final position on the blending board until the rule for soft "g" (/j/) is taught. The card pack contains an extra "g" so that it can be used in both the initial and final position after teaching soft "g."

Phonological Awareness:

Materials Needed:
tokens, sound boxes, one-minute activities, or Zgonc PA book

Use the PAST assessment to determine a starting point for instruction. Incorporate daily phonological awareness activities by using Zgonc's tiered activities and/or Kilpatrick's One-Minute Activities in *Equipped for Reading Success*.

Phonemic awareness warm-up: Use tokens (or letter tiles once concepts have been taught) and sound boxes to do a quick phonemic awareness activity that ties in with the new concept, if appropriate.

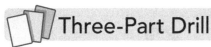

Three-Part Drill

Materials Needed:
review cards, sand, blending board, vowel tents or sticks

Do this at least 3x per week. Use the Flip Chart for steps. Include the new concept after Day 1.

- Remember to use the vowel grid, green crayon, and screen for the Auditory/Kinesthetic part of the drill instead of sand until students have the letter formation skills needed for writing in the sand.

- Include the Vowel Intensive with "a" and "o."

V	VC	CVC
a	ag, ap, ab	lat, cad, zan
e	et, en, eb	zeg, ren, med
i	ig, ib, im	lin, hib, fid
o	ob, ot, oz	rom, hob, cog
u	un, ud, ub	sup, pum, dut

- Below is a sample script. Remember to use all of the review concepts.

1. **Visual:**
   (T) Tell me the sounds you know for these letters.
   (S) /m/, /l/, etc.
   Alternative:
   (T) Tell me the names and sounds you know for these letters.
   (S) m says /m/, l says /l/, etc.

2. **Auditory/Kinesthetic:**
   (T) Eyes on me. Spell /m/. Repeat.
   (S) /m/ m says m.

3. **Blending:**
   (T) Tell me the sound for each letter as I point. Then blend the sounds together to read the word or syllable. Give me a thumbs up if it is a real word.
   (S) /mmm/ /ŏŏŏ/ /mmm/ *mom* (thumbs up)
   Alternative:
   (T) Watch me first. /mmm/ /ŏŏŏ/ /mmm/ *mom*
   (T) Do it with me. (T&S) /mmm/ /ŏŏŏ/ /mmm/ *mom*
   (T) Your turn. (S) /mmm/ /ŏŏŏ/ /mmm/ *mom* (thumbs up)

   *Vowel Intensive: Model the visual cue while calling out the sound. Students will do the visual cue as they repeat the sound. Students will then hold up the vowel tent while stating the letter name and sound.
   - (T): Eyes on me. The sound is /ă/. Repeat.
   - (S): /ă/ a says /ă/

🧠 Teaching a New Concept

Materials Needed:
concept card, screen, green crayon, object, sand, decodable readers (beginning with the "t" lesson), literature, P/G chart

Introduce on Monday, and practice daily.

1. (T) Reads alliteration sentences. (S) Identify the target sound.
   a. Great girls get green gum.
   b. Gorillas get gooey, gluey glitter.
2. (T) Shows the new concept card.
   a. (T) Tells students the letter name and sound. Have (S) repeat, 3 times (g says /g/).
   b. (T) Tells students that "g" is a consonant.
   c. (T) Tells students it is a voiced sound.
   d. (T) Asks students where they find "g" in the alphabet.
   e. (T) Uses mirrors to discuss the mouth, tongue, and teeth placement.
3. (T) Shows an object.
   a. (T) Allows students to manipulate the object and discuss prior knowledge. Reminds (S) that the object has the target sound spelled with the target letter.
4. (S) Brainstorm.
   a. Brainstorm words that have the target sound. (Accept all answers, but place incorrect answers in a "thought bubble" to discuss.) The brainstorming can be a teacher-directed activity if students need extra support.
5. (T) Teaches Letter Formation. Use house paper to teach lowercase letters.
   a. (T) models with the solid letter. The letter "g" starts at the ceiling and goes around, touches the floor, and comes back to the ceiling. Then come down through the house and into the basement. Curve around.
   b. Using the screen and green crayon, (T&S) trace the solid while saying, "g says /g/" (3x).
   c. (T&S) use their finger to trace the solid while saying, "g says /g/" (3x).
   d. (S) trace the dotted letter and complete the remainder of the row independently.
   e. (S) move to smaller house and repeat process if needed.
   f. Teach capital letters throughout the week using the same process. Capital letters go outside the house.
6. (T) Dictates target sound. (S) Practice in the sand or other medium.
   a. Practice writing the letter using a different medium, such as sand, shaving cream, finger paint, gel board, iPad app, air writing, etc.
   b. Do this while stating: g says /g/, 3 times.
7. (T) Connects with literature.
   a. Have students signal when they hear the /g/ sound for the first page or two.
   b. Read again for language comprehension.
   c. Continue to work on language comprehension with rich literature throughout the week.
8. Use decodable readers beginning with the "t" lesson.
9. (T&S) Mark the Phoneme/Grapheme (P/G) chart by highlighting the target sound.

Word Dictation

Materials Needed:
fingertapping hand, dictation paper, pencil

Create any syllables using the new concept and previously taught concepts. Practice daily. Use the Flip Chart to follow the steps for word dictation.

Day 1:	1. gag	2. log	3. gal	4. ham	5. lag
Day 2:	1. lag	2. gag	3. hog	4. mom	5. gal
Day 3:	1. am	2. log	3. gal	4. lag	5. gag
Days 4-5:	Review prior words. Optional additional words: Al, Hal				

Below is a sample script:

1. (T) States word: *mom*. Uses it in a sentence: My *mom* is a wonderful lady. (Pounds) *mom*. (T) Models fingertapping if needed: /m/ /ŏ/ /m/. (Pounds) *mom*.
2. (S) State while pounding: *mom*. (Fingertap) /m/ /ŏ/ /m/. (Pound) *mom*. Write the letters known for the sounds.
3. (T) When yours looks like mine, rewrite the word.
4. (S) Rewrite.
5. Repeat the process for each word.
6. (S) Read the list of words multiple times to build automaticity.

Sentence Dictation

(After teaching Tt /t/)

Weekly Red Words

Materials Needed:
screen, red crayon, red word paper

Introduce on Tuesday, and practice daily. Use the Flip Chart for steps.

New:	Review:	New Read-Only:	Review Read-Only:
and	the, was, is, a, on		

Steps for Teaching a New Red Word:

1. (T) States the word. (*and*)
2. (T&S) Use tokens to determine how many sounds are in the word. (/ă/ /n/ /d/; 3)
3. (T&S) Discuss how we would expect to spell each sound as the teacher writes the grapheme(s) correctly. Identify what is unexpected or irregular about the spelling of the word. It could also be expected, but the concept hasn't been taught yet.
4. (T&S) Discuss the etymology of the word, if appropriate (lexical words). Visit www. etymonline.com for more information on the word.

5. (T) Defines the word, and writes a sentence using the word.

6. (T) Writes the word on Red Word paper with the screen underneath, using red crayon.

7. (S) Write the word on Red Word paper with the screen underneath, using red crayon. (S) Show the word to the teacher.
(**NOTE:** The teacher should have students chunk the word if it has more than four letters.)

8. (T&S) Stand up, holding the Red Word in the nondominant hand. Armtap word while naming each letter. Then "underline" the word by sweeping left to right while stating the word, 3x. (**NOTE:** Left-handed students will place their left hand on their right wrist. They tap to their right shoulder. Underline from wrist to shoulder. Right-handed students place their right hand on their left shoulder. They tap to their left wrist. Underline shoulder to wrist.)

9. (T&S) Trace crayon bumps with the pointer finger while naming the letters, 3x.

10. (T&S) Place the screen over the paper and trace the word with the pointer finger while naming the letters, 3x.

11. (S) Turn paper over. With red crayon, write the word without the screen one time, and hold up the word for the teacher to check. (S) Write the word two more times.

12. (S) Write an original sentence in pencil and underline the Red Word with a red crayon. (**NOTE:** The sentence can also be dictated by the teacher while the student writes or dictated by the student while the teacher writes it.)

Review Ideas for Red Words:

- Sculpt the word using red Play-Doh or clay. Have students spell the word as they smash each letter.
- Print flashcards from IOG, and practice reading.
- Armtap the word to review.
- Cross-clap the word to review.
- Do Spelling Aerobics.

Fluency, Vocabulary, and Comprehension

- Incorporate fluency into your literacy lessons daily/weekly (minimum 30 min/week) by using Rapid Word Charts, IMSE Decodable Readers, words and sentences, Acadience Reading K-6 or DIBELS 8th Edition, repeated reading, and other activities.
- Incorporate vocabulary into your literacy lessons daily/weekly (minimum 50 min/week) by choosing 3-5 appropriate tier two words (can pull from rich literature or decodable readers). Teach the words through explicit, direct instruction using student-friendly definitions, word webs, vocabulary charts, illustrations, and other activities.
- Incorporate oral language comprehension into your literacy lessons daily/weekly (approximately 100 min/week). Comprehension instruction should be explicit, direct instruction that includes teacher modeling, guided practice, and independent practice. Plan ahead to build on students' background knowledge, language structures, verbal reasoning, and literacy knowledge.

Extension Activity Ideas

- Continue to add to the multi-sensory ABC book. Have students glue glitter (or another object) in the shape of the target letter.
- Have students compare and contrast gum and gummy bears using a Venn Diagram.
- Make a paper gumdrop. Have students glue pictures of words that begin with the /g/ sound on the gumdrop.
- Divide students into teams of 3 and have them lie on the ground to form the target letter. Take pictures to hang around the classroom.
- Create the target letter out of green Play-Doh or clay.
- Have students use a bingo dauber to find the target letter on a page with various letters.
- Have students go on a "sound hunt" around the room or outside to find objects that begin with the target sound.
- Coding activity: Have students underline and label the letters in words or syllables with a "v" for vowels and a "c" for consonants. For example, when using the word *mom*, each letter should be underlined with the labels "cvc" underneath the word. This activity will help prepare students for decoding multisyllabic words later in the sequence.
- Visit IMSE's Orton-Gillingham's Pinterest page for more ideas.

Weekly Lesson Reminders

- Any of the above extension activities
- Daily practice writing the target letter (capital and lowercase) using a screen, green crayon, and house paper
- Practice writing the target letter using another medium (sand, paint, shaving cream, pudding, iPad app, etc.).
- Practice writing the target letter using age-appropriate paper and pencil.
- Daily practice with writing the weekly Red Word(s)
- Kilpatrick's "One-Minute Activities" for daily phonological awareness practice
- Zgonc's phonological awareness activities
- Listen to rich literature to work on oral language comprehension.
- Target letter practice sheets from IMSE's practice books and handwriting books
- Practice test on Thursday and test on Friday

Cc as in cat

Card Pack #7	
Object Ideas:	**Literature Ideas:**
cotton, candy, cotton candy, cut, cap, carrot, coin, cone	▪ *The Colors of Us* by Karen Katz ▪ *Cool Cuts* by Mechal Renee Roe ▪ *Corduroy* by Don Freeman ▪ *The Very Hungry Caterpillar* by Eric Carle ▪ *Millions of Cats* by Wanda Gág ▪ *The Carrot Seed* by Ruth Krauss ▪ *Caps for Sale* by Esphyr Slobodkina ▪ *Crown: An Ode to the Fresh Cut* by Derrick Barnes ▪ *Eyes That Kiss in the Corners* by Joanna Ho

Notes

- Use the Comprehensive Flip Chart for the steps on how to teach each part of IMSE's Lesson Plan.
- Cc /k/ is an unvoiced, stopped consonant created with the lips parted and the back of the tongue on the back roof of the mouth.
- Keep "c" in the initial position until after the -ck rule is taught. Then, you can move it to the final position to help establish syllables like "pic" in *picnic*.

Phonological Awareness:

Materials Needed:
tokens, sound boxes, one-minute activities, or Zgonc PA book

Use the PAST assessment to determine a starting point for instruction. Incorporate daily phonological awareness activities by using Zgonc's tiered activities and/or Kilpatrick's One-Minute Activities in *Equipped for Reading Success.*

Phonemic awareness warm-up: Use tokens (or letter tiles once concepts have been taught) and sound boxes to do a quick phonemic awareness activity that ties in with the new concept, if appropriate.

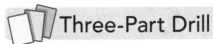

Three-Part Drill

Materials Needed:
review cards, sand, blending board, vowel tents or sticks

Do this at least 3x per week. Use the Flip Chart for steps. Include the new concept after Day 1.

- Remember to use the vowel grid, green crayon, and screen for the Auditory/ Kinesthetic part of the drill instead of sand until students have the letter formation skills needed for writing in the sand.

- Include the Vowel Intensive with "a" and "o."

V	VC	CVC
a	ag, ap, ab	lat, cad, zan
e	et, en, eb	zeg, ren, med
i	ig, ib, im	lin, hib, fid
o	ob, ot, oz	rom, hob, cog
u	un, ud, ub	sup, pum, dut

- Below is a sample script. Remember to use all of the review concepts.

1. **Visual:**
   (T) Tell me the sounds you know for these letters.
   (S) /m/, /l/, etc.
   Alternative:
   (T) Tell me the names and sounds you know for these letters.
   (S) m says /m/, l says /l/, etc.

2. **Auditory/Kinesthetic:**
   (T) Eyes on me. Spell /m/. Repeat.
   (S) /m/ m says m.

3. **Blending:**
   (T) Tell me the sound for each letter as I point. Then blend the sounds together to read the word or syllable. Give me a thumbs up if it is a real word.
   (S) /mmm/ /ŏŏŏ/ /mmm/ *mom* (thumbs up)
   Alternative:
   (T) Watch me first. /mmm/ /ŏŏŏ/ /mmm/ *mom*
   (T) Do it with me. (T&S) /mmm/ /ŏŏŏ/ /mmm/ *mom*
   (T) Your turn. (S) /mmm/ /ŏŏŏ/ /mmm/ *mom* (thumbs up)

   Vowel Intensive: Model the visual cue while calling out the sound. Students will do the visual cue as they repeat the sound. Students will then hold up the vowel tent while stating the letter name and sound.
   - (T): Eyes on me. The sound is /ă/. Repeat.
   - (S): /ă/ a says /ă/

Teaching a New Concept

Materials Needed:
concept card, screen, green crayon, object, sand, decodable readers (beginning with the "t" lesson), literature, P/G chart

Introduce on Monday, and practice daily.

1. (T) Reads alliteration sentences. (S) Identify the target sound.
   a. Can Casey cook carrots?
   b. Crunchy, crispy cookies can crumble.
2. (T) Shows the new concept card.
   a. (T) Tells students the letter name and sound. Have (S) repeat, 3 times (c says /k/).
   b. (T) Tells students that "c" is a consonant.
   c. (T) Tells students it is an unvoiced sound.
   d. (T) Asks students where they find "c" in the alphabet.
   e. (T) Uses mirrors to discuss the mouth, tongue, and teeth placement.
3. (T) Shows an object.
   a. (T) Allows students to manipulate the object and discuss prior knowledge. Reminds (S) that the object has the target sound spelled with the target letter.
4. (S) Brainstorm.
   a. Brainstorm words that have the target sound. (Accept all answers, but place incorrect answers in a "thought bubble" to discuss.) The brainstorming can be a teacher-directed activity if students need extra support.
5. (T) Teaches Letter Formation. Use house paper to teach lowercase letters.
   a. (T) models with the solid letter. The letter "c" starts below the ceiling and goes around, touches the floor, and stops just above the floor.
   b. Using the screen and green crayon, (T&S) trace the solid while saying, "c says /k/" (3x).
   c. (T&S) use their finger to trace the solid while saying, "c says /k/" (3x).
   d. (S) trace the dotted letter and complete the remainder of the row independently.
   e. (S) move to smaller house and repeat process if needed.
   f. Teach capital letters throughout the week using the same process. Capital letters go outside the house.
6. (T) Dictates target sound. (S) Practice in the sand or other medium.
   a. Practice writing the letter using a different medium, such as sand, shaving cream, finger paint, gel board, iPad app, air writing, etc.
   b. Do this while stating: c says /k/, 3 times.
7. (T) Connects with literature.
   a. Have students signal when they hear the /k/ sound for the first page or two.
   b. Read again for language comprehension.
   c. Continue to work on language comprehension with rich literature throughout the week.
8. Use decodable readers beginning with the "t" lesson.
9. (T&S) Mark the Phoneme/Grapheme (P/G) chart by highlighting the target sound.

Word Dictation

Materials Needed:
fingertapping hand, dictation paper, pencil

Create any syllables using the new concept and previously taught concepts. Practice daily. Use the Flip Chart to follow the steps for word dictation.

Day 1:	1. Cam	2. hog	3. cog	4. mom	5. gag
Day 2:	1. ham	2. Cam	3. lag	4. gal	5. cog
Day 3:	1. Hal	2. am	3. cog	4. Cam	5. log
Days 4-5:	Review prior words. Optional additional word: Al

Below is a sample script:

1. (T) States word: *mom*. Uses it in a sentence: My *mom* is a wonderful lady. (Pounds) *mom*. (T) Models fingertapping if needed: /m/ /ŏ/ /m/. (Pounds) *mom*.
2. (S) State while pounding: *mom*. (Fingertap) /m/ /ŏ/ /m/. (Pound) *mom*. Write the letters known for the sounds.
3. (T) When yours looks like mine, rewrite the word.
4. (S) Rewrite.
5. Repeat the process for each word.
6. (S) Read the list of words multiple times to build automaticity.

Sentence Dictation

(After teaching Tt /t/)

Weekly Red Words

Materials Needed:
screen, red crayon, red word paper

Introduce on Tuesday, and practice daily. Use the Flip Chart for steps.

New:	**Review:**	**New Read-Only:**	**Review Read-Only:**
to	the, was, is, a, on, and		

Steps for Teaching a New Red Word:

1. (T) States the word. (*to*)
2. (T&S) Use tokens to determine how many sounds are in the word. (/t/ / $\overline{oo}$ /; 2)
3. (T&S) Discuss how we would expect to spell each sound as the teacher writes the grapheme(s) correctly. Identify what is unexpected or irregular about the spelling of the word. It could also be expected, but the concept hasn't been taught yet.

4. (T&S) Discuss the etymology of the word, if appropriate (lexical words). Visit www. etymonline.com for more information on the word.

5. (T) Defines the word, and writes a sentence using the word.

6. (T) Writes the word on Red Word paper with the screen underneath, using red crayon.

7. (S) Write the word on Red Word paper with the screen underneath, using red crayon. (S) Show the word to the teacher.
   (**NOTE:** The teacher should have students chunk the word if it has more than four letters.)

8. (T&S) Stand up, holding the Red Word in the nondominant hand. Armtap word while naming each letter. Then "underline" the word by sweeping left to right while stating the word, 3x. (**NOTE:** Left-handed students will place their left hand on their right wrist. They tap to their right shoulder. Underline from wrist to shoulder. Right-handed students place their right hand on their left shoulder. They tap to their left wrist. Underline shoulder to wrist.)

9. (T&S) Trace crayon bumps with the pointer finger while naming the letters, 3x.

10. (T&S) Place the screen over the paper and trace the word with the pointer finger while naming the letters, 3x.

11. (S) Turn paper over. With red crayon, write the word without the screen one time, and hold up the word for the teacher to check. (S) Write the word two more times.

12. (S) Write an original sentence in pencil and underline the Red Word with a red crayon. (**NOTE:** The sentence can also be dictated by the teacher while the student writes or dictated by the student while the teacher writes it.)

Review Ideas for Red Words:

- Sculpt the word using red Play-Doh or clay. Have students spell the word as they smash each letter.
- Print flashcards from IOG, and practice reading.
- Armtap the word to review.
- Cross-clap the word to review.
- Do Spelling Aerobics.

 # Fluency, Vocabulary, and Comprehension

- Incorporate fluency into your literacy lessons daily/weekly (minimum 30 min/ week) by using Rapid Word Charts, IMSE Decodable Readers, words and sentences, Acadience Reading K-6 or DIBELS 8th Edition, repeated reading, and other activities.

- Incorporate vocabulary into your literacy lessons daily/weekly (minimum 50 min/ week) by choosing 3-5 appropriate tier two words (can pull from rich literature or decodable readers). Teach the words through explicit, direct instruction using student-friendly definitions, word webs, vocabulary charts, illustrations, and other activities.

- Incorporate oral language comprehension into your literacy lessons daily/weekly (approximately 100 min/week). Comprehension instruction should be explicit, direct instruction that includes teacher modeling, guided practice, and independent practice. Plan ahead to build on students' background knowledge, language structures, verbal reasoning, and literacy knowledge.

Extension Activity Ideas

- Continue to add to the multi-sensory ABC book. Have students glue cotton balls (or another object) in the shape of the target letter.
- Have students compare and contrast cotton with cotton candy using a Venn Diagram.
- Glue candy on a pre-cut letter "c," or cut out pictures from magazines of objects that start with the target letter and sound.
- Divide students into teams of 3 and have them lie on the ground to form the target letter. Take pictures to hang around the classroom.
- Create the target letter out of green Play-Doh or clay.
- Have students use a bingo dauber to find the target letter on a page with various letters.
- Have students go on a "sound hunt" around the room or outside to find objects that begin with the target sound.
- Coding activity: Have students underline and label the letters in words or syllables with a "v" for vowels and a "c" for consonants. For example, when using the word *mom*, each letter should be underlined with the labels "cvc" underneath the word. This activity will help prepare students for decoding multisyllabic words later in the sequence.
- Visit IMSE's Orton-Gillingham's Pinterest page for more ideas.

Weekly Lesson Reminders

- Any of the above extension activities
- Daily practice writing the target letter (capital and lowercase) using a screen, green crayon, and house paper
- Practice writing the target letter using another medium (sand, paint, shaving cream, pudding, iPad app, etc.).
- Practice writing the target letter using age-appropriate paper and pencil.
- Daily practice with writing the weekly Red Word(s)
- Kilpatrick's "One-Minute Activities" for daily phonological awareness practice
- Zgonc's phonological awareness activities
- Listen to rich literature to work on oral language comprehension.
- Target letter practice sheets from IMSE's practice books and handwriting books
- Practice test on Thursday and test on Friday

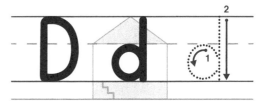

Dd as in dog

Card Pack #8	
Object Ideas:	**Literature Ideas:**
doughnut, dough, dog, dime, drum, dinosaur, drama, dancing, dragon	▪ *Dim Sum for Everyone!* by Grace Lin ▪ *Daisy Comes Home* by Jan Brett ▪ *Go, Dog. Go!* by P. D. Eastman ▪ *No, David!* by David Shannon ▪ *Bones, Bones, Dinosaur Bones* by Byron Barton ▪ *The Dinosaur Who Lived in My Backyard* by B. G. Hennessy ▪ *In a Dark, Dark Wood* by Ruth Ware ▪ *It's Called Dyslexia* by Jennifer Moore-Mallinos ▪ *Going Down Home With Daddy* by Kelly Starling Lyons ▪ *Dreamers* by Yuyi Morales

Notes

- Use the Comprehensive Flip Chart for the steps on how to teach each part of IMSE's Lesson Plan.
- Dd /d/ is a voiced, stopped consonant. It is created with the lips parted and the tongue on the ridge behind the front teeth while tapping out the air.
- Use the Drum/Drumstick master to help with letter formation.
- Can teach this song (to the tune of "The Farmer in the Dell"):

  A doorknob and a door,
  A doorknob and a door,
  This is how we make a "d,"
  A doorknob and a door.

- If needed, the card pack contains an extra "d" so it can be used in both the initial and final position on the blending board.

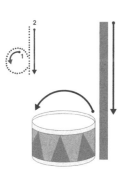

Phonological Awareness:

Materials Needed:
tokens, sound boxes, one-minute activities, or Zgonc PA book

Use the PAST assessment to determine a starting point for instruction. Incorporate daily phonological awareness activities by using Zgonc's tiered activities and/or Kilpatrick's One-Minute Activities in *Equipped for Reading Success*.

Phonemic awareness warm-up: Use tokens (or letter tiles once concepts have been taught) and sound boxes to do a quick phonemic awareness activity that ties in with the new concept, if appropriate.

Three-Part Drill

Materials Needed:
review cards, sand, blending board, vowel tents or sticks

Do this at least 3x per week. Use the Flip Chart for steps. Include the new concept after Day 1.

- Remember to use the vowel grid, green crayon, and screen for the Auditory/Kinesthetic part of the drill instead of sand until students have the letter formation skills needed for writing in the sand.
- Include the Vowel Intensive with "a" and "o."

V	VC	CVC
a	ag, ap, ab	lat, cad, zan
e	et, en, eb	zeg, ren, med
i	ig, ib, im	lin, hib, fid
o	ob, ot, oz	rom, hob, cog
u	un, ud, ub	sup, pum, dut

- Below is a sample script. Remember to use all of the review concepts.

1. **Visual:**
   (T) Tell me the sounds you know for these letters.
   (S) /m/, /l/, etc.
   Alternative:
   (T) Tell me the names and sounds you know for these letters.
   (S) m says /m/, l says /l/, etc.

2. **Auditory/Kinesthetic:**
   (T) Eyes on me. Spell /m/. Repeat.
   (S) /m/ m says m.

3. **Blending:**
   (T) Tell me the sound for each letter as I point. Then blend the sounds together to read the word or syllable. Give me a thumbs up if it is a real word.
   (S) /mmm/ /ŏŏŏ/ /mmm/ *mom* (thumbs up)
   Alternative:
   (T) Watch me first. /mmm/ /ŏŏŏ/ /mmm/ *mom*
   (T) Do it with me. (T&S) /mmm/ /ŏŏŏ/ /mmm/ *mom*
   (T) Your turn. (S) /mmm/ /ŏŏŏ/ /mmm/ *mom* (thumbs up)

Vowel Intensive: Model the visual cue while calling out the sound. Students will do the visual cue as they repeat the sound. Students will then hold up the vowel tent while stating the letter name and sound.
- (T): Eyes on me. The sound is /ă/. Repeat.
- (S): /ă/ a says /ă/

Teaching a New Concept

Materials Needed:
concept card, screen, green crayon, object, sand, decodable readers (beginning with the "t" lesson), literature, P/G chart

Introduce on Monday, and practice daily.

1. (T) Reads alliteration sentences. (S) Identify the target sound.
   a. Dan did dig deep.
   b. Dragons defy dirty ditches.
2. (T) Shows the new concept card.
   a. (T) Tells students the letter name and sound. Have (S) repeat, 3 times (d says /d/).
   b. (T) Tells students that "d" is a consonant.
   c. (T) Tells students it is a voiced sound.
   d. (T) Asks students where they find "d" in the alphabet.
   e. (T) Uses mirrors to discuss the mouth, tongue, and teeth placement.
3. (T) Shows an object.
   a. (T) Allows students to manipulate the object and discuss prior knowledge. Reminds (S) that the object has the target sound spelled with the target letter.
4. (S) Brainstorm.
   a. Brainstorm words that have the target sound. (Accept all answers, but place incorrect answers in a "thought bubble" to discuss.) The brainstorming can be a teacher-directed activity if students need extra support.
5. (T) Teaches Letter Formation. Use house paper to teach lowercase letters.
   a. (T) models with the solid letter. The letter "d" starts at the ceiling and goes around to the floor. Then it goes up to the top of the attic and straight back down to the floor.
   b. Using the screen and green crayon, (T&S) trace the solid while saying, "d says /d/" (3x).
   c. (T&S) use their finger to trace the solid while saying, "d says /d/" (3x).
   d. (S) trace the dotted letter and complete the remainder of the row independently.
   e. (S) move to smaller house and repeat process if needed.
   f. Teach capital letters throughout the week using the same process. Capital letters go outside the house.
6. (T) Dictates target sound. (S) Practice in the sand or other medium.
   a. Practice writing the letter using a different medium, such as sand, shaving cream, finger paint, gel board, iPad app, air writing, etc.
   b. Do this while stating: d says /d/, 3 times.
7. (T) Connects with literature.
   a. Have students signal when they hear the /d/ sound for the first page or two.
   b. Read again for language comprehension.
   c. Continue to work on language comprehension with rich literature throughout the week.
8. Use decodable readers beginning with the "t" lesson.
9. (T&S) Mark the Phoneme/Grapheme (P/G) chart by highlighting the target sound.

Word Dictation

Materials Needed:
fingertapping hand, dictation paper, pencil

Create any syllables using the new concept and previously taught concepts. Practice daily. Use the Flip Chart to follow the steps for word dictation.

Day 1:	1. dog	2. cad	3. cod	4. lad	5. hog
Day 2:	1. dad	2. gag	3. dog	4. mad	5. had
Day 3:	1. cod	2. lad	3. am	4. dam	5. dad
Days 4-5:	Review prior words. Optional additional words: Al, Cam, cog, gal, hag, Hal, ham, lag, mom				

Below is a sample script:

1. (T) States word: *mom.* Uses it in a sentence: My *mom* is a wonderful lady. (Pounds) *mom.* (T) Models fingertapping if needed: /m/ /ŏ/ /m/. (Pounds) *mom.*
2. (S) State while pounding: *mom.* (Fingertap) /m/ /ŏ/ /m/. (Pound) *mom.* Write the letters known for the sounds.
3. (T) When yours looks like mine, rewrite the word.
4. (S) Rewrite.
5. Repeat the process for each word.
6. (S) Read the list of words multiple times to build automaticity.

 # Sentence Dictation

(After teaching Tt /t/)

 # Weekly Red Words

Materials Needed:
screen, red crayon, red word paper

Introduce on Tuesday, and practice daily. Use the Flip Chart for steps.

New:	**Review:**	**New Read-Only:**	**Review Read-Only:**
for	the, was, is, a, on, and, to		

Steps for Teaching a New Red Word:

1. (T) States the word. (*for*)
2. (T&S) Use tokens to determine how many sounds are in the word. (/f/ /or/; 2)
3. (T&S) Discuss how we would expect to spell each sound as the teacher writes the grapheme(s) correctly. Identify what is unexpected or irregular about the spelling of the word. It could also be expected, but the concept hasn't been taught yet.

4. (T&S) Discuss the etymology of the word, if appropriate (lexical words). Visit www.etymonline.com for more information on the word.

5. (T) Defines the word, and writes a sentence using the word.

6. (T) Writes the word on Red Word paper with the screen underneath, using red crayon.

7. (S) Write the word on Red Word paper with the screen underneath, using red crayon. (S) Show the word to the teacher.
(**NOTE:** The teacher should have students chunk the word if it has more than four letters.)

8. (T&S) Stand up, holding the Red Word in the nondominant hand. Armtap word while naming each letter. Then "underline" the word by sweeping left to right while stating the word, 3x. (**NOTE:** Left-handed students will place their left hand on their right wrist. They tap to their right shoulder. Underline from wrist to shoulder. Right-handed students place their right hand on their left shoulder. They tap to their left wrist. Underline shoulder to wrist.)

9. (T&S) Trace crayon bumps with the pointer finger while naming the letters, 3x.

10. (T&S) Place the screen over the paper and trace the word with the pointer finger while naming the letters, 3x.

11. (S) Turn paper over. With red crayon, write the word without the screen one time, and hold up the word for the teacher to check. (S) Write the word two more times.

12. (S) Write an original sentence in pencil and underline the Red Word with a red crayon. (**NOTE:** The sentence can also be dictated by the teacher while the student writes or dictated by the student while the teacher writes it.)

Review Ideas for Red Words:

- Sculpt the word using red Play-Doh or clay. Have students spell the word as they smash each letter.
- Print flashcards from IOG, and practice reading.
- Armtap the word to review.
- Cross-clap the word to review.
- Do Spelling Aerobics.

Fluency, Vocabulary, and Comprehension

- Incorporate fluency into your literacy lessons daily/weekly (minimum 30 min/week) by using Rapid Word Charts, IMSE Decodable Readers, words and sentences, Acadience Reading K-6 or DIBELS 8th Edition, repeated reading, and other activities.

- Incorporate vocabulary into your literacy lessons daily/weekly (minimum 50 min/week) by choosing 3-5 appropriate tier two words (can pull from rich literature or decodable readers). Teach the words through explicit, direct instruction using student-friendly definitions, word webs, vocabulary charts, illustrations, and other activities.

- Incorporate oral language comprehension into your literacy lessons daily/weekly (approximately 100 min/week). Comprehension instruction should be explicit, direct instruction that includes teacher modeling, guided practice, and independent practice. Plan ahead to build on students' background knowledge, language structures, verbal reasoning, and literacy knowledge.

Extension Activity Ideas

- Continue the multi-sensory ABC book. Have students glue Play-Doh (or another object) in the shape of the target letter.
- Have students compare and contrast dough and doughnuts using a Venn Diagram.
- Make a paper dinosaur. Have students glue pictures of words that have the /d/ sound on the dinosaur.
- Divide students into teams of 3 and have them lie on the ground to form the target letter. Take pictures to hang around the classroom.
- Create the target letter out of green Play-Doh or clay.
- Have students use a bingo dauber to find the target letter on a page with various letters.
- Have students go on a "sound hunt" around the room or outside to find objects that begin with the target sound.
- Coding activity: Have students underline and label the letters in words or syllables with a "v" for vowels and a "c" for consonants. For example, when using the word *mom*, each letter should be underlined with the labels "cvc" underneath the word. This activity will help prepare students for decoding multisyllabic words later in the sequence.
- Visit IMSE's Orton-Gillingham's Pinterest page for more ideas.

Weekly Lesson Reminders

- Any of the above extension activities
- Daily practice writing the target letter (capital and lowercase) using a screen, green crayon, and house paper
- Practice writing the target letter using another medium (sand, paint, shaving cream, pudding, iPad app, etc.).
- Practice writing the target letter using age-appropriate paper and pencil.
- Daily practice with writing the weekly Red Word(s)
- Kilpatrick's "One-Minute Activities" for daily phonological awareness practice
- Zgonc's phonological awareness activities
- Listen to rich literature to work on oral language comprehension.
- Target letter practice sheets from IMSE's practice books and handwriting books
- Practice test on Thursday and test on Friday

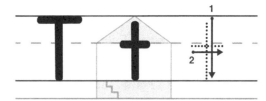

Tt as in turtle

Card Pack #9 Decodable Reader #1	
Object Ideas:	**Literature Ideas:**
tiptoe, table, tape, toe, turtle, tent, toothbrush, top, teeth, Tootsie Roll, tiger, Tic Tac, tape, tic-tac-toe, teapot	▪ *Little Taco Truck* by Tanya Valentine ▪ *Tikki Tikki Tembo* by Arlene Mosel ▪ *Yertle the Turtle* by Dr. Seuss ▪ *The Foolish Tortoise* by Richard Buckley ▪ *The Tortoise and the Hare* ▪ Frog and Toad series by Arnold Lobel ▪ *The Tooth Book* by Dr. Seuss ▪ *I Want to Ride the Tap Tap* by Danielle Joseph

 ## Notes

- Use the Comprehensive Flip Chart for the steps on how to teach each part of IMSE's Lesson Plan.
- Tt /t/ is an unvoiced, stopped consonant. It is created with the lips parted and the tongue on the ridge behind the front teeth while tapping out air.
- If needed, the card pack contains an extra "t" so it can be used in both the initial and final position on the blending board.
- After you teach "t," you can start sentence dictation. You can save this for Tuesday if needed.

After Teaching "t"

1. Students are able to write sentences. Provide word lines with visual cues.

   △ = capital letter

   ☐ = punctuation

   ═══ = Red Word

   ──── = word line

   Example:

   △Tom had the cat☐

2. Begin implementing CUPS for self-editing.

3. Sentence Dictation*
- (T) States the sentence. (e.g., "The lid is hot.")
- (T) Pounds the syllables in the sentence with the off hand.
- (T&S) pound syllables in the sentence.
- (S) Pound on their own.
- (T) Models pointing to word lines while saying sentence.
- (S) Point to word lines while saying sentence. Then write, check (CUPS), rewrite, and read.

*(T) can also have (S) write their own sentences.

Capitalization
Understanding
Punctuation
Spelling

Phonological Awareness:

Materials Needed:
tokens, sound boxes, one-minute activities, or Zgonc PA book

Use the PAST assessment to determine a starting point for instruction. Incorporate daily phonological awareness activities by using Zgonc's tiered activities and/or Kilpatrick's One-Minute Activities in *Equipped for Reading Success*.

Phonemic awareness warm-up: Use tokens (or letter tiles once concepts have been taught) and sound boxes to do a quick phonemic awareness activity that ties in with the new concept, if appropriate.

Three-Part Drill

Materials Needed:
review cards, sand, blending board, vowel tents or sticks

Do this at least 3x per week. Use the Flip Chart for steps. Include the new concept after Day 1.

- Remember to use the grid, green crayon, and screen for the Auditory/Kinesthetic part of the drill instead of sand until students have the letter formation skills needed for writing in the sand.
- Include the Vowel Intensive drill with "a" and "o."

V	VC	CVC
a	ag, ap, ab	lat, cad, zan
e	et, en, eb	zeg, ren, med
i	ig, ib, im	lin, hib, fid
o	ob, ot, oz	rom, hob, cog
u	un, ud, ub	sup, pum, dut

- Below is a sample script. Remember to use all of the review concepts.

1. **Visual:**
   (T) Tell me the sounds you know for these letters.
   (S) /m/, /l/, etc.
   Alternative:
   (T) Tell me the names and sounds you know for these letters.
   (S) m says /m/, l says /l/, etc.

2. **Auditory/Kinesthetic:**
   (T) Eyes on me. Spell /m/. Repeat.
   (S) /m/ m says m.

3. **Blending:**
   (T) Tell me the sound for each letter as I point. Then blend the sounds together to read the word or syllable. Give me a thumbs up if it is a real word.
   (S) /mmm/ /ŏŏŏ/ /mmm/ *mom* (thumbs up)
   Alternative:
   (T) Watch me first. /mmm/ /ŏŏŏ/ /mmm/ *mom*
   (T) Do it with me. (T&S) /mmm/ /ŏŏŏ/ /mmm/ *mom*
   (T) Your turn. (S) /mmm/ /ŏŏŏ/ /mmm/ *mom* (thumbs up)

Vowel Intensive: Model the visual cue while calling out the sound. Students will do the visual cue as they repeat the sound. Students will then hold up the vowel tent while stating the letter name and sound.

- (T): Eyes on me. The sound is /ă/. Repeat.
- (S): /ă/ a says /ă/

 ## Teaching a New Concept

Materials Needed:
concept card, screen, green crayon, object, sand, decodable readers, literature, P/G chart

Introduce on Monday, and practice daily.

1. (T) Reads alliteration sentences. (S) Identify the target sound.
   a. Tim told Tammy to tell Tina.
   b. Tom took turtles to Timbuktu.
2. (T) Shows the new concept card.
   a. (T) Tells students the letter name and sound. Have (S) repeat, 3 times (t says /t/).
   b. (T) Tells students that "t" is a consonant.
   c. (T) Tells students it is an unvoiced sound.
   d. (T) Asks students where they find "t" in the alphabet.
   e. (T) Uses mirrors to discuss the mouth, tongue, and teeth placement.
3. (T) Shows an object.
   a. (T) Allows students to manipulate the object and discuss prior knowledge. Reminds (S) that the object has the target sound spelled with the target letter.
4. (S) Brainstorm.
   a. Brainstorm words that have the target sound. (Accept all answers, but place

incorrect answers in a "thought bubble" to discuss.) The brainstorming can be a teacher-directed activity if students need extra support.

5. (T) Teaches Letter Formation. Use house paper to teach lowercase letters.

   a. (T) models with the solid letter. The letter "t" starts in the attic and goes to the floor. Cross it on the ceiling.

   b. Using the screen and green crayon, (T&S) trace the solid while saying, "t says /t/" (3x).

   c. (T&S) use their finger to trace the solid while saying, "t says /t/" (3x).

   d. (S) trace the dotted letter and complete the remainder of the row independently.

   e. (S) move to smaller house and repeat process if needed.

   f. Teach capital letters throughout the week using the same process. Capital letters go outside the house.

6. (T) Dictates target sound. (S) Practice in the sand or other medium.

   a. Practice writing the letter using a different medium, such as sand, shaving cream, finger paint, gel board, iPad app, air writing, etc.

   b. Do this while stating: t says /t/, 3 times.

7. (T) Connects with literature.

   a. Have students signal when they hear the /t/ sound for the first page or two.

   b. Read again for language comprehension.

   c. Continue to work on language comprehension with rich literature throughout the week.

8. (S) Use decodable readers to practice the concepts learned.

   a. (S) Highlight words with the new concept. Read those words.

   b. (S) Highlight Red Words. Read those words.

   c. (S) Start reading the decodable reader.

   d. (S) Continue reading throughout the week.

   e. (S) Read a clean copy on Friday.

9. (T&S) Mark the Phoneme/Grapheme (P/G) chart by highlighting the target sound.

 ## Word Dictation

Materials Needed:
fingertapping hand, dictation paper, pencil

Create any syllables using the new concept and previously taught concepts. Practice daily. Use the Flip Chart to follow the steps for word dictation.

Day 1:	1. tot	2. cat	3. tag	4. got	5. mat
Day 2:	1. dot	2. mat	3. Tad	4. lot	5. hat
Day 3:	1. cot	2. Tom	3. tag	4. hot	5. cat
Days 4-5:	Review prior words. Optional additional words: cad, Cam, cod, cog, dad, dog, gag, gal, had, hag, hog, lad, lag, log, mad				

Below is a sample script:

> 1. (T) States word: *mom*. Uses it in a sentence: My *mom* is a wonderful lady. (Pounds) *mom*. (T) Models fingertapping if needed: /m/ /ŏ/ /m/. (Pounds) *mom*.
> 2. (S) State while pounding: *mom*. (Fingertap) /m/ /ŏ/ /m/. (Pound) *mom*. Write the letters known for the sounds.
> 3. (T) When yours looks like mine, rewrite the word.
> 4. (S) Rewrite.
> 5. Repeat the process for each word.
> 6. (S) Read the list of words multiple times to build automaticity.

Sentence Dictation

Red Words are underlined. Students can fingertap the green words. Use the Flip Chart to follow the steps for sentence dictation.

1. Tad had a cat.
2. The dog got hot.
3. The mat was hot.
4. Dad got the ham.
5. Mom was mad at Tom.
6. Is Tad mad at Dad?
7. Is the log hot?
8. Tad got a hot ham.
9. Mom is mad at the cat.
10. The hat had a tag.
11. The lad is hot.
12. Mom was mad at Tom.
13. The cot was hot.

- Below is a sample script for sentence dictation.

> 1. (T): Listen to the sentence. *Tad had a cat.*
> 2. (T): Listen while I pound the syllables. *Tad had a cat.*
> 3. (T): Pound it with me. (T&S): *Tad had a cat.*
> 4. (T): You pound the sentence. (S): *Tad had a cat.*
> 5. (T): Watch me as I point to the lines while stating the sentence. *Tad had a cat.*
> 6. (T): You point to the lines while stating the sentence.
> 7. (S): *Tad had a cat.*
> 8. (T): Now write the sentence. Fingertap if needed.

- Below is a sample script to check CUPS*.

> 1. (T): C stands for capitalization. Did you remember a capital letter at the beginning of your sentence? It's also a name. *Tad* would always be capitalized. If you forgot, fix it. If you remembered, put a tally mark above the capital letter. Add a mark in the box for C.
>
> 2. (T): U stands for understanding. Is your sentence neat? Reread it to yourself. Does it make sense? Could someone else understand it? If not, fix it. Add a mark in the box for U.
>
> 3. (T): P stands for punctuation. Did you remember a period at the end? If not, fix it. If you remembered, put a tally mark above the period. Add a mark in the box for P.
>
> 4. (T): S stands for spelling. Did you spell your words correctly? Check them. Now, check yours with mine (show the teacher's copy). Fix any words you spelled incorrectly. Put a tally mark above the words you spelled correctly. Add a mark in the box for S.
>
> 5. (T): Rewrite your sentence with all of the corrections.
>
> 6. (T): Check for CUPS again. Put another mark in the boxes.
>
> 7. (T): Let's read the sentences.
>
> 8. (S) Read the sentences for fluency and automaticity.
>
> ***Please note:** Once students understand how to use CUPS, transition to letting them check their sentence independently before showing the teacher's copy.

Weekly Red Words

Materials Needed:
screen, red crayon, red word paper

Introduce on Tuesday, and practice daily. Use the Flip Chart for steps.

New:	Review:	New Read-Only:	Review Read-Only:
go	the, was, is, a, on, and, to, for	orange, white	

Steps for Teaching a New Red Word:

1. (T) States the word. (*go*)
2. (T&S) Use tokens to determine how many sounds are in the word. (/g/ /ō/; 2)
3. (T&S) Discuss how we would expect to spell each sound as the teacher writes the grapheme(s) correctly. Identify what is unexpected or irregular about the spelling of the word. It could also be expected, but the concept hasn't been taught yet.
4. (T&S) Discuss the etymology of the word, if appropriate (lexical words). Visit www. etymonline.com for more information on the word.
5. (T) Defines the word, and writes a sentence using the word.

6. (T) Writes the word on Red Word paper with the screen underneath, using red crayon.

7. (S) Write the word on Red Word paper with the screen underneath, using red crayon. (S) Show the word to the teacher.
(**NOTE:** The teacher should have students chunk the word if it has more than four letters.)

8. (T&S) Stand up, holding the Red Word in the nondominant hand. Armtap word while naming each letter. Then "underline" the word by sweeping left to right while stating the word, 3x. (**NOTE:** Left-handed students will place their left hand on their right wrist. They tap to their right shoulder. Underline from wrist to shoulder. Right-handed students place their right hand on their left shoulder. They tap to their left wrist. Underline shoulder to wrist.)

9. (T&S) Trace crayon bumps with the pointer finger while naming the letters, 3x.

10. (T&S) Place the screen over the paper and trace the word with the pointer finger while naming the letters, 3x.

11. (S) Turn paper over. With red crayon, write the word without the screen one time, and hold up the word for the teacher to check. (S) Write the word two more times.

12. (S) Write an original sentence in pencil and underline the Red Word with a red crayon. (**NOTE:** The sentence can also be dictated by the teacher while the student writes or dictated by the student while the teacher writes it.)

Review Ideas for Red Words:

- Sculpt the word using red Play-Doh or clay. Have students spell the word as they smash each letter.
- Print flashcards from IOG, and practice reading.
- Armtap the word to review.
- Cross-clap the word to review.
- Do Spelling Aerobics.

Fluency, Vocabulary, and Comprehension

- Incorporate fluency into your literacy lessons daily/weekly (minimum 30 min/week) by using Rapid Word Charts, IMSE Decodable Readers, words and sentences, Acadience Reading K-6 or DIBELS 8th Edition, repeated reading, and other activities.
- Incorporate vocabulary into your literacy lessons daily/weekly (minimum 50 min/week) by choosing 3-5 appropriate tier two words (can pull from rich literature or decodable readers). Teach the words through explicit, direct instruction using student-friendly definitions, word webs, vocabulary charts, illustrations, and other activities.
- Incorporate oral language comprehension into your literacy lessons daily/weekly (approximately 100 min/week). Comprehension instruction should be explicit, direct instruction that includes teacher modeling, guided practice, and independent practice. Plan ahead to build on students' background knowledge, language structures, verbal reasoning, and literacy knowledge.

Extension Activity Ideas

- Continue to add to the multi-sensory ABC book. Have students glue Tic Tacs (or another object) in the shape of the target letter.
- Have students compare and contrast a turtle and a tiger using a Venn Diagram.
- Make a paper tooth. Have students glue pictures of words that begin with the /t/ sound on the tooth.
- Divide students into teams of 3 and have them lie on the ground to form the target letter. Take pictures to hang around the classroom.
- Create the target letter out of green Play-Doh or clay.
- Have students use a bingo dauber to find the target letter on a page with various letters.
- Have students go on a "sound hunt" around the room or outside to find objects that begin with the target sound.
- Coding activity: Have students underline and label the letters in words or syllables with a "v" for vowels and a "c" for consonants. For example, when using the word *mom*, each letter should be underlined with the labels "cvc" underneath the word. This activity will help prepare students for decoding multisyllabic words later in the sequence.
- Visit IMSE's Orton-Gillingham's Pinterest page for more ideas.

Weekly Lesson Reminders

- Any of the above extension activities
- Daily practice writing the target letter (capital and lowercase) using a screen, green crayon, and house paper
- Practice writing the target letter using another medium (sand, paint, shaving cream, pudding, iPad app, etc.).
- Practice writing the target letter using age-appropriate paper and pencil.
- Daily practice with writing the weekly Red Word(s)
- Kilpatrick's "One-Minute Activities" for daily phonological awareness practice
- Zgonc's phonological awareness activities
- Listen to rich literature to work on oral language comprehension.
- Target letter practice sheets from IMSE's practice books and handwriting books
- Practice test on Thursday and test on Friday

Review for Concepts m–t

After teaching the first 9 concepts, the following words and sentences may be utilized for review. Teachers can dictate a different list (A, B, C, or D) and three sentences each day of the review. Teachers can spend up to a week on review *if needed*. If a review is not needed, this page can be skipped or partially utilized. Students can use IMSE workbooks or age-appropriate paper for recording their answers.

List A	List B	List C	List D
1. got	1. cat	1. lot	1. mat
2. Tad	2. dot	2. lam	2. lag
3. am	3. gag	3. tag	3. cat
4. dad	4. mad	4. dad	4. hot
5. tot	5. Cam	5. dog	5. gal
6. hog	6. lad	6. am	6. dot
7. mom	7. cot	7. log	7. hat
8. cod	8. gal	8. ham	8. mad
9. Hal	9. hag	9. Tom	9. cad
10. had	10. hot	10. mom	10. Al

Sentences:
1. Dad got <u>the</u> ham.
2. Mom <u>was</u> mad at Tom.
3. <u>Is the</u> log hot?
4. <u>The</u> hat had <u>a</u> tag.
5. Tad had <u>a</u> cat.
6. <u>The</u> lad <u>is</u> hot.
7. Tad got <u>a</u> hot ham.
8. <u>The</u> mat <u>was</u> hot.
9. Mom <u>is</u> mad at <u>the</u> cat.
10. <u>The</u> dog got hot.
11. <u>The</u> cot <u>was</u> hot.
12. <u>Is</u> Tad mad at Dad?

Notes:

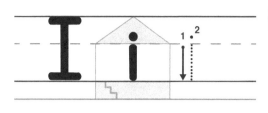

Ii as in igloo

Card Pack #10 Decodable Reader #2	
Object Ideas:	**Literature Ideas:**
Initial position: insect, igloo, itch, iguana, icky	▪ *India (On the Way to School)* by Obiols and Subi
	▪ *If You Give a Pig a Pancake* by Laura Numeroff
	▪ *I Wanna Iguana* by Karen Kaufman Orloff
Medial position: pig, fig, six, mix	▪ *The Legend of the Indian Paintbrush* by Tomie dePaola
	▪ *Itsy Bitsy Spider*

Notes

- Use the Comprehensive Flip Chart for the steps on how to teach each part of IMSE's Lesson Plan.
- Ii /ĭ/ is a voiced, continuant vowel. To produce vowel sounds, articulators hold a shape but do not obstruct air. Refer to the Vowel Valley on sound production.
- Make a vowel stick or tent.
- Teach the visual cue: scrunch nose and point.

Phonological Awareness:

Materials Needed:
tokens, sound boxes, one-minute activities, or Zgonc PA book

Use the PAST assessment to determine a starting point for instruction. Incorporate daily phonological awareness activities by using Zgonc's tiered activities and/or Kilpatrick's One-Minute Activities in *Equipped for Reading Success*.

Phonemic awareness warm-up: Use tokens (or letter tiles once concepts have been taught) and sound boxes to do a quick phonemic awareness activity that ties in with the new concept, if appropriate.

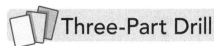

Three-Part Drill

Materials Needed:
review cards, sand, blending board, vowel tents or sticks

Do this at least 3x per week. Use the Flip Chart for steps. Include the new concept after Day 1.

- Include the Vowel Intensive with "a" and "o." Include "i" after it has been taught.

V	VC	CVC
a	ag, ap, ab	lat, cad, zan
e	et, en, eb	zeg, ren, med
i	ig, ib, im	lin, hib, fid
o	ob, ot, oz	rom, hob, cog
u	un, ud, ub	sup, pum, dut

- Below is a sample script. Remember to use all of the review concepts.

1. **Visual:**
   (T) Tell me the sounds you know for these letters.
   (S) /m/, /l/, etc.
   Alternative:
   (T) Tell me the names and sounds you know for these letters.
   (S) m says /m/, l says /l/, etc.

2. **Auditory/Kinesthetic:**
   (T) Eyes on me. Spell /m/. Repeat.
   (S) /m/ m says m.

3. **Blending:**
   (T) Tell me the sound for each letter as I point. Then blend the sounds together to read the word or syllable. Give me a thumbs up if it is a real word.
   (S) /mmm/ /ŏŏŏ/ /mmm/ *mom* (thumbs up)
   Alternative:
   (T) Watch me first. /mmm/ /ŏŏŏ/ /mmm/ *mom*
   (T) Do it with me. (T&S) /mmm/ /ŏŏŏ/ /mmm/ *mom*
   (T) Your turn. (S) /mmm/ /ŏŏŏ/ /mmm/ *mom* (thumbs up)

Vowel Intensive: Model the visual cue while calling out the sound. Students will do the visual cue as they repeat the sound. Students will then hold up the vowel tent while stating the letter name and sound.

- (T): Eyes on me. The sound is /ă/. Repeat.
- (S): /ă/ a says /ă/

Teaching a New Concept

Materials Needed:
concept card, screen, green crayon, object, sand, decodable readers, literature, P/G chart

Introduce on Monday, and practice daily.

1. (T) Reads alliteration sentence. (S) Identify the target sound.

   a. Icky Izzy is inside.

   (T) Reads the following sentence in which /ĭ/ is in the medial position. (S) Identify the target sound.

   b. Tim hid six wigs.

2. (T) Shows the new concept card.

   a. (T) Tells students the letter name and sound. Have (S) repeat, 3 times (i says /ĭ/).

   b. (T) Tells students that "i" is a vowel.

   c. (T) Tells students it is a voiced sound.

   d. (T) Asks students where they find "i" in the alphabet.

   e. (T) Uses mirrors to discuss the mouth, tongue, and teeth placement.

3. (T) Shows an object.

   a. (T) Allows students to manipulate the object and discuss prior knowledge. Reminds (S) that the object has the target sound spelled with the target letter.

4. (S) Brainstorm.

   a. Brainstorm words that have the target sound. (Accept all answers, but place incorrect answers in a "thought bubble" to discuss.) The brainstorming can be a teacher-directed activity if students need extra support. (**Note:** For short vowels, students can brainstorm word families or rhyming words containing the vowel sound.)

5. (T) Teaches Letter Formation. Use house paper to teach lowercase letters.

   a. (T) models with the solid letter. The letter "i" starts at the ceiling and goes to the floor. Dot it in the attic.

   b. Using the screen and green crayon, (T&S) trace the solid while saying, "i says /ĭ/" (3x).

   c. (T&S) use their finger to trace the solid while saying, "i says /ĭ/" (3x).

   d. (S) trace the dotted letter and complete the remainder of the row independently.

   e. (S) move to smaller house and repeat process if needed.

   f. Teach capital letters throughout the week using the same process. Capital letters go outside the house.

6. (T) Dictates target sound. (S) Practice in the sand or other medium.

   a. Practice writing the letter using a different medium, such as sand, shaving cream, finger paint, gel board, iPad app, air writing, etc.

   b. Do this while stating: i says /ĭ/, 3 times.

7. (T) Connects with literature.

   a. Have students signal when they hear the /ĭ/ sound for the first page or two.

   b. Read again for language comprehension.

c. Continue to work on language comprehension with rich literature throughout the week.

8. (S) Use decodable readers to practice the concepts learned.

    a. (S) Highlight words with the new concept. Read those words.

    b. (S) Highlight Red Words. Read those words.

    c. (S) Start reading the decodable reader.

    d. (S) Continue reading throughout the week.

    e. (S) Read a clean copy on Friday.

9. (T&S) Mark the Phoneme/Grapheme (P/G) chart by highlighting the target sound.

 ## Word Dictation

Materials Needed:
fingertapping hand, dictation paper, pencil

Create any syllables using the new concept and previously taught concepts. Practice daily. Use the Flip Chart to follow the steps for word dictation.

Day 1:	1. dig	2. mid	3. him	4. did	5. it
Day 2:	1. Tim	2. lit	3. mit	4. hid	5. lid
Day 3:	1. hit	2. lig	3. dim	4. dig	5. lid
Days 4-5:	Review prior words.				

Below is a sample script:

1. (T) States word: *mom*. Uses it in a sentence: My *mom* is a wonderful lady. (Pounds) *mom*. (T) Models fingertapping if needed: /m/ /ŏ/ /m/. (Pounds) *mom*.

2. (S) State while pounding: *mom*. (Fingertap) /m/ /ŏ/ /m/. (Pound) *mom*. Write the letters known for the sounds.

3. (T) When yours looks like mine, rewrite the word.

4. (S) Rewrite.

5. Repeat the process for each word.

6. (S) Read the list of words multiple times to build automaticity.

 ## Sentence Dictation

Red Words are underlined. Students can fingertap the green words. Use the Flip Chart to follow the steps for sentence dictation.

1. The log was lit.
2. Mom was mad at him.
3. Dad hid the hot cat.
4. The lad hit the lid.
5. Dot had the hot lid.

6. Tom <u>and</u> <u>I</u> did <u>like</u> <u>the</u> hat.
7. Tim did dig.
8. Tom got <u>the</u> lid.
9. Mom lit <u>the</u> log.
10. Did Dot hit <u>the</u> log?

- Below is a sample script for sentence dictation.

> 1. (T): Listen to the sentence. *Tad had a cat.*
> 2. (T): Listen while I pound the syllables. *Tad had a cat.*
> 3. (T): Pound it with me. (T&S): *Tad had a cat.*
> 4. (T): You pound the sentence. (S): *Tad had a cat.*
> 5. (T): Watch me as I point to the lines while stating the sentence. *Tad had a cat.*
> 6. (T): You point to the lines while stating the sentence.
> 7. (S): *Tad had a cat.*
> 8. (T): Now write the sentence. Fingertap if needed.

- Below is a sample script to check CUPS*.

> 1. (T): C stands for capitalization. Did you remember a capital letter at the beginning of your sentence? It's also a name. *Tad* would always be capitalized. If you forgot, fix it. If you remembered, put a tally mark above the capital letter. Add a mark in the box for C.
> 2. (T): U stands for understanding. Is your sentence neat? Reread it to yourself. Does it make sense? Could someone else understand it? If not, fix it. Add a mark in the box for U.
> 3. (T): P stands for punctuation. Did you remember a period at the end? If not, fix it. If you remembered, put a tally mark above the period. Add a mark in the box for P.
> 4. (T): S stands for spelling. Did you spell your words correctly? Check them. Now, check yours with mine (show the teacher's copy). Fix any words you spelled incorrectly. Put a tally mark above the words you spelled correctly. Add a mark in the box for S.
> 5. (T): Rewrite your sentence with all of the corrections.
> 6. (T): Check for CUPS again. Put another mark in the boxes.
> 7. (T): Let's read the sentences.
> 8. (S) Read the sentences for fluency and automaticity.
>
> **Please note:** Once students understand how to use CUPS, transition to letting them check their sentence independently before showing the teacher's copy.

Weekly Red Words

Materials Needed:
screen, red crayon, red word paper

Introduce on Tuesday, and practice daily. Use the Flip Chart for steps.

New:	Review:	New Read-Only:	Review Read-Only:
I, like	the, was, is, a, on, and, to, for, go	brown, stop	orange, white

Steps for Teaching a New Red Word:

1. (T) States the word. (*I*)
2. (T&S) Use tokens to determine how many sounds are in the word. (/ī/; 1)
3. (T&S) Discuss how we would expect to spell each sound as the teacher writes the grapheme(s) correctly. Identify what is unexpected or irregular about the spelling of the word. It could also be expected, but the concept hasn't been taught yet.
4. (T&S) Discuss the etymology of the word, if appropriate (lexical words). Visit www.etymonline.com for more information on the word.
5. (T) Defines the word, and writes a sentence using the word.
6. (T) Writes the word on Red Word paper with the screen underneath, using red crayon.
7. (S) Write the word on Red Word paper with the screen underneath, using red crayon. (S) Show the word to the teacher.
   (**NOTE:** The teacher should have students chunk the word if it has more than four letters.)
8. (T&S) Stand up, holding the Red Word in the nondominant hand. Armtap word while naming each letter. Then "underline" the word by sweeping left to right while stating the word, 3x. (**NOTE:** Left-handed students will place their left hand on their right wrist. They tap to their right shoulder. Underline from wrist to shoulder. Right-handed students place their right hand on their left shoulder. They tap to their left wrist. Underline shoulder to wrist.)
9. (T&S) Trace crayon bumps with the pointer finger while naming the letters, 3x.
10. (T&S) Place the screen over the paper and trace the word with the pointer finger while naming the letters, 3x.
11. (S) Turn paper over. With red crayon, write the word without the screen one time, and hold up the word for the teacher to check. (S) Write the word two more times.
12. (S) Write an original sentence in pencil and underline the Red Word with a red crayon. (**NOTE:** The sentence can also be dictated by the teacher while the student writes or dictated by the student while the teacher writes it.)
13. Repeat the steps for *like*. (/l/ /ī/ /k/; 3)

Review Ideas for Red Words:

- Sculpt the word using red Play-Doh or clay. Have students spell the word as they smash each letter.
- Print flashcards from IOG, and practice reading.
- Armtap the word to review.
- Cross-clap the word to review.
- Do Spelling Aerobics.

Fluency, Vocabulary, and Comprehension

- Incorporate fluency into your literacy lessons daily/weekly (minimum 30 min/week) by using Rapid Word Charts, IMSE Decodable Readers, words and sentences, Acadience Reading K-6 or DIBELS 8th Edition, repeated reading, and other activities.
- Incorporate vocabulary into your literacy lessons daily/weekly (minimum 50 min/week) by choosing 3-5 appropriate tier two words (can pull from rich literature or decodable readers). Teach the words through explicit, direct instruction using student-friendly definitions, word webs, vocabulary charts, illustrations, and other activities.
- Incorporate oral language comprehension into your literacy lessons daily/weekly (approximately 100 min/week). Comprehension instruction should be explicit, direct instruction that includes teacher modeling, guided practice, and independent practice. Plan ahead to build on students' background knowledge, language structures, verbal reasoning, and literacy knowledge.

Extension Activity Ideas

- Continue to add to the multi-sensory ABC book. Have students glue insect pictures or stickers (or another object) in the shape of the target letter.
- Have students compare and contrast an iguana and a pig using a Venn Diagram.
- Make a paper igloo. Have students glue pictures of words that begin with the /ĭ/ sound on the igloo.
- Divide students into teams of 3 and have them lie on the ground to form the target letter. Take pictures to hang around the classroom.
- Create the target letter out of green Play-Doh or clay.
- Have students use a bingo dauber to find the target letter on a page with various letters.
- Have students go on a "sound hunt" around the room or outside to find objects that begin with the target sound.
- Coding activity: Have students underline and label the letters in words or syllables with a "v" for vowels and a "c" for consonants. For example, when using the word *mom*, each letter should be underlined with the labels "cvc" underneath the word. This activity will help prepare students for decoding multisyllabic words later in the sequence.
- Visit IMSE's Orton-Gillingham's Pinterest page for more ideas.

Weekly Lesson Reminders

- Any of the above extension activities
- Practice writing the target letter (capital and lowercase) using a screen, green crayon, and house paper.
- Practice writing the target letter using another medium (sand, paint, shaving cream, pudding, iPad app, etc.).
- Practice writing the target letter using age-appropriate paper and pencil.
- Daily practice with writing the weekly Red Word(s)
- Kilpatrick's "One-Minute Activities" for daily phonological awareness practice
- Zgonc's phonological awareness activities
- Listen to rich literature to work on oral language comprehension.
- Target letter practice sheets from IMSE's practice books and handwriting books
- Practice test on Thursday and test on Friday

Jj as in jam

Card Pack #11   Decodable Reader #3

Object Ideas:	Literature Ideas:
jelly beans, jam, Jell-O, jacket, jump rope, jack-o'-lantern, jelly, jumping jacks, jacks, juggle, juice	▪ *Jump, Frog, Jump!* by Robert Kalan ▪ *The Jacket I Wear in the Snow* by Shirley Neitzel ▪ *Johnny Appleseed* ▪ *Jack and the Beanstalk* ▪ *Jamberry* by Bruce Degen ▪ *Bread and Jam for Frances* by Russell Hoban ▪ *Norma Jean, Jumping Bean* by Joanna Cole ▪ *Just Like Me* by Vanessa Brantley-Newton ▪ *Jabari Jumps* by Gaia Cornwall ▪ *Julian Is a Mermaid* by Jessica Love

Notes

- Use the Comprehensive Flip Chart for the steps on how to teach each part of IMSE's Lesson Plan.
- Jj /j/ is a voiced consonant that is an affricate. It is formed with the lips forward and tongue pulled back on the roof of the mouth.
- Keep "j" in the initial position. English words do not end with "j."

Phonological Awareness:

Materials Needed:
tokens, sound boxes, one-minute activities, or Zgonc PA book

Use the PAST assessment to determine a starting point for instruction. Incorporate daily phonological awareness activities by using Zgonc's tiered activities and/or Kilpatrick's One-Minute Activities in *Equipped for Reading Success.*

Phonemic awareness warm-up: Use tokens (or letter tiles once concepts have been taught) and sound boxes to do a quick phonemic awareness activity that ties in with the new concept, if appropriate.

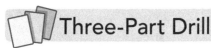

Three-Part Drill

Materials Needed:
review cards, sand, blending board, vowel tents or sticks

Do this at least 3x per week. Use the Flip Chart for steps. Include the new concept after Day 1.

- Include the Vowel Intensive with "a," "i," and "o."

V	VC	CVC
a	ag, ap, ab	lat, cad, zan
e	et, en, eb	zeg, ren, med
i	ig, ib, im	lin, hib, fid
o	ob, ot, oz	rom, hob, cog
u	un, ud, ub	sup, pum, dut

- Below is a sample script. Remember to use all of the review concepts.

1. **Visual:**
   (T) Tell me the sounds you know for these letters.
   (S) /m/, /l/, etc.
   Alternative:
   (T) Tell me the names and sounds you know for these letters.
   (S) m says /m/, l says /l/, etc.

2. **Auditory/Kinesthetic:**
   (T) Eyes on me. Spell /m/. Repeat.
   (S) /m/ m says m.

3. **Blending:**
   (T) Tell me the sound for each letter as I point. Then blend the sounds together to read the word or syllable. Give me a thumbs up if it is a real word.
   (S) /mmm/ /ŏŏŏ/ /mmm/ *mom* (thumbs up)
   Alternative:
   (T) Watch me first. /mmm/ /ŏŏŏ/ /mmm/ *mom*
   (T) Do it with me. (T&S) /mmm/ /ŏŏŏ/ /mmm/ *mom*
   (T) Your turn. (S) /mmm/ /ŏŏŏ/ /mmm/ *mom* (thumbs up)

Vowel Intensive: Model the visual cue while calling out the sound. Students will do the visual cue as they repeat the sound. Students will then hold up the vowel tent while stating the letter name and sound.

- (T): Eyes on me. The sound is /ă/. Repeat.
- (S): /ă/ a says /ă/

Teaching a New Concept

Materials Needed:
concept card, screen, green crayon, object, sand, decodable readers, literature, P/G chart

Introduce on Monday, and practice daily.

1. (T) Reads alliteration sentences. (S) Identify the target sound.
   a. Jed jogs jollily.
   b. Joking Jim joined jumping Joan.

2. (T) Shows the new concept card.
   a. (T) Tells students the letter name and sound. Have (S) repeat, 3 times (j says /j/).
   b. (T) Tells students that "j" is a consonant.
   c. (T) Tells students it is a voiced sound.
   d. (T) Asks students where they find "j" in the alphabet.
   e. (T) Uses mirrors to discuss the mouth, tongue, and teeth placement.

3. (T) Shows an object.
   a. (T) Allows students to manipulate the object and discuss prior knowledge. Reminds (S) that the object has the target sound spelled with the target letter.

4. (S) Brainstorm.
   a. Brainstorm words that have the target sound. (Accept all answers, but place incorrect answers in a "thought bubble" to discuss.) The brainstorming can be a teacher-directed activity if students need extra support.

5. (T) Teaches Letter Formation. Use house paper to teach lowercase letters.
   a. (T) models with the solid letter. The letter "j" starts in the middle of the house and goes into the basement and curves, then stops. Dot it in the attic.
   b. Using the screen and green crayon, (T&S) trace the solid while saying, "j says /j/" (3x).
   c. (T&S) use their finger to trace the solid while saying, "j says /j/" (3x).
   d. (S) trace the dotted letter and complete the remainder of the row independently.
   e. (S) move to smaller house and repeat process if needed.
   f. Teach capital letters throughout the week using the same process. Capital letters go outside the house.

6. (T) Dictates target sound. (S) Practice in the sand or other medium.
   a. Practice writing the letter using a different medium, such as sand, shaving cream, finger paint, gel board, iPad app, air writing, etc.
   b. Do this while stating: j says /j/, 3 times.

7. (T) Connects with literature.
   a. Have students signal when they hear the /j/ sound for the first page or two.
   b. Read again for language comprehension.
   c. Continue to work on language comprehension with rich literature throughout the week.

8. (S) Use decodable readers to practice the concepts learned.

a. (S) Highlight words with the new concept. Read those words.

b. (S) Highlight Red Words. Read those words.

c. (S) Start reading the decodable reader.

d. (S) Continue reading throughout the week.

e. (S) Read a clean copy on Friday.

9. (T&S) Mark the Phoneme/Grapheme (P/G) chart by highlighting the target sound.

 ## Word Dictation

Materials Needed:
fingertapping hand, dictation paper, pencil

Create any syllables using the new concept and previously taught concepts. Practice daily. Use the Flip Chart to follow the steps for word dictation.

Day 1:	1. jam	2. did	3. jig	4. jot	5. jog
Day 2:	1. jog	2. lid	3. jam	4. jig	5. Jim
Day 3:	1. Jim	2. jot	3. dig	4. jam	5. jag
Days 4-5:	Review prior words.				

Below is a sample script:

1. (T) States word: *mom*. Uses it in a sentence: My *mom* is a wonderful lady. (Pounds) *mom*. (T) Models fingertapping if needed: /m/ /ŏ/ /m/. (Pounds) *mom*.

2. (S) State while pounding: *mom*. (Fingertap) /m/ /ŏ/ /m/. (Pound) *mom*. Write the letters known for the sounds.

3. (T) When yours looks like mine, rewrite the word.

4. (S) Rewrite.

5. Repeat the process for each word.

6. (S) Read the list of words multiple times to build automaticity.

 ## Sentence Dictation

Red Words are underlined. Students can fingertap the green words. Use the Flip Chart to follow the steps for sentence dictation.

1. Mom and Tom jog.

2. I did a jig.

3. Did Dad jog to the log?

4. Jim had the hat.

5. Will the cat and dog jog?

6. Will the lid go on the jam?

7. Did Jim dig a dam?

8. Tom did a jig for Mom.

© IMSE 2022

9. Tom did jig <u>and</u> jog.

10. Did Tim jam <u>the</u> log?

- Below is a sample script for sentence dictation.

> 1. (T): Listen to the sentence. *Tad had a cat.*
> 2. (T): Listen while I pound the syllables. *Tad had a cat.*
> 3. (T): Pound it with me. (T&S): *Tad had a cat.*
> 4. (T): You pound the sentence. (S): *Tad had a cat.*
> 5. (T): Watch me as I point to the lines while stating the sentence. *Tad had a cat.*
> 6. (T): You point to the lines while stating the sentence.
> 7. (S): *Tad had a cat.*
> 8. (T): Now write the sentence. Fingertap if needed.

- Below is a sample script to check CUPS*.

> 1. (T): C stands for capitalization. Did you remember a capital letter at the beginning of your sentence? It's also a name. *Tad* would always be capitalized. If you forgot, fix it. If you remembered, put a tally mark above the capital letter. Add a mark in the box for C.
> 2. (T): U stands for understanding. Is your sentence neat? Reread it to yourself. Does it make sense? Could someone else understand it? If not, fix it. Add a mark in the box for U.
> 3. (T): P stands for punctuation. Did you remember a period at the end? If not, fix it. If you remembered, put a tally mark above the period. Add a mark in the box for P.
> 4. (T): S stands for spelling. Did you spell your words correctly? Check them. Now, check yours with mine (show the teacher's copy). Fix any words you spelled incorrectly. Put a tally mark above the words you spelled correctly. Add a mark in the box for S.
> 5. (T): Rewrite your sentence with all of the corrections.
> 6. (T): Check for CUPS again. Put another mark in the boxes.
> 7. (T): Let's read the sentences.
> 8. (S) Read the sentences for fluency and automaticity.
>
> ***Please note:*** Once students understand how to use CUPS, transition to letting them check their sentence independently before showing the teacher's copy.

Weekly Red Words

Materials Needed:
screen, red crayon, red word paper

Introduce on Tuesday, and practice daily. Use the Flip Chart for steps.

New:	Review:	New Read-Only:	Review Read-Only:
of, will	the, was, is, a, on, and, to, for, go, I, like	said	orange, white, brown, stop

Steps for Teaching a New Red Word:

1. (T) States the word. (*of*)

2. (T&S) Use tokens to determine how many sounds are in the word. (/ŭ/ /v/; 2)

3. (T&S) Discuss how we would expect to spell each sound as the teacher writes the grapheme(s) correctly. Identify what is unexpected or irregular about the spelling of the word. It could also be expected, but the concept hasn't been taught yet.

4. (T&S) Discuss the etymology of the word, if appropriate (lexical words). Visit www.etymonline.com for more information on the word.

5. (T) Defines the word, and writes a sentence using the word.

6. (T) Writes the word on Red Word paper with the screen underneath, using red crayon.

7. (S) Write the word on Red Word paper with the screen underneath, using red crayon. (S) Show the word to the teacher.
   (**NOTE:** The teacher should have students chunk the word if it has more than four letters.)

8. (T&S) Stand up, holding the Red Word in the nondominant hand. Armtap word while naming each letter. Then "underline" the word by sweeping left to right while stating the word, 3x. (**NOTE:** Left-handed students will place their left hand on their right wrist. They tap to their right shoulder. Underline from wrist to shoulder. Right-handed students place their right hand on their left shoulder. They tap to their left wrist. Underline shoulder to wrist.)

9. (T&S) Trace crayon bumps with the pointer finger while naming the letters, 3x.

10. (T&S) Place the screen over the paper and trace the word with the pointer finger while naming the letters, 3x.

11. (S) Turn paper over. With red crayon, write the word without the screen one time, and hold up the word for the teacher to check. (S) Write the word two more times.

12. (S) Write an original sentence in pencil and underline the Red Word with a red crayon. (**NOTE:** The sentence can also be dictated by the teacher while the student writes or dictated by the student while the teacher writes it.)

13. Repeat the steps for *will*. (/w/ /ĭ/ /l/; 3)

© IMSE 2022

Review Ideas for Red Words:

- Sculpt the word using red Play-Doh or clay. Have students spell the word as they smash each letter.
- Print flashcards from IOG, and practice reading.
- Armtap the word to review.
- Cross-clap the word to review.
- Do Spelling Aerobics.

Fluency, Vocabulary, and Comprehension

- Incorporate fluency into your literacy lessons daily/weekly (minimum 30 min/week) by using Rapid Word Charts, IMSE Decodable Readers, words and sentences, Acadience Reading K-6 or DIBELS 8th Edition, repeated reading, and other activities.
- Incorporate vocabulary into your literacy lessons daily/weekly (minimum 50 min/week) by choosing 3-5 appropriate tier two words (can pull from rich literature or decodable readers). Teach the words through explicit, direct instruction using student-friendly definitions, word webs, vocabulary charts, illustrations, and other activities.
- Incorporate oral language comprehension into your literacy lessons daily/weekly (approximately 100 min/week). Comprehension instruction should be explicit, direct instruction that includes teacher modeling, guided practice, and independent practice. Plan ahead to build on students' background knowledge, language structures, verbal reasoning, and literacy knowledge.

Extension Activity Ideas

- Continue to add to the multi-sensory ABC book. Have students glue jelly beans (or another object) in the shape of the target letter.
- Have students compare and contrast jelly and jelly beans using a Venn Diagram.
- Make a paper jack-o'-lantern. Have students glue pictures of words that begin with the /j/ sound on the jack-o'-lantern.
- Divide students into teams of 3 and have them lie on the ground to form the target letter. Take pictures to hang around the classroom.
- Create the target letter out of green Play-Doh or clay.
- Have students use a bingo dauber to find the target letter on a page with various letters.
- Have students go on a "sound hunt" around the room or outside to find objects that begin with the target sound.
- Coding activity: Have students underline and label the letters in words or syllables with a "v" for vowels and a "c" for consonants. For example, when using the word *mom*, each letter should be underlined with the labels "cvc" underneath the word. This activity will help prepare students for decoding multisyllabic words later in the sequence.
- Visit IMSE's Orton-Gillingham's Pinterest page for more ideas.

Weekly Lesson Reminders

- Any of the above extension activities
- Practice writing the target letter (capital and lowercase) using a screen, green crayon, and house paper.
- Practice writing the target letter using another medium (sand, paint, shaving cream, pudding, iPad app, etc.).
- Practice writing the target letter using age-appropriate paper and pencil.
- Daily practice with writing the weekly Red Word(s)
- Kilpatrick's "One-Minute Activities" for daily phonological awareness practice
- Zgonc's phonological awareness activities
- Listen to rich literature to work on oral language comprehension.
- Target letter practice sheets from IMSE's practice books and handwriting books
- Practice test on Thursday and test on Friday

Kk as in kite

Card Pack #12 Decodable Reader #4	
Object Ideas:	**Literature Ideas:**
kite, ketchup, kick, kitten, king, key, kiwi	▪ *The Kissing Hand* by Audrey Penn ▪ *Ella McKeen, Kickball Queen* by Beth Mills ▪ *The One in the Middle Is the Green Kangaroo* by Judy Blume ▪ *A Computer Called Katherine: How Katherine Johnson Helped Put America on the Moon* by Suzanne Slade ▪ *One Kitten for Kim* by Adelaide Holl ▪ *The King of Kindergarten* by Derrick Barnes ▪ *Mommy's Khimar* by Jamilah Thompkins-Bigelow

Notes

- Use the Comprehensive Flip Chart for the steps on how to teach each part of IMSE's Lesson Plan.
- Kk /k/ is an unvoiced, stopped consonant sound. This is formed with the lips parted and the back of the tongue on the back roof of the mouth.
- Draw the cat/kite image to help teach the spelling rule.

- Show the cat/kite poster.
- From now on, your students will know 2 ways to spell the /k/ sound during the Auditory/Kinesthetic part of the Three-Part Drill. (T): You know 2 ways to spell this. Spell /k/. Repeat. (S): /k/ c says /k/ and k says /k/.
- Keep "k" in the initial position on the blending board at first. At the end of a one-syllable word with one short vowel, the /k/ sound is spelled "-ck." The "k" can go at the end of the blending board after vowel teams are introduced for words like *sneak*.

c/k/   k/k/

cat, cot, cut, clap   kit, kept, smoke

Phonological Awareness:

Materials Needed:
tokens, sound boxes, one-minute activities, or Zgonc PA book

Use the PAST assessment to determine a starting point for instruction. Incorporate daily phonological awareness activities by using Zgonc's tiered activities and/or Kilpatrick's One-Minute Activities in *Equipped for Reading Success*.

Phonemic awareness warm-up: Use tokens (or letter tiles once concepts have been taught) and sound boxes to do a quick phonemic awareness activity that ties in with the new concept, if appropriate.

Three-Part Drill

Materials Needed:
review cards, sand, blending board, vowel tents or sticks

Do this at least 3x per week. Use the Flip Chart for steps. Include the new concept after Day 1.

- Include the Vowel Intensive with "a," "i," and "o."

V	VC	CVC
a	ag, ap, ab	lat, cad, zan
e	et, en, eb	zeg, ren, med
i	ig, ib, im	lin, hib, fid
o	ob, ot, oz	rom, hob, cog
u	un, ud, ub	sup, pum, dut

- Below is a sample script. Remember to use all of the review concepts.

1. **Visual:**
   (T) Tell me the sounds you know for these letters.
   (S) /m/, /l/, etc.
   Alternative:
   (T) Tell me the names and sounds you know for these letters.
   (S) m says /m/, l says /l/, etc.

2. **Auditory/Kinesthetic:**
   (T) Eyes on me. Spell /m/. Repeat
   (S) /m/ m says m.

3. **Blending:**
   (T) Tell me the sound for each letter as I point. Then blend the sounds together to read the word or syllable. Give me a thumbs up if it is a real word.
   (S) /mmm/ /ŏŏŏ/ /mmm/ *mom* (thumbs up)
   Alternative:
   (T) Watch me first. /mmm/ /ŏŏŏ/ /mmm/ *mom*
   (T) Do it with me. (T&S) /mmm/ /ŏŏŏ/ /mmm/ *mom*
   (T) Your turn. (S) /mmm/ /ŏŏŏ/ /mmm/ *mom* (thumbs up)

Vowel Intensive: Model the visual cue while calling out the sound. Students will do the visual cue as they repeat the sound. Students will then hold up the vowel tent while stating the letter name and sound.

- (T): Eyes on me. The sound is /ă/. Repeat.
- (S): /ă/ a says /ă/

Teaching a New Concept

Materials Needed:
concept card, screen, green crayon, object, sand, decodable readers, literature, P/G chart

Introduce on Monday, and practice daily.

1. (T) Reads alliteration sentences. (S) Identify the target sound.
   a. Kit kept Kim's kangaroo kite.
   b. Kip kissed Kathy's koala.
2. (T) Shows the new concept card.
   a. (T) Tells students the letter name and sound. Have (S) repeat, 3 times (k says /k/).
   b. (T) Tells students that "k" is a consonant.
   c. (T) Tells students it is an unvoiced sound.
   d. (T) Asks students where they find "k" in the alphabet.
   e. (T) Uses mirrors to discuss the mouth, tongue, and teeth placement.
3. (T) Shows an object.
   a. (T) Allows students to manipulate the object and discuss prior knowledge. Reminds (S) that the object has the target sound spelled with the target letter.
   b. (T) Uses the cat/kite poster to teach the c/k rule.

4. (S) Brainstorm.
   a. Brainstorm words that have the target sound. (Accept all answers, but place incorrect answers in a "thought bubble" to discuss.) The brainstorming can be a teacher-directed activity if students need extra support.

5. (T) Teaches Letter Formation. Use house paper to teach lowercase letters.
   a. (T) models with the solid letter. The letter "k" starts in the attic and goes to the floor. Then start at the ceiling, kiss the line, and come back to the floor.
   b. Using the screen and green crayon, (T&S) trace the solid while saying, "k says /k/" (3x).
   c. (T&S) use their finger to trace the solid while saying, "k says /k/" (3x).
   d. (S) trace the dotted letter and complete the remainder of the row independently.
   e. (S) move to smaller house and repeat process if needed.
   f. Teach capital letters throughout the week using the same process. Capital letters go outside the house.

6. (T) Dictates target sound. (S) Practice in the sand or other medium.
   a. Practice writing the letter using a different medium, such as sand, shaving cream, finger paint, gel board, iPad app, air writing, etc.
   b. Do this while stating: c says /k/; k says /k/ (3 times). (Because this is the second spelling learned for /k/, students should write all known spellings for the sound [i.e., c, k]).

7. (T) Connects with literature.
   a. Have students signal when they hear the /k/ sound for the first page or two.
   b. Read again for language comprehension.
   c. Continue to work on language comprehension with rich literature throughout the week.

8. (S) Use decodable readers to practice the concepts learned.
   a. (S) Highlight words with the new concept. Read those words.
   b. (S) Highlight Red Words. Read those words.
   c. (S) Start reading the decodable reader.
   d. (S) Continue reading throughout the week.
   e. (S) Read a clean copy on Friday.

9. (T&S) Mark the Phoneme/Grapheme (P/G) chart by highlighting the target sound.

Word Dictation

Materials Needed:
fingertapping hand, dictation paper, pencil

Create any syllables using the new concept and previously taught concepts. Practice daily. Use the Flip Chart to follow the steps for word dictation.

Day 1:	1. kid	2. cat	3. kit	4. cad	5. cod
Day 2:	1. Kim	2. cod	3. kid	4. gag	5. cat
Day 3:	1. Cam	2. Kim	3. cad	4. kit	5. jam
Days 4-5:	Review prior words.				

Below is a sample script:

> 1. (T) States word: *mom*. Uses it in a sentence: My *mom* is a wonderful lady. (Pounds) *mom*. (T) Models fingertapping if needed: /m/ /ŏ/ /m/. (Pounds) *mom*.
> 2. (S) State while pounding: *mom*. (Fingertap) /m/ /ŏ/ /m/. (Pound) *mom*. Write the letters known for the sounds.
> 3. (T) When yours looks like mine, rewrite the word.
> 4. (S) Rewrite.
> 5. Repeat the process for each word.
> 6. (S) Read the list of words multiple times to build automaticity.
>
> **NOTE:** To handle miscues with the /k/ sound, ask students to look at the letter that comes after the /k/ sound. Refer to the poster. If the next letter is "a," "o," "u," or a consonant, the /k/ sound is spelled with a "c." If the next letter is an "i" or "e," the /k/ sound is spelled with a "k."

Sentence Dictation

Red Words are underlined. Students can fingertap the green words. Use the Flip Chart to follow the steps for sentence dictation.

1. The kid was mad.
2. Did Dad and Kim jig and jog?
3. The kit had ham and jam.
4. Mom and Kim hid the kit.
5. The kid got jam on the hat.
6. Kim will get the hot dog for Tad.
7. The kit is for Mom.
8. I like the hat for Kit.
9. Kim did get the dog.
10. The kid had a tag on the mat.

- Below is a sample script for sentence dictation.

> 1. (T): Listen to the sentence. *Tad had a cat.*
> 2. (T): Listen while I pound the syllables. *Tad had a cat.*
> 3. (T): Pound it with me. (T&S): *Tad had a cat.*
> 4. (T): You pound the sentence. (S): *Tad had a cat.*
> 5. (T): Watch me as I point to the lines while stating the sentence. *Tad had a cat.*
> 6. (T): You point to the lines while stating the sentence.
> 7. (S): *Tad had a cat.*
> 8. (T): Now write the sentence. Fingertap if needed.

- Below is a sample script to check CUPS*.

1. (T): C stands for capitalization. Did you remember a capital letter at the beginning of your sentence? It's also a name. *Tad* would always be capitalized. If you forgot, fix it. If you remembered, put a tally mark above the capital letter. Add a mark in the box for C.

2. (T): U stands for understanding. Is your sentence neat? Reread it to yourself. Does it make sense? Could someone else understand it? If not, fix it. Add a mark in the box for U.

3. (T): P stands for punctuation. Did you remember a period at the end? If not, fix it. If you remembered, put a tally mark above the period. Add a mark in the box for P.

4. (T): S stands for spelling. Did you spell your words correctly? Check them. Now, check yours with mine (show the teacher's copy). Fix any words you spelled incorrectly. Put a tally mark above the words you spelled correctly. Add a mark in the box for S.

5. (T): Rewrite your sentence with all of the corrections.

6. (T): Check for CUPS again. Put another mark in the boxes.

7. (T): Let's read the sentences.

8. (S) Read the sentences for fluency and automaticity.

*Please note:** Once students understand how to use CUPS, transition to letting them check their sentence independently before showing the teacher's copy.

Weekly Red Words

Materials Needed:
screen, red crayon, red word paper

Introduce on Tuesday, and practice daily. Use the Flip Chart for steps.

New:	Review:	New Read-Only:	Review Read-Only:
get, no	the, was, is, a, on, and, to, for, go, I, like, of, will	red, see	orange, white, brown, stop, said

Steps for Teaching a New Red Word:

1. (T) States the word. (*get*)

2. (T&S) Use tokens to determine how many sounds are in the word. (/g/ /ĕ/ /t/; 3)

3. (T&S) Discuss how we would expect to spell each sound as the teacher writes the grapheme(s) correctly. Identify what is unexpected or irregular about the spelling of the word. It could also be expected, but the concept hasn't been taught yet.

4. (T&S) Discuss the etymology of the word, if appropriate (lexical words). Visit www.etymonline.com for more information on the word.

5. (T) Defines the word, and writes a sentence using the word.

6. (T) Writes the word on Red Word paper with the screen underneath, using red crayon.

7. (S) Write the word on Red Word paper with the screen underneath, using red crayon. (S) Show the word to the teacher.
(**NOTE:** The teacher should have students chunk the word if it has more than four letters.)

8. (T&S) Stand up, holding the Red Word in the nondominant hand. Armtap word while naming each letter. Then "underline" the word by sweeping left to right while stating the word, 3x. (**NOTE:** Left-handed students will place their left hand on their right wrist. They tap to their right shoulder. Underline from wrist to shoulder. Right-handed students place their right hand on their left shoulder. They tap to their left wrist. Underline shoulder to wrist.)

9. (T&S) Trace crayon bumps with the pointer finger while naming the letters, 3x.

10. (T&S) Place the screen over the paper and trace the word with the pointer finger while naming the letters, 3x.

11. (S) Turn paper over. With red crayon, write the word without the screen one time, and hold up the word for the teacher to check. (S) Write the word two more times.

12. (S) Write an original sentence in pencil and underline the Red Word with a red crayon. (**NOTE:** The sentence can also be dictated by the teacher while the student writes or dictated by the student while the teacher writes it.)

13. Repeat the steps for *no.* (/n/ /ō/; 2)

Review Ideas for Red Words:

- Sculpt the word using red Play-Doh or clay. Have students spell the word as they smash each letter.
- Print flashcards from IOG, and practice reading.
- Armtap the word to review.
- Cross-clap the word to review.
- Do Spelling Aerobics.

Fluency, Vocabulary, and Comprehension

- Incorporate fluency into your literacy lessons daily/weekly (minimum 30 min/week) by using Rapid Word Charts, IMSE Decodable Readers, words and sentences, Acadience Reading K-6 or DIBELS 8th Edition, repeated reading, and other activities.
- Incorporate vocabulary into your literacy lessons daily/weekly (minimum 50 min/week) by choosing 3-5 appropriate tier two words (can pull from rich literature or decodable readers). Teach the words through explicit, direct instruction using student-friendly definitions, word webs, vocabulary charts, illustrations, and other activities.
- Incorporate oral language comprehension into your literacy lessons daily/weekly (approximately 100 min/week). Comprehension instruction should be explicit, direct instruction that includes teacher modeling, guided practice, and independent practice. Plan ahead to build on students' background knowledge, language structures, verbal reasoning, and literacy knowledge.

Extension Activity Ideas

- Continue to add to the multi-sensory ABC book. Have students glue kites (or another object) in the shape of the target letter.
- Teach students the following rhyme: "C goes with a, o, and u. K goes with the other two."
- Have students compare and contrast a koala and a kangaroo using a Venn Diagram. ***Note:** Koala and kangaroo are Aboriginal words. Therefore, they do not fit the c/k rule, which is a rule for English spelling.
- Make a paper kite. Have students glue pictures of words that begin with the /k/ sound on the kite.
- Divide students into teams of 3 and have them lie on the ground to form the target letter. Take pictures to hang around the classroom.
- Create the target letter out of green Play-Doh or clay.
- Have students use a bingo dauber to find the target letter on a page with various letters.
- Have students go on a "sound hunt" around the room or outside to find objects that begin with the target sound.
- Coding activity: Have students underline and label the letters in words or syllables with a "v" for vowels and a "c" for consonants. For example, when using the word *mom*, each letter should be underlined with the labels "cvc" underneath the word. This activity will help prepare students for decoding multisyllabic words later in the sequence.
- Visit IMSE's Orton-Gillingham's Pinterest page for more ideas.

Weekly Lesson Reminders

- Any of the above extension activities
- Practice writing the target letter (capital and lowercase) using a screen, green crayon, and house paper.
- Practice writing the target letter using another medium (sand, paint, shaving cream, pudding, iPad app, etc.).
- Practice writing the target letter using age-appropriate paper and pencil.
- Daily practice with writing the weekly Red Word(s)
- Kilpatrick's "One-Minute Activities" for daily phonological awareness practice
- Zgonc's phonological awareness activities
- Listen to rich literature to work on oral language comprehension.
- Target letter practice sheets from IMSE's practice books and handwriting books
- Practice test on Thursday and test on Friday

Pp as in pig

Card Pack #13 Decodable Reader #5	
Object Ideas:	**Literature Ideas:**
pig, pancake, popcorn, penguin, penny, polar bear, pie, pencil, pizza, Pop-Tart, pinecone, park, pasta, polygon, parallel, perpendicular, pumpkin, pan, play putty, ping-pong	<ul><li>*Peter's Chair* by Ezra Jack Keats</li><li>*Pink Is for Boys* by Robb Pearlman</li><li>*Pet Show!* by Ezra Jack Keats</li><li>*Mama Panya's Pancakes: A Village Tale From Kenya* by Mary and Rich Chamberlin</li><li>*If You Give a Pig a Pancake* by Laura Numeroff</li><li>*The Popcorn Book* by Tomie dePaola</li><li>*The Biggest Pumpkin Ever* by Steven Kroll</li><li>*The Polar Express* by Chris Van Allsburg</li><li>*Mr. Popper's Penguins* by Florence and Richard Atwater</li><li>*Lilly's Purple Plastic Purse* by Kevin Henkes</li><li>*The True Story of the Three Little Pigs* by Jon Scieszka</li><li>*Don't Let the Pigeon Drive the Bus!* by Mo Willems</li><li>*Lubna and Pebble* by Wendy Meddour</li><li>*The Piñata That the Farm Maiden Hung* by Samantha R. Vamos</li><li>*The Paper Kingdom* by Helena Ku Rhee</li></ul>

Notes

- Use the Comprehensive Flip Chart for the steps on how to teach each part of IMSE's Lesson Plan.
- Pp /p/ is an unvoiced, stopped consonant sound. This is formed with the lips together and a pop of air.
- If needed, the card pack contains an extra "p" so it can be used in both the initial and final position on the blending board.

Phonological Awareness:

Materials Needed:
tokens, sound boxes, one-minute activities, or Zgonc PA book

Use the PAST assessment to determine a starting point for instruction. Incorporate daily phonological awareness activities by using Zgonc's tiered activities and/or Kilpatrick's One-Minute Activities in *Equipped for Reading Success.*

Phonemic awareness warm-up: Use tokens (or letter tiles once concepts have been taught) and sound boxes to do a quick phonemic awareness activity that ties in with the new concept, if appropriate.

Three-Part Drill

Materials Needed:
review cards, sand, blending board, vowel tents or sticks

Do this at least 3x per week. Use the Flip Chart for steps. Include the new concept after Day 1.

- Include the Vowel Intensive with "a," "i," and "o."

V	VC	CVC
a	ag, ap, ab	lat, cad, zan
e	et, en, eb	zeg, ren, med
i	ig, ib, im	lin, hib, fid
o	ob, ot, oz	rom, hob, cog
u	un, ud, ub	sup, pum, dut

- Below is a sample script now that students know more than one way to spell a concept. Remember to use all of the review concepts.

1. **Visual:**
   (T) Tell me the sounds you know for these letters.
   (S) /m/, /l/, etc.
   Alternative:
   (T) Tell me the names and sounds you know for these letters.
   (S) m says /m/, l says /l/, etc.

2. **Auditory/Kinesthetic:**
   (T) You know two ways to spell this. (S) split trays. (T) Eyes on me.
   Spell /k/. Repeat.
   (S) /k/ c says /k/; k says /k/

3. **Blending:**
   (T) Tell me the sound for each letter as I point. Then blend the sounds together to read the word or syllable. Give me a thumbs up if it is a real word.
   (S) /mmm/ /ŏŏŏ/ /mmm/ *mom* (thumbs up)
   Alternative:
   (T) Watch me first. /mmm/ /ŏŏŏ/ /mmm/ *mom*
   (T) Do it with me. (T&S) /mmm/ /ŏŏŏ/ /mmm/ *mom*
   (T) Your turn. (S) /mmm/ /ŏŏŏ/ /mmm/ *mom* (thumbs up)

   *Vowel Intensive: Model the visual cue while calling out the sound. Students will do the visual cue as they repeat the sound. Students will then hold up the vowel tent while stating the letter name and sound.
   - (T): Eyes on me. The sound is /ă/. Repeat.
   - (S): /ă/ a says /ă/

Teaching a New Concept

Materials Needed:
concept card, screen, green crayon, object, sand, decodable readers, literature, P/G chart

Introduce on Monday, and practice daily.

1. (T) Reads alliteration sentences. (S) Identify the target sound.
   a. Peter Piper picked a peck of pickled peppers.
   b. Pip placed pears perfectly.
2. (T) Shows the new concept card.
   a. (T) Tells students the letter name and sound. Have (S) repeat, 3 times (p says /p/).
   b. (T) Tells students that "p" is a consonant.
   c. (T) Tells students it is an unvoiced sound.
   d. (T) Asks students where they find "p" in the alphabet.
   e. (T) Uses mirrors to discuss the mouth, tongue, and teeth placement.
3. (T) Shows an object.
   a. (T) Allows students to manipulate the object and discuss prior knowledge. Reminds (S) that the object has the target sound spelled with the target letter.
4. (S) Brainstorm.
   a. Brainstorm words that have the target sound. (Accept all answers, but place incorrect answers in a "thought bubble" to discuss.) The brainstorming can be a teacher-directed activity if students need extra support.
5. (T) Teaches Letter Formation. Use house paper to teach lowercase letters.
   a. (T) models with the solid letter. The letter "p" starts at the ceiling and goes into the basement. Trace back up to the ceiling, come around, hit the floor, and stop.
   b. Using the screen and green crayon, (T&S) trace the solid while saying, "p says /p/" (3x).
   c. (T&S) use their finger to trace the solid while saying, "p says /p/" (3x).
   d. (S) trace the dotted letter and complete the remainder of the row independently.

e. (S) move to smaller house and repeat process if needed.

f. Teach capital letters throughout the week using the same process. Capital letters go outside the house.

6. (T) Dictates target sound. (S) Practice in the sand or other medium.

   a. Practice writing the letter using a different medium, such as sand, shaving cream, finger paint, gel board, iPad app, air writing, etc.

   b. Do this while stating: p says /p/, 3 times.

7. (T) Connects with literature.

   a. Have students signal when they hear the /p/ sound for the first page or two.

   b. Read again for language comprehension.

   c. Continue to work on language comprehension with rich literature throughout the week.

8. (S) Use decodable readers to practice the concepts learned.

   a. (S) Highlight words with the new concept. Read those words.

   b. (S) Highlight Red Words. Read those words.

   c. (S) Start reading the decodable reader.

   d. (S) Continue reading throughout the week.

   e. (S) Read a clean copy on Friday.

9. (T&S) Mark the Phoneme/Grapheme (P/G) chart by highlighting the target sound.

 ## Word Dictation

Materials Needed:
fingertapping hand, dictation paper, pencil

Create any syllables using the new concept and previously taught concepts. Practice daily. Use the Flip Chart to follow the steps for word dictation.

Day 1:	1. gap	2. lip	3. tap	4. pad	5. pop
Day 2:	1. map	2. pat	3. hip	4. pot	5. tip
Day 3:	1. Kip	2. lap	3. pit	4. dip	5. pig
Days 4-5:	Review prior words. Optional additional words: hap, mop, Pam, pip, pom, top				

Below is a sample script:

1. (T) States word: *mom*. Uses it in a sentence: My *mom* is a wonderful lady. (Pounds) *mom*. (T) Models fingertapping if needed: /m/ /ŏ/ /m/. (Pounds) *mom*.

2. (S) State while pounding: *mom*. (Fingertap) /m/ /ŏ/ /m/. (Pound) *mom*. Write the letters known for the sounds.

3. (T) When yours looks like mine, rewrite the word.

4. (S) Rewrite.

5. Repeat the process for each word.

6. (S) Read the list of words multiple times to build automaticity.

Sentence Dictation

Red Words are underlined. Students can fingertap the green words. Use the Flip Chart to follow the steps for sentence dictation.

1. The lot was on the map.
2. The mop is on the mat.
3. Dot got Pam a pig and a hog.
4. Did Dad tap the lad?
5. Pam did want to dip the mop.
6. Did Kip tap Pam with the cap?
7. The cap is on the pig.
8. A cat was on top of the hat.
9. The pot was hot.
10. Did Jim tap the pot?

- Below is a sample script for sentence dictation.

> 1. (T): Listen to the sentence. *Tad had a cat.*
> 2. (T): Listen while I pound the syllables. *Tad had a cat.*
> 3. (T): Pound it with me. (T&S): *Tad had a cat.*
> 4. (T): You pound the sentence. (S): *Tad had a cat.*
> 5. (T): Watch me as I point to the lines while stating the sentence. *Tad had a cat.*
> 6. (T): You point to the lines while stating the sentence.
> 7. (S): *Tad had a cat.*
> 8. (T): Now write the sentence. Fingertap if needed.

- Below is a sample script to check CUPS*.

> 1. (T): C stands for capitalization. Did you remember a capital letter at the beginning of your sentence? It's also a name. *Tad* would always be capitalized. If you forgot, fix it. If you remembered, put a tally mark above the capital letter. Add a mark in the box for C.
> 2. (T): U stands for understanding. Is your sentence neat? Reread it to yourself. Does it make sense? Could someone else understand it? If not, fix it. Add a mark in the box for U.
> 3. (T): P stands for punctuation. Did you remember a period at the end? If not, fix it. If you remembered, put a tally mark above the period. Add a mark in the box for P.
> 4. (T): S stands for spelling. Did you spell your words correctly? Check them. Now, check yours with mine (show the teacher's copy). Fix any words you spelled incorrectly. Put a tally mark above the words you spelled correctly. Add a mark in the box for S.

5. (T): Rewrite your sentence with all of the corrections.

6. (T): Check for CUPS again. Put another mark in the boxes.

7. (T): Let's read the sentences.

8. (S) Read the sentences for fluency and automaticity.

***Please note:** Once students understand how to use CUPS, transition to letting them check their sentence independently before showing the teacher's copy.

Weekly Red Words

Materials Needed:
screen, red crayon, red word paper

Introduce on Tuesday, and practice daily. Use the Flip Chart for steps.

New:	Review:	New Read-Only:	Review Read-Only:
want, with	the, was, is, a, on, and, to, for, go, I, like, of, will, get, no	yellow	orange, white, brown, stop, said, red, see

Steps for Teaching a New Red Word:

1. (T) States the word. (*want*)

2. (T&S) Use tokens to determine how many sounds are in the word. (/w/ /ŏ/ /n/ /t/; 4)

3. (T&S) Discuss how we would expect to spell each sound as the teacher writes the grapheme(s) correctly. Identify what is unexpected or irregular about the spelling of the word. It could also be expected, but the concept hasn't been taught yet.

4. (T&S) Discuss the etymology of the word, if appropriate (lexical words). Visit www.etymonline.com for more information on the word.

5. (T) Defines the word, and writes a sentence using the word.

6. (T) Writes the word on Red Word paper with the screen underneath, using red crayon.

7. (S) Write the word on Red Word paper with the screen underneath, using red crayon. (S) Show the word to the teacher.
(**NOTE:** The teacher should have students chunk the word if it has more than four letters.)

8. (T&S) Stand up, holding the Red Word in the nondominant hand. Armtap word while naming each letter. Then "underline" the word by sweeping left to right while stating the word, 3x. (**NOTE:** Left-handed students will place their left hand on their right wrist. They tap to their right shoulder. Underline from wrist to shoulder. Right-handed students place their right hand on their left shoulder. They tap to their left wrist. Underline shoulder to wrist.)

9. (T&S) Trace crayon bumps with the pointer finger while naming the letters, 3x.

10. (T&S) Place the screen over the paper and trace the word with the pointer finger while naming the letters, 3x.

11. (S) Turn paper over. With red crayon, write the word without the screen one time, and hold up the word for the teacher to check. (S) Write the word two more times.

12. (S) Write an original sentence in pencil and underline the Red Word with a red crayon. (**NOTE:** The sentence can also be dictated by the teacher while the student writes or dictated by the student while the teacher writes it.)

13. Repeat the steps for *with*. (/w/ /ĭ/ /th/; 3)

Review Ideas for Red Words:

- Sculpt the word using red Play-Doh or clay. Have students spell the word as they smash each letter.
- Print flashcards from IOG, and practice reading.
- Armtap the word to review.
- Cross-clap the word to review.
- Do Spelling Aerobics.

Fluency, Vocabulary, and Comprehension

- Incorporate fluency into your literacy lessons daily/weekly (minimum 30 min/week) by using Rapid Word Charts, IMSE Decodable Readers, words and sentences, Acadience Reading K-6 or DIBELS 8th Edition, repeated reading, and other activities.
- Incorporate vocabulary into your literacy lessons daily/weekly (minimum 50 min/week) by choosing 3-5 appropriate tier two words (can pull from rich literature or decodable readers). Teach the words through explicit, direct instruction using student-friendly definitions, word webs, vocabulary charts, illustrations, and other activities.
- Incorporate oral language comprehension into your literacy lessons daily/weekly (approximately 100 min/week). Comprehension instruction should be explicit, direct instruction that includes teacher modeling, guided practice, and independent practice. Plan ahead to build on students' background knowledge, language structures, verbal reasoning, and literacy knowledge.

Extension Activity Ideas

- Continue to add to the multi-sensory ABC book. Have students glue popcorn (or another object) in the shape of the target letter.
- Have students compare and contrast pencils and pens using a Venn Diagram.
- Make a paper pig. Have students glue pictures of words that begin with the /p/ sound on the pig.
- Divide students into teams of 3 and have them lie on the ground to form the target letter. Take pictures to hang around the classroom.
- Create the target letter out of green Play-Doh or clay.
- Have students use a bingo dauber to find the target letter on a page with various letters.
- Have students go on a "sound hunt" around the room or outside to find objects that begin with the target sound.
- Coding activity: Have students underline and label the letters in words or syllables with a "v" for vowels and a "c" for consonants. For example, when using the word *mom*, each letter should be underlined with the labels "cvc" underneath the word. This activity will help prepare students for decoding multisyllabic words later in the sequence.
- Visit IMSE's Orton-Gillingham's Pinterest page for more ideas.

Weekly Lesson Reminders

- Any of the above extension activities
- Practice writing the target letter (capital and lowercase) using a screen, green crayon, and house paper.
- Practice writing the target letter using another medium (sand, paint, shaving cream, pudding, iPad app, etc.).
- Practice writing the target letter using age-appropriate paper and pencil.
- Daily practice with writing the weekly Red Word(s)
- Kilpatrick's "One-Minute Activities" for daily phonological awareness practice
- Zgonc's phonological awareness activities
- Listen to rich literature to work on oral language comprehension.
- Target letter practice sheets from IMSE's practice books and handwriting books
- Practice test on Thursday and test on Friday

Uu as in umbrella

Card Pack #14 Decodable Reader #6	
Object Ideas:	**Literature Ideas:**
Initial position: positional words (up/down, under/over), uncle, usher, umbrella, umpire, upside-down cake **Medial position:** hut, cut, mutt, rut	▪ *The Umbrella* by Jan Brett ▪ *Mr. Digby's Bad Day* by Jerry Smath ▪ *Get Up, Stand Up* by Bob Marley and Cedella Marley ▪ *Unspoken: A Story From the Underground Railroad* by Henry Cole ▪ *The Ugly Duckling* ▪ *Humpty Dumpty* ▪ *Under My Hijab* by Hena Khan

 ## Notes

- Use the Comprehensive Flip Chart for the steps on how to teach each part of IMSE's Lesson Plan.
- Uu /ŭ/ is a voiced vowel sound. To produce vowel sounds, articulators hold a shape but do not obstruct air. Refer to the Vowel Valley on sound production.
- Make a vowel stick or tent.
- Teach the visual cue: push in on the stomach with the fist (gently).

 ## Phonological Awareness:

Materials Needed:
tokens, sound boxes, one-minute activities, or Zgonc PA book

Use the PAST assessment to determine a starting point for instruction. Incorporate daily phonological awareness activities by using Zgonc's tiered activities and/or Kilpatrick's One-Minute Activities in *Equipped for Reading Success.*

Phonemic awareness warm-up: Use tokens (or letter tiles once concepts have been taught) and sound boxes to do a quick phonemic awareness activity that ties in with the new concept, if appropriate.

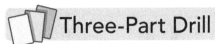

Three-Part Drill

Materials Needed:
review cards, sand, blending board, vowel tents or sticks

Do this at least 3x per week. Use the Flip Chart for steps. Include the new concept after Day 1.

- Include the Vowel Intensive with "a," "i," and "o." Include "u" after it has been taught.

V	VC	CVC
a	ag, ap, ab	lat, cad, zan
e	et, en, eb	zeg, ren, med
i	ig, ib, im	lin, hib, fid
o	ob, ot, oz	rom, hob, cog
u	un, ud, ub	sup, pum, dut

- Below is a sample script now that students know more than one way to spell a concept. Remember to use all of the review concepts.

1. **Visual:**
   (T) Tell me the sounds you know for these letters.
   (S) /m/, /l/, etc.
   Alternative:
   (T) Tell me the names and sounds you know for these letters.
   (S) m says /m/, l says /l/, etc.

2. **Auditory/Kinesthetic:**
   (T) You know two ways to spell this. (S) split trays. (T) Eyes on me.
   Spell /k/. Repeat.
   (S) /k/ c says /k/; k says /k/

3. **Blending:**
   (T) Tell me the sound for each letter as I point. Then blend the sounds together to read the word or syllable. Give me a thumbs up if it is a real word.
   (S) /mmm/ /ŏŏŏ/ /mmm/ *mom* (thumbs up)
   Alternative:
   (T) Watch me first. /mmm/ /ŏŏŏ/ /mmm/ *mom*
   (T) Do it with me. (T&S) /mmm/ /ŏŏŏ/ /mmm/ *mom*
   (T) Your turn. (S) /mmm/ /ŏŏŏ/ /mmm/ *mom* (thumbs up)

Vowel Intensive: Model the visual cue while calling out the sound. Students will do the visual cue as they repeat the sound. Students will then hold up the vowel tent while stating the letter name and sound.

- (T): Eyes on me. The sound is /ă/. Repeat.
- (S): /ă/ a says /ă/

Teaching a New Concept

Materials Needed:
concept card, screen, green crayon, object, sand, decodable readers, literature, P/G chart

Introduce on Monday, and practice daily.

1. (T) Reads alliteration sentence. (S) Identify the target sound.

    a. Uncle umpired under the umbrella.

    (T) Reads the following sentence in which /ŭ/ is in the medial position. (S) Identify the target sound.

    b. Run, bud! Hug a bug!

2. (T) Shows the new concept card.

    a. (T) Tells students the letter name and sound. Have (S) repeat, 3 times (u says /ŭ/).

    b. (T) Tells students that "u" is a vowel.

    c. (T) Tells students it is a voiced sound.

    d. (T) Asks students where they find "u" in the alphabet.

    e. (T) Uses mirrors to discuss the mouth, tongue, and teeth placement.

3. (T) Shows an object.

    a. (T) Allows students to manipulate the object and discuss prior knowledge. Reminds (S) that the object has the target sound spelled with the target letter.

4. (S) Brainstorm.

    a. Brainstorm words that have the target sound. (Accept all answers, but place incorrect answers in a "thought bubble" to discuss.) The brainstorming can be a teacher-directed activity if students need extra support. (**Note:** For short vowels, students can brainstorm word families or rhyming words containing the vowel sound.)

5. (T) Teaches Letter Formation. Use house paper to teach lowercase letters.

    a. (T) models with the solid letter. The letter "u" starts at the ceiling, touches the floor, comes back up to the ceiling, and back down to the floor.

    b. Using the screen and green crayon, (T&S) trace the solid while saying, "u says /ŭ/" (3x).

    c. (T&S) use their finger to trace the solid while saying, "u says /ŭ/" (3x).

    d. (S) trace the dotted letter and complete the remainder of the row independently.

    e. (S) move to smaller house and repeat process if needed.

    f. Teach capital letters throughout the week using the same process. Capital letters go outside the house.

6. (T) Dictates target sound. (S) Practice in the sand or other medium.

    a. Practice writing the letter using a different medium, such as sand, shaving cream, finger paint, gel board, iPad app, air writing, etc.

    b. Do this while stating: u says /ŭ/, 3 times.

7. (T) Connects with literature.

    a. Have students signal when they hear the /ŭ/ sound for the first page or two.

    b. Read again for language comprehension.

    c. Continue to work on language comprehension with rich literature throughout the week.

8. (S) Use decodable readers to practice the concepts learned.

   a. (S) Highlight words with the new concept. Read those words.

   b. (S) Highlight Red Words. Read those words.

   c. (S) Start reading the decodable reader.

   d. (S) Continue reading throughout the week.

   e. (S) Read a clean copy on Friday.

9. (T&S) Mark the Phoneme/Grapheme (P/G) chart by highlighting the target sound.

Word Dictation

Materials Needed:
fingertapping hand, dictation paper, pencil

Create any syllables using the new concept and previously taught concepts. Practice daily. Use the Flip Chart to follow the steps for word dictation.

Day 1:	1. hug	2. lug	3. cut	4. pug	5. up
Day 2:	1. cup	2. hut	3. jut	4. pup	5. gut
Day 3:	1. gum	2. jug	3. tug	4. mud	5. mug
Days 4-5:	Review prior words. Optional additional word: tum				

Below is a sample script:

1. (T) States word: *mom*. Uses it in a sentence: My *mom* is a wonderful lady. (Pounds) *mom*. (T) Models fingertapping if needed: /m/ /ŏ/ /m/. (Pounds) *mom*.

2. (S) State while pounding: *mom*. (Fingertap) /m/ /ŏ/ /m/. (Pound) *mom*. Write the letters known for the sounds.

3. (T) When yours looks like mine, rewrite the word.

4. (S) Rewrite.

5. Repeat the process for each word.

6. (S) Read the list of words multiple times to build automaticity.

Sentence Dictation

Red Words are underlined. Students can fingertap the green words. Use the Flip Chart to follow the steps for sentence dictation.

1. The pig had mud on him.

2. Tad did tug the gum.

3. The jug had a lid on it.

4. The pup was a pug.

5. Dad said to cut the log.

6. Tim had to lug the jug.

7. Did you cut the ham?

8. The tip of the jug is cut.
9. The cap is on the pup.
10. Tom dug up a mug.
11. Will you go to the hot tub?

- Below is a sample script for sentence dictation.

> 1. (T): Listen to the sentence. *Tad had a cat.*
> 2. (T): Listen while I pound the syllables. *Tad had a cat.*
> 3. (T): Pound it with me. (T&S): *Tad had a cat.*
> 4. (T): You pound the sentence. (S): *Tad had a cat.*
> 5. (T): Watch me as I point to the lines while stating the sentence. *Tad had a cat.*
> 6. (T): You point to the lines while stating the sentence.
> 7. (S): *Tad had a cat.*
> 8. (T): Now write the sentence. Fingertap if needed.

- Below is a sample script to check CUPS*.

> 1. (T): C stands for capitalization. Did you remember a capital letter at the beginning of your sentence? It's also a name. *Tad* would always be capitalized. If you forgot, fix it. If you remembered, put a tally mark above the capital letter. Add a mark in the box for C.
> 2. (T): U stands for understanding. Is your sentence neat? Reread it to yourself. Does it make sense? Could someone else understand it? If not, fix it. Add a mark in the box for U.
> 3. (T): P stands for punctuation. Did you remember a period at the end? If not, fix it. If you remembered, put a tally mark above the period. Add a mark in the box for P.
> 4. (T): S stands for spelling. Did you spell your words correctly? Check them. Now, check yours with mine (show the teacher's copy). Fix any words you spelled incorrectly. Put a tally mark above the words you spelled correctly. Add a mark in the box for S.
> 5. (T): Rewrite your sentence with all of the corrections.
> 6. (T): Check for CUPS again. Put another mark in the boxes.
> 7. (T): Let's read the sentences.
> 8. (S) Read the sentences for fluency and automaticity.
>
> **Please note:** Once students understand how to use CUPS, transition to letting them check their sentence independently before showing the teacher's copy.

Weekly Red Words

Materials Needed:
screen, red crayon, red word paper

Introduce on Tuesday, and practice daily. Use the Flip Chart for steps.

New:	Review:	New Read-Only:	Review Read-Only:
said, you	the, was, is, a, on, and, to, for, go, I, like, of, will, get, no, want, with		orange, white, brown, stop, red, see, yellow

Steps for Teaching a New Red Word:

1. (T) States the word. (*said*)

2. (T&S) Use tokens to determine how many sounds are in the word. (/s/ /ĕ/ /d; 3)

3. (T&S) Discuss how we would expect to spell each sound as the teacher writes the grapheme(s) correctly. Identify what is unexpected or irregular about the spelling of the word. It could also be expected, but the concept hasn't been taught yet.

4. (T&S) Discuss the etymology of the word, if appropriate (lexical words). Visit www.etymonline.com for more information on the word.

5. (T) Defines the word, and writes a sentence using the word.

6. (T) Writes the word on Red Word paper with the screen underneath, using red crayon.

7. (S) Write the word on Red Word paper with the screen underneath, using red crayon. (S) Show the word to the teacher.
(**NOTE:** The teacher should have students chunk the word if it has more than four letters.)

8. (T&S) Stand up, holding the Red Word in the nondominant hand. Armtap word while naming each letter. Then "underline" the word by sweeping left to right while stating the word, 3x. (**NOTE:** Left-handed students will place their left hand on their right wrist. They tap to their right shoulder. Underline from wrist to shoulder. Right-handed students place their right hand on their left shoulder. They tap to their left wrist. Underline shoulder to wrist.)

9. (T&S) Trace crayon bumps with the pointer finger while naming the letters, 3x.

10. (T&S) Place the screen over the paper and trace the word with the pointer finger while naming the letters, 3x.

11. (S) Turn paper over. With red crayon, write the word without the screen one time, and hold up the word for the teacher to check. (S) Write the word two more times.

12. (S) Write an original sentence in pencil and underline the Red Word with a red crayon. (**NOTE:** The sentence can also be dictated by the teacher while the student writes or dictated by the student while the teacher writes it.)

13. Repeat the steps for *you*. (/y/ / $\overline{oo}$ /; 2)

Review Ideas for Red Words:

- Sculpt the word using red Play-Doh or clay. Have students spell the word as they smash each letter.
- Print flashcards from IOG, and practice reading.
- Armtap the word to review.
- Cross-clap the word to review.
- Do Spelling Aerobics.

Fluency, Vocabulary, and Comprehension

- Incorporate fluency into your literacy lessons daily/weekly (minimum 30 min/week) by using Rapid Word Charts, IMSE Decodable Readers, words and sentences, Acadience Reading K-6 or DIBELS 8th Edition, repeated reading, and other activities.
- Incorporate vocabulary into your literacy lessons daily/weekly (minimum 50 min/week) by choosing 3-5 appropriate tier two words (can pull from rich literature or decodable readers). Teach the words through explicit, direct instruction using student-friendly definitions, word webs, vocabulary charts, illustrations, and other activities.
- Incorporate oral language comprehension into your literacy lessons daily/weekly (approximately 100 min/week). Comprehension instruction should be explicit, direct instruction that includes teacher modeling, guided practice, and independent practice. Plan ahead to build on students' background knowledge, language structures, verbal reasoning, and literacy knowledge.

Extension Activity Ideas

- Continue to add to the multi-sensory ABC book. Have students glue umbrellas (or another object) in the shape of the target letter.
- Have students compare and contrast up and under using a Venn Diagram.
- Make a paper umbrella. Have students glue pictures of words that begin with the /ŭ/ sound on the umbrella.
- Divide students into teams of 3 and have them lie on the ground to form the target letter. Take pictures to hang around the classroom.
- Create the target letter out of green Play-Doh or clay.
- Have students use a bingo dauber to find the target letter on a page with various letters.
- Have students go on a "sound hunt" around the room or outside to find objects that begin with the target sound.
- Coding activity: Have students underline and label the letters in words or syllables with a "v" for vowels and a "c" for consonants. For example, when using the word *mom*, each letter should be underlined with the labels "cvc" underneath the word. This activity will help prepare students for decoding multisyllabic words later in the sequence.
- Visit IMSE's Orton-Gillingham's Pinterest page for more ideas.

Weekly Lesson Reminders

- Any of the above extension activities
- Practice writing the target letter (capital and lowercase) using a screen, green crayon, and house paper.
- Practice writing the target letter using another medium (sand, paint, shaving cream, pudding, iPad app, etc.)
- Practice writing the target letter using age-appropriate paper and pencil.
- Daily practice with writing the weekly Red Word(s)
- Kilpatrick's "One-Minute Activities" for daily phonological awareness practice
- Zgonc's phonological awareness activities
- Listen to rich literature to work on oral language comprehension.
- Target letter practice sheets from IMSE's practice books and handwriting books
- Practice test on Thursday and test on Friday

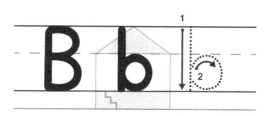

Bb as in bat

Card Pack #15 Decodable Reader #7	
Object Ideas:	**Literature Ideas:**
baby, bubble, button, book, biscuit, bell, bat, ball, balloon, basketball, basket, Band-Aid, bubble gum, blink, black, blue, banana, beach, bead, boss	▪ *Buzzy the Bumblebee* by Denise Brennan-Nelson ▪ *Little Bear* by Else Holmelund Minarik ▪ *Biscuit Goes to School* by Alyssa Satin Capucilli ▪ *The Big Bed* by Bunmi Laditan ▪ *Bee-bim Bop!* by Linda Sue Park ▪ Encyclopedia Brown series by Donald J. Sobol ▪ *Bridge to Terabithia* by Katherine Paterson ▪ *The Button Box* by Margarette S. Reid ▪ *Brown Bear, Brown Bear, What Do You See?* by Bill Martin, Jr. ▪ *Baa, Baa, Black Sheep* ▪ *Black Is a Rainbow Color* by Angela Joy ▪ *My Two Blankets* by Irena Kobald

Notes

- Use the Comprehensive Flip Chart for the steps on how to teach each part of IMSE's Lesson Plan.
- Bb /b/ is a voiced, stopped consonant sound. It is formed with the lips together and a pop of air.
- If needed, the card pack contains an extra "b" so it can be used in both the initial and final position on the blending board.
- Use the bat and ball image to help with reversals.

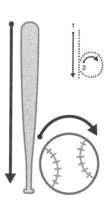

- Teach the strategy of "Make Your Bed Pretty Quickly." Have students put their thumbs up and knuckles together. Have students look at their hands. The left hand looks like the first sound in "bed" (*b*). The right hand looks like the last sound in "bed" (*d*). Then have students flip their thumbs upside down. The left hand looks like a *p* (as in "pretty"). The right hand looks like a *q* (as in "quickly"). (See the Masters for a color copy of this visual.)

Make your bed pretty quickly!

Phonological Awareness:

Materials Needed:
tokens, sound boxes, one-minute activities, or Zgonc PA book

Use the PAST assessment to determine a starting point for instruction. Incorporate daily phonological awareness activities by using Zgonc's tiered activities and/or Kilpatrick's One-Minute Activities in *Equipped for Reading Success*.

Phonemic awareness warm-up: Use tokens (or letter tiles once concepts have been taught) and sound boxes to do a quick phonemic awareness activity that ties in with the new concept, if appropriate.

Three-Part Drill

Materials Needed:
review cards, sand, blending board, vowel tents or sticks

Do this at least 3x per week. Use the Flip Chart for steps. Include the new concept after Day 1.

- Include the Vowel Intensive with "a," "i," "o," and "u."

V	VC	CVC
a	ag, ap, ab	lat, cad, zan
e	et, en, eb	zeg, ren, med
i	ig, ib, im	lin, hib, fid
o	ob, ot, oz	rom, hob, cog
u	un, ud, ub	sup, pum, dut

▪ Below is a sample script now that students know more than one way to spell a concept. Remember to use all of the review concepts.

1. **Visual:**
   (T) Tell me the sounds you know for these letters.
   (S) /m/, /l/, etc.
   Alternative:
   (T) Tell me the names and sounds you know for these letters.
   (S) m says /m/, l says /l/, etc.

2. **Auditory/Kinesthetic:**
   (T) You know two ways to spell this. (S) split trays. (T) Eyes on me.
   Spell /k/. Repeat.
   (S) /k/ c says /k/; k says /k/

3. **Blending:**
   (T) Tell me the sound for each letter as I point. Then blend the sounds together to read the word or syllable. Give me a thumbs up if it is a real word.
   (S) /mmm/ /ŏŏŏ/ /mmm/ *mom* (thumbs up)
   Alternative:
   (T) Watch me first. /mmm/ /ŏŏŏ/ /mmm/ *mom*
   (T) Do it with me. (T&S) /mmm/ /ŏŏŏ/ /mmm/ *mom*
   (T) Your turn. (S) /mmm/ /ŏŏŏ/ /mmm/ *mom* (thumbs up)

*Vowel Intensive: Model the visual cue while calling out the sound. Students will do the visual cue as they repeat the sound. Students will then hold up the vowel tent while stating the letter name and sound.
   ▪ (T): Eyes on me. The sound is /ă/. Repeat.
   ▪ (S): /ă/ a says /ă/

Teaching a New Concept

Materials Needed:
concept card, screen, green crayon, object, sand, decodable readers, literature, P/G chart

Introduce on Monday, and practice daily.

1. (T) Reads alliteration sentences. (S) Identify the target sound.
   a. Buzzy the Bumblebee believed and buzzed.
   b. Baby buggies broke badly.
2. (T) Shows the new concept card.
   a. (T) Tells students the letter name and sound. Have (S) repeat, 3 times (b says /b/).
   b. (T) Tells students that "b" is a consonant.
   c. (T) Tells students it is a voiced sound.
   d. (T) Asks students where they find "b" in the alphabet.
   e. (T) Uses mirrors to discuss the mouth, tongue, and teeth placement.
3. (T) Shows an object.
   a. (T) Allows students to manipulate the object and discuss prior knowledge. Reminds (S) that the object has the target sound spelled with the target letter.

4. (S) Brainstorm.
   a. Brainstorm words that have the target sound. (Accept all answers, but place incorrect answers in a "thought bubble" to discuss.) The brainstorming can be a teacher-directed activity if students need extra support.
5. (T) Teaches Letter Formation. Use house paper to teach lowercase letters.
   a. (T) models with the solid letter. The letter "b" starts in the attic and comes down to the floor. Then trace back up and around to bump the ceiling. Come around, bump the floor, and touch the line.
   b. Using the screen and green crayon, (T&S) trace the solid while saying, "b says /b/" (3x).
   c. (T&S) use their finger to trace the solid while saying, "b says /b/" (3x).
   d. (S) trace the dotted letter and complete the remainder of the row independently.
   e. (S) move to smaller house and repeat process if needed.
   f. Teach capital letters throughout the week using the same process. Capital letters go outside the house.
6. (T) Dictates target sound. (S) Practice in the sand or other medium.
   a. Practice writing the letter using a different medium, such as sand, shaving cream, finger paint, gel board, iPad app, air writing, etc.
   b. Do this while stating: b says /b/, 3 times.
7. (T) Connects with literature.
   a. Have students signal when they hear the /b/ sound for the first page or two.
   b. Read again for language comprehension.
   c. Continue to work on language comprehension with rich literature throughout the week.
8. (S) Use decodable readers to practice the concepts learned.
   a. (S) Highlight words with the new concept. Read those words.
   b. (S) Highlight Red Words. Read those words.
   c. (S) Start reading the decodable reader.
   d. (S) Continue reading throughout the week.
   e. (S) Read a clean copy on Friday.
9. (T&S) Mark the Phoneme/Grapheme (P/G) chart by highlighting the target sound.

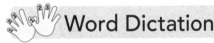 ## Word Dictation

Materials Needed:
fingertapping hand, dictation paper, pencil

Create any syllables using the new concept and previously taught concepts. Practice daily. Use the Flip Chart to follow the steps for word dictation.

Day 1:	1. bad	2. bug	3. dab	4. lob	5. bit
Day 2:	1. bid	2. tub	3. lab	4. bog	5. cob
Day 3:	1. bag	2. hub	3. bop	4. tab	5. big
Days 4-5:	Review prior words. Optional additional words: bat, bob, bud, but, cab, cub, dub, gab, jab, job, pub				

Below is a sample script:

> 1. (T) States word: *mom*. Uses it in a sentence: My *mom* is a wonderful lady. (Pounds) *mom*. (T) Models fingertapping if needed: /m/ /ŏ/ /m/. (Pounds) *mom*.
> 2. (S) State while pounding: *mom*. (Fingertap) /m/ /ŏ/ /m/. (Pound) *mom*. Write the letters known for the sounds.
> 3. (T) When yours looks like mine, rewrite the word.
> 4. (S) Rewrite.
> 5. Repeat the process for each word.
> 6. (S) Read the list of words multiple times to build automaticity.

Sentence Dictation

Red Words are underlined. Students can fingertap the green words. Use the Flip Chart to follow the steps for sentence dictation.

1. Jim and Kim had a big tub.
2. The bad bug bit Bob.
3. Did the cub tug on the bag?
4. Bob had a job to get the cub.
5. Tom got a cab with Tad.
6. Did the kid put the bug on the mat?
7. Jim had to lug the pug to the tub.
8. Did Bob want the bag?
9. Kim lit the big log.
10. Tab got in the cab.
11. The dog bit the bug.
12. Bob had gum.

- Below is a sample script for sentence dictation.

> 1. (T): Listen to the sentence. *Tad had a cat.*
> 2. (T): Listen while I pound the syllables. *Tad had a cat.*
> 3. (T): Pound it with me. (T&S): *Tad had a cat.*
> 4. (T): You pound the sentence. (S): *Tad had a cat.*
> 5. (T): Watch me as I point to the lines while stating the sentence. *Tad had a cat.*
> 6. (T): You point to the lines while stating the sentence.
> 7. (S): *Tad had a cat.*
> 8. (T): Now write the sentence. Fingertap if needed.

- Below is a sample script to check CUPS*.

---

1. (T): C stands for capitalization. Did you remember a capital letter at the beginning of your sentence? It's also a name. *Tad* would always be capitalized. If you forgot, fix it. If you remembered, put a tally mark above the capital letter. Add a mark in the box for C.

2. (T): U stands for understanding. Is your sentence neat? Reread it to yourself. Does it make sense? Could someone else understand it? If not, fix it. Add a mark in the box for U.

3. (T): P stands for punctuation. Did you remember a period at the end? If not, fix it. If you remembered, put a tally mark above the period. Add a mark in the box for P.

4. (T): S stands for spelling. Did you spell your words correctly? Check them. Now, check yours with mine (show the teacher's copy). Fix any words you spelled incorrectly. Put a tally mark above the words you spelled correctly. Add a mark in the box for S.

5. (T): Rewrite your sentence with all of the corrections.

6. (T): Check for CUPS again. Put another mark in the boxes.

7. (T): Let's read the sentences.

8. (S) Read the sentences for fluency and automaticity.

*Please note: Once students understand how to use CUPS, transition to letting them check their sentence independently before showing the teacher's copy.

Weekly Red Words

Materials Needed:
screen, red crayon, red word paper

Introduce on Tuesday, and practice daily. Use the Flip Chart for steps.

New:	Review:	New Read-Only:	Review Read-Only:
in, put	the, was, is, a, on, and, to, for, go, I, like, of, will, get, no, want, with, said, you	bus	orange, white, brown, stop, red, see, yellow

Steps for Teaching a New Red Word:

1. (T) States the word. (*in*)

2. (T&S) Use tokens to determine how many sounds are in the word. (/ĭ/ /n/; 2)

3. (T&S) Discuss how we would expect to spell each sound as the teacher writes the grapheme(s) correctly. Identify what is unexpected or irregular about the spelling of the word. It could also be expected, but the concept hasn't been taught yet.

4. (T&S) Discuss the etymology of the word, if appropriate (lexical words).

Visit www.etymonline.com for more information on the word.

5. (T) Defines the word, and writes a sentence using the word.

6. (T) Writes the word on Red Word paper with the screen underneath, using red crayon.

7. (S) Write the word on Red Word paper with the screen underneath, using red crayon. (S) Show the word to the teacher.
   (**NOTE:** The teacher should have students chunk the word if it has more than four letters.)

8. (T&S) Stand up, holding the Red Word in the nondominant hand. Armtap word while naming each letter. Then "underline" the word by sweeping left to right while stating the word, 3x. (**NOTE:** Left-handed students will place their left hand on their right wrist. They tap to their right shoulder. Underline from wrist to shoulder. Right-handed students place their right hand on their left shoulder. They tap to their left wrist. Underline shoulder to wrist.)

9. (T&S) Trace crayon bumps with the pointer finger while naming the letters, 3x.

10. (T&S) Place the screen over the paper and trace the word with the pointer finger while naming the letters, 3x.

11. (S) Turn paper over. With red crayon, write the word without the screen one time, and hold up the word for the teacher to check. (S) Write the word two more times.

12. (S) Write an original sentence in pencil and underline the Red Word with a red crayon. (**NOTE:** The sentence can also be dictated by the teacher while the student writes or dictated by the student while the teacher writes it.)

13. Repeat the steps for *put*. (/p/ /o͝o/ /t/; 3)

Review Ideas for Red Words:

- Sculpt the word using red Play-Doh or clay. Have students spell the word as they smash each letter.
- Print flashcards from IOG, and practice reading.
- Armtap the word to review.
- Cross-clap the word to review.
- Do Spelling Aerobics.

Fluency, Vocabulary, and Comprehension

- Incorporate fluency into your literacy lessons daily/weekly (minimum 30 min/week) by using Rapid Word Charts, IMSE Decodable Readers, words and sentences, Acadience Reading K-6 or DIBELS 8th Edition, repeated reading, and other activities.
- Incorporate vocabulary into your literacy lessons daily/weekly (minimum 50 min/week) by choosing 3-5 appropriate tier two words (can pull from rich literature or decodable readers). Teach the words through explicit, direct instruction using student-friendly definitions, word webs, vocabulary charts, illustrations, and other activities.
- Incorporate oral language comprehension into your literacy lessons daily/weekly (approximately 100 min/week). Comprehension instruction should be explicit, direct instruction that includes teacher modeling, guided practice, and independent practice. Plan ahead to build on students' background knowledge, language structures, verbal reasoning, and literacy knowledge.

Extension Activity Ideas

- Continue to add to the multi-sensory ABC book. Have students glue bees (or another object) in the shape of the target letter.
- Have students compare and contrast bumblebees and honeybees using a Venn Diagram.
- Make a paper boot. Have students glue pictures of words that begin with the /b/ sound on the boot.
- Divide students into teams of 3 and have them lie on the ground to form the target letter. Take pictures to hang around the classroom.
- Create the target letter out of green Play-Doh or clay.
- Have students use a bingo dauber to find the target letter on a page with various letters.
- Have students go on a "sound hunt" around the room or outside to find objects that begin with the target sound.
- Coding activity: Have students underline and label the letters in words or syllables with a "v" for vowels and a "c" for consonants. For example, when using the word *mom*, each letter should be underlined with the labels "cvc" underneath the word. This activity will help prepare students for decoding multisyllabic words later in the sequence.
- Visit IMSE's Orton-Gillingham's Pinterest page for more ideas.

Weekly Lesson Reminders

- Any of the above extension activities
- Practice writing the target letter (capital and lowercase) using a screen, green crayon, and house paper.
- Practice writing the target letter using another medium (sand, paint, shaving cream, pudding, iPad app, etc.).
- Practice writing the target letter using age-appropriate paper and pencil.
- Daily practice with writing the weekly Red Word(s)
- Kilpatrick's "One-Minute Activities" for daily phonological awareness practice
- Zgonc's phonological awareness activities
- Listen to rich literature to work on oral language comprehension.
- Target letter practice sheets from IMSE's practice books and handwriting books
- Practice test on Thursday and test on Friday

Rr as in raccoon

Object Ideas:	Literature Ideas:
rabbit, raccoon, race, robot, river, rainbow, rocket, ring, rope, rake, ribbon, rectangle, round, recycle, rhombus, run, rubber band, rug, rat, rose, red, rice, raisin	<ul><li>*The Rainbow Fish* by Marcus Pfister</li><li>*The Red Racer* by Audrey Wood</li><li>*Rotten Ralph* by Jack Gantos</li><li>*Ralph S. Mouse* by Beverly Cleary</li><li>*The Runaway Rabbit* by Margaret Wise Brown</li><li>Ramona series by Beverly Cleary</li><li>*Runaway Ralph* by Beverly Cleary</li><li>*Big Red Lollipop* by Rukhsana Khan</li><li>*Rosa* by Nikki Giovanni</li><li>*Remarkably You* by Pat Zietlow Miller</li></ul>

Notes

- Use the Comprehensive Flip Chart for the steps on how to teach each part of IMSE's Lesson Plan.
- Rr /r/ is a voiced consonant sound. The lips pucker together and the sides of the tongue touch the roof of the mouth.
- The /r/ sound is a liquid consonant sound. Liquid sounds can sometimes result in a resonant, vowel-like quality. These can be tricky for students.
- "R" in the initial position does not say /er/. Be sure that students are looking in a mirror for proper mouth formation.
- Be careful that students are not saying /ruh/. Cut off the /uh/.
- Keep "r" in the initial position. Otherwise, it will create an R-Controlled Vowel (Bossy R).

Phonological Awareness:

Materials Needed:
tokens, sound boxes, one-minute activities, or Zgonc PA book

Use the PAST assessment to determine a starting point for instruction. Incorporate daily phonological awareness activities by using Zgonc's tiered activities and/or Kilpatrick's One-Minute Activities in *Equipped for Reading Success*.

Phonemic awareness warm-up: Use tokens (or letter tiles once concepts have been taught) and sound boxes to do a quick phonemic awareness activity that ties in with the new concept, if appropriate.

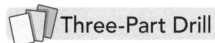

Three-Part Drill

Materials Needed:
review cards, sand, blending board, vowel tents or sticks

Do this at least 3x per week. Use the Flip Chart for steps. Include the new concept after Day 1.

- Include the Vowel Intensive with "a," "i," "o," and "u."

V	VC	CVC
a	ag, ap, ab	lat, cad, zan
e	et, en, eb	zeg, ren, med
i	ig, ib, im	lin, hib, fid
o	ob, ot, oz	rom, hob, cog
u	un, ud, ub	sup, pum, dut

- Below is a sample script now that students know more than one way to spell a concept. Remember to use all of the review concepts.

1. **Visual:**
   (T) Tell me the sounds you know for these letters.
   (S) /m/, /l/, etc.
   Alternative:
   (T) Tell me the names and sounds you know for these letters.
   (S) m says /m/, l says /l/, etc.

2. **Auditory/Kinesthetic:**
   (T) You know two ways to spell this. (S) split trays. (T) Eyes on me.
   Spell /k/. Repeat.
   (S) /k/ c says /k/; k says /k/

3. **Blending:**
   (T) Tell me the sound for each letter as I point. Then blend the sounds together to read the word or syllable. Give me a thumbs up if it is a real word.
   (S) /mmm/ /ŏŏŏ/ /mmm/ *mom* (thumbs up)
   Alternative:
   (T) Watch me first. /mmm/ /ŏŏŏ/ /mmm/ *mom*
   (T) Do it with me. (T&S) /mmm/ /ŏŏŏ/ /mmm/ *mom*
   (T) Your turn. (S) /mmm/ /ŏŏŏ/ /mmm/ *mom* (thumbs up)

Vowel Intensive: Model the visual cue while calling out the sound. Students will do the visual cue as they repeat the sound. Students will then hold up the vowel tent while stating the letter name and sound.

- (T): Eyes on me. The sound is /ă/. Repeat.
- (S): /ă/ a says /ă/

Teaching a New Concept

Materials Needed:
concept card, screen, green crayon, object, sand, decodable readers, literature, P/G chart

Introduce on Monday, and practice daily.

1. (T) Reads alliteration sentences. (S) Identify the target sound.
   a. Rabbits rarely run really rapidly.
   b. Roger ran right on Rexford.
2. (T) Shows the new concept card.
   a. (T) Tells students the letter name and sound. Have (S) repeat, 3 times (r says /r/).
   b. (T) Tells students that "r" is a consonant.
   c. (T) Tells students it is a voiced sound.
   d. (T) Asks students where they find "r" in the alphabet.
   e. (T) Uses mirrors to discuss the mouth, tongue, and teeth placement.
3. (T) Shows an object.
   a. (T) Allows students to manipulate the object and discuss prior knowledge. Reminds (S) that the object has the target sound spelled with the target letter.
4. (S) Brainstorm.
   a. Brainstorm words that have the target sound. (Accept all answers, but place incorrect answers in a "thought bubble" to discuss.) The brainstorming can be a teacher-directed activity if students need extra support.
5. (T) Teaches Letter Formation. Use house paper to teach lowercase letters.
   a. (T) models with the solid letter. The letter "r" starts at the ceiling and comes down to the floor. Then trace back up and around to bump the ceiling, and stop.
   b. Using the screen and green crayon, (T&S) trace the solid while saying, "r says /r/" (3x).
   c. (T&S) use their finger to trace the solid while saying, "r says /r/" (3x).
   d. (S) trace the dotted letter and complete the remainder of the row independently.
   e. (S) move to smaller house and repeat process if needed.
   f. Teach capital letters throughout the week using the same process. Capital letters go outside the house.
6. (T) Dictates target sound. (S) Practice in the sand or other medium.
   a. Practice writing the letter using a different medium, such as sand, shaving cream, finger paint, gel board, iPad app, air writing, etc.
   b. Do this while stating: r says /r/, 3 times.

7. (T) Connects with literature.

   a. Have students signal when they hear the /r/ sound for the first page or two.

   b. Read again for language comprehension.

   c. Continue to work on language comprehension with rich literature throughout the week.

8. (S) Use decodable readers to practice the concepts learned.

   a. (S) Highlight words with the new concept. Read those words.

   b. (S) Highlight Red Words. Read those words.

   c. (S) Start reading the decodable reader.

   d. (S) Continue reading throughout the week.

   e. (S) Read a clean copy on Friday.

9. (T&S) Mark the Phoneme/Grapheme (P/G) chart by highlighting the target sound.

 # Word Dictation

Materials Needed:
fingertapping hand, dictation paper, pencil

Create any syllables using the new concept and previously taught concepts. Practice daily. Use the Flip Chart to follow the steps for word dictation.

Day 1:	1. rap	2. rid	3. rot	4. rag	5. rub
Day 2:	1. rip	2. ram	3. rat	4. rig	5. rut
Day 3:	1. rod	2. rib	3. rad	4. rim	5. rug
Days 4-5:	Review prior words.				

Below is a sample script:

1. (T) States word: *mom.* Uses it in a sentence: My *mom* is a wonderful lady. (Pounds) *mom.* (T) Models fingertapping if needed: /m/ /ŏ/ /m/. (Pounds) *mom.*

2. (S) State while pounding: *mom.* (Fingertap) /m/ /ŏ/ /m/. (Pound) *mom.* Write the letters known for the sounds.

3. (T) When yours looks like mine, rewrite the word.

4. (S) Rewrite.

5. Repeat the process for each word.

6. (S) Read the list of words multiple times to build automaticity.

 # Sentence Dictation

Red Words are underlined. Students can fingertap the green words. Use the Flip Chart to follow the steps for sentence dictation.

1. The cat got rid of the rat.

2. Tad was hit on the rib.

3. It was up to Mom to rub the rat.

4. The ram was in the mud.
5. See the rip on the rug!
6. Mom said to rub the cat.
7. The cap got a big rip.
8. The ram hit the log.
9. Is the rim of the pot big?
10. The bug in the rug did stop.
11. The rig was in a big rut.
12. The ram did rip the rug.

- Below is a sample script for sentence dictation.

  1. (T): Listen to the sentence. *Tad had a cat.*
  2. (T): Listen while I pound the syllables. *Tad had a cat.*
  3. (T): Pound it with me. (T&S): *Tad had a cat.*
  4. (T): You pound the sentence. (S): *Tad had a cat.*
  5. (T): Watch me as I point to the lines while stating the sentence. *Tad had a cat.*
  6. (T): You point to the lines while stating the sentence.
  7. (S): *Tad had a cat.*
  8. (T): Now write the sentence. Fingertap if needed.

- Below is a sample script to check CUPS*.

  1. (T): C stands for capitalization. Did you remember a capital letter at the beginning of your sentence? It's also a name. *Tad* would always be capitalized. If you forgot, fix it. If you remembered, put a tally mark above the capital letter. Add a mark in the box for C.
  2. (T): U stands for understanding. Is your sentence neat? Reread it to yourself. Does it make sense? Could someone else understand it? If not, fix it. Add a mark in the box for U.
  3. (T): P stands for punctuation. Did you remember a period at the end? If not, fix it. If you remembered, put a tally mark above the period. Add a mark in the box for P.
  4. (T): S stands for spelling. Did you spell your words correctly? Check them. Now, check yours with mine (show the teacher's copy). Fix any words you spelled incorrectly. Put a tally mark above the words you spelled correctly. Add a mark in the box for S.
  5. (T): Rewrite your sentence with all of the corrections.
  6. (T): Check for CUPS again. Put another mark in the boxes.
  7. (T): Let's read the sentences.
  8. (S) Read the sentences for fluency and automaticity.

  ***Please note:** Once students understand how to use CUPS, transition to letting them check their sentence independently before showing the teacher's copy.

Weekly Red Words

Materials Needed:
screen, red crayon, red word paper

Introduce on Tuesday, and practice daily. Use the Flip Chart for steps.

New:	Review:	New Read-Only:	Review Read-Only:
see, stop	the, was, is, a, on, and, to, for, go, I, like, of, will, get, no, want, with, said, you, in, put	blue, eek	orange, white, brown, stop, red, yellow, bus

Steps for Teaching a New Red Word:

1. (T) States the word. (*see*)

2. (T&S) Use tokens to determine how many sounds are in the word. (/s/ /ē/; 2)

3. (T&S) Discuss how we would expect to spell each sound as the teacher writes the grapheme(s) correctly. Identify what is unexpected or irregular about the spelling of the word. It could also be expected, but the concept hasn't been taught yet.

4. (T&S) Discuss the etymology of the word, if appropriate (lexical words). Visit www.etymonline.com for more information on the word.

5. (T) Defines the word, and writes a sentence using the word.

6. (T) Writes the word on Red Word paper with the screen underneath, using red crayon.

7. (S) Write the word on Red Word paper with the screen underneath, using red crayon. (S) Show the word to the teacher.
   (**NOTE:** The teacher should have students chunk the word if it has more than four letters.)

8. (T&S) Stand up, holding the Red Word in the nondominant hand. Armtap word while naming each letter. Then "underline" the word by sweeping left to right while stating the word, 3x. (**NOTE:** Left-handed students will place their left hand on their right wrist. They tap to their right shoulder. Underline from wrist to shoulder. Right-handed students place their right hand on their left shoulder. They tap to their left wrist. Underline shoulder to wrist.)

9. (T&S) Trace crayon bumps with the pointer finger while naming the letters, 3x.

10. (T&S) Place the screen over the paper and trace the word with the pointer finger while naming the letters, 3x.

11. (S) Turn paper over. With red crayon, write the word without the screen one time, and hold up the word for the teacher to check. (S) Write the word two more times.

12. (S) Write an original sentence in pencil and underline the Red Word with a red crayon. (**NOTE:** The sentence can also be dictated by the teacher while the student writes or dictated by the student while the teacher writes it.)

13. Repeat the steps for *stop*. (/s/ /t/ /ŏ/ /p/; 4)

Review Ideas for Red Words:

- Sculpt the word using red Play-Doh or clay. Have students spell the word as they smash each letter.
- Print flashcards from IOG, and practice reading.
- Armtap the word to review.
- Cross-clap the word to review.
- Do Spelling Aerobics.

Fluency, Vocabulary, and Comprehension

- Incorporate fluency into your literacy lessons daily/weekly (minimum 30 min/week) by using Rapid Word Charts, IMSE Decodable Readers, words and sentences, Acadience Reading K-6 or DIBELS 8th Edition, repeated reading, and other activities.
- Incorporate vocabulary into your literacy lessons daily/weekly (minimum 50 min/week) by choosing 3-5 appropriate tier two words (can pull from rich literature or decodable readers). Teach the words through explicit, direct instruction using student-friendly definitions, word webs, vocabulary charts, illustrations, and other activities.
- Incorporate oral language comprehension into your literacy lessons daily/weekly (approximately 100 min/week). Comprehension instruction should be explicit, direct instruction that includes teacher modeling, guided practice, and independent practice. Plan ahead to build on students' background knowledge, language structures, verbal reasoning, and literacy knowledge.

Extension Activity Ideas

- Continue to add to the multi-sensory ABC book. Have students glue rice (or another object) in the shape of the target letter.
- Have students compare and contrast a rope and a ribbon using a Venn Diagram.
- Make a paper rainbow. Have students glue pictures of words that begin with the /r/ sound on the rainbow.
- Divide students into teams of 3 and have them lie on the ground to form the target letter. Take pictures to hang around the classroom.
- Create the target letter out of green Play-Doh or clay.
- Have students use a bingo dauber to find the target letter on a page with various letters.
- Have students go on a "sound hunt" around the room or outside to find objects that begin with the target sound.
- Coding activity: Have students underline and label the letters in words or syllables with a "v" for vowels and a "c" for consonants. For example, when using the word *mom*, each letter should be underlined with the labels "cvc" underneath the word. This activity will help prepare students for decoding multisyllabic words later in the sequence.
- Visit IMSE's Orton-Gillingham's Pinterest page for more ideas.

Weekly Lesson Reminders

- Any of the above extension activities
- Practice writing the target letter (capital and lowercase) using a screen, green crayon, and house paper.
- Practice writing the target letter using another medium (sand, paint, shaving cream, pudding, iPad app, etc.).
- Practice writing the target letter using age-appropriate paper and pencil.
- Daily practice with writing the weekly Red Word(s)
- Kilpatrick's "One-Minute Activities" for daily phonological awareness practice
- Zgonc's phonological awareness activities
- Listen to rich literature to work on oral language comprehension.
- Target letter practice sheets from IMSE's practice books and handwriting books
- Practice test on Thursday and test on Friday

Ff  as in fish

Card Pack #17 Decodable Reader #9

Object Ideas:	Literature Ideas:
fish, football, feather, fox, fan, foot, footprint, felt, foam, Frisbee, freeze pop, fur, fruit, fuzzy, flower, flour	▪ *Tales of a Fourth Grade Nothing* by Judy Blume ▪ *Freckle Juice* by Judy Blume ▪ *One Fish, Two Fish, Red Fish, Blue Fish* by Dr. Seuss ▪ *The Foot Book* by Dr. Seuss ▪ Frog and Toad series by Arnold Lobel ▪ *Flossie and the Fox* by Patricia McKissack ▪ *Stone Fox* by John Reynolds Gardiner

 ## Notes

- Use the Comprehensive Flip Chart for the steps on how to teach each part of IMSE's Lesson Plan.
- Ff /f/ is an unvoiced, fricative consonant sound. The teeth are on the bottom lip.
- Keep "f" in the initial position at first. If /f/ is at the end of a one-syllable word with one short vowel, it is spelled "-ff." After open and closed syllables have been taught, "f" can be moved to the final position to support syllables such as "muf" in "muffin."

 ## Phonological Awareness:

Materials Needed:
tokens, sound boxes, one-minute activities, or Zgonc PA book

Use the PAST assessment to determine a starting point for instruction. Incorporate daily phonological awareness activities by using Zgonc's tiered activities and/or Kilpatrick's One-Minute Activities in *Equipped for Reading Success.*

Phonemic awareness warm-up: Use tokens (or letter tiles once concepts have been taught) and sound boxes to do a quick phonemic awareness activity that ties in with the new concept, if appropriate.

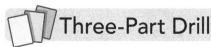

Three-Part Drill

Materials Needed:
review cards, sand, blending board, vowel tents or sticks

Do this at least 3x per week. Use the Flip Chart for steps. Include the new concept after Day 1.

- Include the Vowel Intensive with "a," "i," "o," and "u."

V	VC	CVC
a	ag, ap, ab	lat, cad, zan
e	et, en, eb	zeg, ren, med
i	ig, ib, im	lin, hib, fid
o	ob, ot, oz	rom, hob, cog
u	un, ud, ub	sup, pum, dut

- Below is a sample script now that students know more than one way to spell a concept. Remember to use all of the review concepts.

1. **Visual:**
   (T) Tell me the sounds you know for these letters.
   (S) /m/, /l/, etc.
   Alternative:
   (T) Tell me the names and sounds you know for these letters.
   (S) m says /m/, l says /l/, etc.

2. **Auditory/Kinesthetic:**
   (T) You know two ways to spell this. (S) split trays. (T) Eyes on me.
   Spell /k/. Repeat.
   (S) /k/ c says /k/; k says /k/

3. **Blending:**
   (T) Tell me the sound for each letter as I point. Then blend the sounds together to read the word or syllable. Give me a thumbs up if it is a real word.
   (S) /mmm/ /ŏŏŏ/ /mmm/ *mom* (thumbs up)
   Alternative:
   (T) Watch me first. /mmm/ /ŏŏŏ/ /mmm/ *mom*
   (T) Do it with me. (T&S) /mmm/ /ŏŏŏ/ /mmm/ *mom*
   (T) Your turn. (S) /mmm/ /ŏŏŏ/ /mmm/ *mom* (thumbs up)

*Vowel Intensive: Model the visual cue while calling out the sound. Students will do the visual cue as they repeat the sound. Students will then hold up the vowel tent while stating the letter name and sound.

- (T): Eyes on me. The sound is /ă/. Repeat.
- (S): /ă/ a says /ă/

Teaching a New Concept

Materials Needed:
concept card, screen, green crayon, object, sand, decodable readers, literature, P/G chart

Introduce on Monday, and practice daily.

1. (T) Reads alliteration sentences. (S) Identify the target sound.
   a. Fred fried fish on Friday.
   b. Fat fish fry fabulously.

2. (T) Shows the new concept card.
   a. (T) Tells students the letter name and sound. Have (S) repeat, 3 times (f says /f/).
   b. (T) Tells students that "f" is a consonant.
   c. (T) Tells students it is an unvoiced sound.
   d. (T) Asks students where they find "f" in the alphabet.
   e. (T) Uses mirrors to discuss the mouth, tongue, and teeth placement.

3. (T) Shows an object.
   a. (T) Allows students to manipulate the object and discuss prior knowledge. Reminds (S) that the object has the target sound spelled with the target letter.

4. (S) Brainstorm.
   a. Brainstorm words that have the target sound. (Accept all answers, but place incorrect answers in a "thought bubble" to discuss.) The brainstorming can be a teacher-directed activity if students need extra support.

5. (T) Teaches Letter Formation. Use house paper to teach lowercase letters.
   a. (T) models with the solid letter. The letter "f" starts outside the attic, comes around to the top of the attic, and stops at the floor. Cross it at the ceiling.
   b. Using the screen and green crayon, (T&S) trace the solid while saying, "f says /f/" (3x).
   c. (T&S) use their finger to trace the solid while saying, "f says /f/" (3x).
   d. (S) trace the dotted letter and complete the remainder of the row independently.
   e. (S) move to smaller house and repeat process if needed.
   f. Teach capital letters throughout the week using the same process. Capital letters go outside the house.

6. (T) Dictates target sound. (S) Practice in the sand or other medium.
   a. Practice writing the letter using a different medium, such as sand, shaving cream, finger paint, gel board, iPad app, air writing, etc.
   b. Do this while stating: f says /f/, 3 times.

7. (T) Connects with literature.
   a. Have students signal when they hear the /f/ sound for the first page or two.
   b. Read again for language comprehension.
   c. Continue to work on language comprehension with rich literature throughout the week.

8. (S) Use decodable readers to practice the concepts learned.
    a. (S) Highlight words with the new concept. Read those words.
    b. (S) Highlight Red Words. Read those words.
    c. (S) Start reading the decodable reader.
    d. (S) Continue reading throughout the week.
    e. (S) Read a clean copy on Friday.
9. (T&S) Mark the Phoneme/Grapheme (P/G) chart by highlighting the target sound.

 ## Word Dictation

Materials Needed:
fingertapping hand, dictation paper, pencil

Create any syllables using the new concept and previously taught concepts. Practice daily. Use the Flip Chart to follow the steps for word dictation.

Day 1:	1. fib	2. fat	3. fob	4. tab	5. fig
Day 2:	1. fad	2. bat	3. fig	4. fit	5. fib
Day 3:	1. fit	2. fab	3. bug	4. fad	5. fat
Days 4-5:	Review prior words.				

Below is a sample script:

1. (T) States word: *mom*. Uses it in a sentence: My *mom* is a wonderful lady. (Pounds) *mom*. (T) Models fingertapping if needed: /m/ /ŏ/ /m/. (Pounds) *mom*.
2. (S) State while pounding: *mom*. (Fingertap) /m/ /ŏ/ /m/. (Pound) *mom*. Write the letters known for the sounds.
3. (T) When yours looks like mine, rewrite the word.
4. (S) Rewrite.
5. Repeat the process for each word.
6. (S) Read the list of words multiple times to build automaticity.

 ## Sentence Dictation

Red Words are underlined. Students can fingertap the green words. Use the Flip Chart to follow the steps for sentence dictation.

1. The fat pig was in the rut.
2. The lad is fit.
3. Mom had to jog in the fog.
4. The fig had a bud.
5. The fig is from Kip.
6. Bob, get the rag off the fig.
7. The fat hog was in the rut.

8. Rob had a big, fat lip.
9. It is bad to fib.
10. The fat rat is big.
11. I like fig jam.

- Below is a sample script for sentence dictation.

> 1. (T): Listen to the sentence. *Tad had a cat.*
> 2. (T): Listen while I pound the syllables. *Tad had a cat.*
> 3. (T): Pound it with me. (T&S): *Tad had a cat.*
> 4. (T): You pound the sentence. (S): *Tad had a cat.*
> 5. (T): Watch me as I point to the lines while stating the sentence. *Tad had a cat.*
> 6. (T): You point to the lines while stating the sentence.
> 7. (S): *Tad had a cat.*
> 8. (T): Now write the sentence. Fingertap if needed.

- Below is a sample script to check CUPS*.

> 1. (T): C stands for capitalization. Did you remember a capital letter at the beginning of your sentence? It's also a name. *Tad* would always be capitalized. If you forgot, fix it. If you remembered, put a tally mark above the capital letter. Add a mark in the box for C.
> 2. (T): U stands for understanding. Is your sentence neat? Reread it to yourself. Does it make sense? Could someone else understand it? If not, fix it. Add a mark in the box for U.
> 3. (T): P stands for punctuation. Did you remember a period at the end? If not, fix it. If you remembered, put a tally mark above the period. Add a mark in the box for P.
> 4. (T): S stands for spelling. Did you spell your words correctly? Check them. Now, check yours with mine (show the teacher's copy). Fix any words you spelled incorrectly. Put a tally mark above the words you spelled correctly. Add a mark in the box for S.
> 5. (T): Rewrite your sentence with all of the corrections.
> 6. (T): Check for CUPS again. Put another mark in the boxes.
> 7. (T): Let's read the sentences.
> 8. (S) Read the sentences for fluency and automaticity.
>
> ***Please note:** Once students understand how to use CUPS, transition to letting them check their sentence independently before showing the teacher's copy.

Weekly Red Words

Materials Needed:
screen, red crayon, red word paper

Introduce on Tuesday, and practice daily. Use the Flip Chart for steps.

New:	Review:	New Read-Only:	Review Read-Only:
from, off	the, was, is, a, on, and, to, for, go, I, like, of, will, get, no, want, with, said, you, in, put, see, stop	sun	orange, white, brown, stop, red, yellow, bus, blue, eek

Steps for Teaching a New Red Word:

1. (T) States the word. (*from*)
2. (T&S) Use tokens to determine how many sounds are in the word. (/f/ /r/ /ŭ/ /m/; 4)
3. (T&S) Discuss how we would expect to spell each sound as the teacher writes the grapheme(s) correctly. Identify what is unexpected or irregular about the spelling of the word. It could also be expected, but the concept hasn't been taught yet.
4. (T&S) Discuss the etymology of the word, if appropriate (lexical words). Visit www.etymonline.com for more information on the word.
5. (T) Defines the word, and writes a sentence using the word.
6. (T) Writes the word on Red Word paper with the screen underneath, using red crayon.
7. (S) Write the word on Red Word paper with the screen underneath, using red crayon. (S) Show the word to the teacher.
   (**NOTE:** The teacher should have students chunk the word if it has more than four letters.)
8. (T&S) Stand up, holding the Red Word in the nondominant hand. Armtap word while naming each letter. Then "underline" the word by sweeping left to right while stating the word, 3x. (**NOTE:** Left-handed students will place their left hand on their right wrist. They tap to their right shoulder. Underline from wrist to shoulder. Right-handed students place their right hand on their left shoulder. They tap to their left wrist. Underline shoulder to wrist.)
9. (T&S) Trace crayon bumps with the pointer finger while naming the letters, 3x.
10. (T&S) Place the screen over the paper and trace the word with the pointer finger while naming the letters, 3x.
11. (S) Turn paper over. With red crayon, write the word without the screen one time, and hold up the word for the teacher to check. (S) Write the word two more times.

12. (S) Write an original sentence in pencil and underline the Red Word with a red crayon. (**NOTE:** The sentence can also be dictated by the teacher while the student writes or dictated by the student while the teacher writes it.)

13. Repeat the steps for *off*. (/ŏ/ /f/; 2)

Review Ideas for Red Words:

- Sculpt the word using red Play-Doh or clay. Have students spell the word as they smash each letter.
- Print flashcards from IOG, and practice reading.
- Armtap the word to review.
- Cross-clap the word to review.
- Do Spelling Aerobics.

Fluency, Vocabulary, and Comprehension

- Incorporate fluency into your literacy lessons daily/weekly (minimum 30 min/week) by using Rapid Word Charts, IMSE Decodable Readers, words and sentences, Acadience Reading K-6 or DIBELS 8th Edition, repeated reading, and other activities.

- Incorporate vocabulary into your literacy lessons daily/weekly (minimum 50 min/week) by choosing 3-5 appropriate tier two words (can pull from rich literature or decodable readers). Teach the words through explicit, direct instruction using student-friendly definitions, word webs, vocabulary charts, illustrations, and other activities.

- Incorporate oral language comprehension into your literacy lessons daily/weekly (approximately 100 min/week). Comprehension instruction should be explicit, direct instruction that includes teacher modeling, guided practice, and independent practice. Plan ahead to build on students' background knowledge, language structures, verbal reasoning, and literacy knowledge.

Extension Activity Ideas

- Continue to add to the multi-sensory ABC book. Have students glue felt (or another object) in the shape of the target letter.
- Have students compare and contrast Swedish Fish and Goldfish crackers using a Venn Diagram.
- Make a paper frog. Have students glue pictures of words that begin with the /f/ sound on the frog.
- Divide students into teams of 3 and have them lie on the ground to form the target letter. Take pictures to hang around the classroom.
- Create the target letter out of green Play-Doh or clay.
- Have students use a bingo dauber to find the target letter on a page with various letters.
- Have students go on a "sound hunt" around the room or outside to find objects that begin with the target sound.
- Coding activity: Have students underline and label the letters in words or syllables with a "v" for vowels and a "c" for consonants. For example, when using the word *mom*, each letter should be underlined with the labels "cvc" underneath the word. This activity will help prepare students for decoding multisyllabic words later in the sequence.
- Visit IMSE's Orton-Gillingham's Pinterest page for more ideas.

Weekly Lesson Reminders

- Any of the above extension activities
- Practice writing the target letter (capital and lowercase) using a screen, green crayon, and house paper.
- Practice writing the target letter using another medium (sand, paint, shaving cream, pudding, iPad app, etc.).
- Practice writing the target letter using age-appropriate paper and pencil.
- Daily practice with writing the weekly Red Word(s)
- Kilpatrick's "One-Minute Activities" for daily phonological awareness practice
- Zgonc's phonological awareness activities
- Listen to rich literature to work on oral language comprehension.
- Target letter practice sheets from IMSE's practice books and handwriting books
- Practice test on Thursday and test on Friday

Nn as in nose

Card Pack #18 Decodable Reader #10	
Object Ideas:	**Literature Ideas:**
Nerds, nest, number, nail, nickel, necklace, noodle, Nerf, note, nose, Nintendo, nine, needle, Nestlé Crunch	<ul><li>Nancy Drew series by Carolyn Keene</li><li>*The Napping House* by Audrey Wood</li><li>*Nana Upstairs and Nana Downstairs* by Tomie dePaola</li><li>*No, David!* by David Shannon</li><li>*Goodnight Moon* by Margaret Wise Brown</li><li>*Nelson Mandela* by Kadir Nelson</li><li>*My Name is Brain Brian* by Jeanne Betancourt</li><li>*Strega Nona* by Tomie dePaola</li><li>*Miss Nelson Is Missing!* by Harry Allard</li><li>*Natsumi's Song of Summer* by Robert Paul Weston</li><li>*Not Quite Snow White* by Ashley Franklin</li></ul>

Notes

- Use the Comprehensive Flip Chart for the steps on how to teach each part of IMSE's Lesson Plan.
- Nn /n/ is a voiced, nasal consonant sound. The lips are parted and the tongue is on the ridge behind the teeth.
- If needed, the card pack contains an extra "n" so it can be used in both the initial and final position on the blending board.

Phonological Awareness:

Materials Needed:
tokens, sound boxes, one-minute activities, or Zgonc PA book

Use the PAST assessment to determine a starting point for instruction. Incorporate daily phonological awareness activities by using Zgonc's tiered activities and/or Kilpatrick's One-Minute Activities in *Equipped for Reading Success*.

Phonemic awareness warm-up: Use tokens (or letter tiles once concepts have been taught) and sound boxes to do a quick phonemic awareness activity that ties in with the new concept, if appropriate.

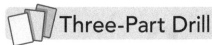

Three-Part Drill

Materials Needed:
review cards, sand, blending board, vowel tents or sticks

Do this at least 3x per week. Use the Flip Chart for steps. Include the new concept after Day 1.

- Include the Vowel Intensive with "a," "i," "o," and "u."

V	VC	CVC
a	ag, ap, ab	lat, cad, zan
e	et, en, eb	zeg, ren, med
i	ig, ib, im	lin, hib, fid
o	ob, ot, oz	rom, hob, cog
u	un, ud, ub	sup, pum, dut

- Below is a sample script now that students know more than one way to spell a concept. Remember to use all of the review concepts.

1. **Visual:**
   (T) Tell me the sounds you know for these letters.
   (S) /m/, /l/, etc.
   Alternative:
   (T) Tell me the names and sounds you know for these letters.
   (S) m says /m/, l says /l/, etc.

2. **Auditory/Kinesthetic:**
   (T) You know two ways to spell this. (S) split trays. (T) Eyes on me.
   Spell /k/. Repeat.
   (S) /k/ c says /k/; k says /k/

3. **Blending:**
   (T) Tell me the sound for each letter as I point. Then blend the sounds together to read the word or syllable. Give me a thumbs up if it is a real word.
   (S) /mmm/ /ŏŏŏ/ /mmm/ *mom* (thumbs up)
   Alternative:
   (T) Watch me first. /mmm/ /ŏŏŏ/ /mmm/ *mom*
   (T) Do it with me. (T&S) /mmm/ /ŏŏŏ/ /mmm/ *mom*
   (T) Your turn. (S) /mmm/ /ŏŏŏ/ /mmm/ *mom* (thumbs up)

*Vowel Intensive: Model the visual cue while calling out the sound. Students will do the visual cue as they repeat the sound. Students will then hold up the vowel tent while stating the letter name and sound.

- (T): Eyes on me. The sound is /ă/. Repeat.
- (S): /ă/ a says /ă/

Teaching a New Concept

Materials Needed:
concept card, screen, green crayon, object, sand, decodable readers, literature, P/G chart

Introduce on Monday, and practice daily.

1. (T) Reads alliteration sentences. (S) Identify the target sound.
   a. Nettie nestled noodles.
   b. Nick nailed nine nails.

2. (T) Shows the new concept card.
   a. (T) Tells students the letter name and sound. Have (S) repeat, 3 times (n says /n/).
   b. (T) Tells students that "n" is a consonant.
   c. (T) Tells students it is a voiced sound.
   d. (T) Asks students where they find "n" in the alphabet.
   e. (T) Uses mirrors to discuss the mouth, tongue, and teeth placement.

3. (T) Shows an object.
   a. (T) Allows students to manipulate the object and discuss prior knowledge. Reminds (S) that the object has the target sound spelled with the target letter.

4. (S) Brainstorm.
   a. Brainstorm words that have the target sound. (Accept all answers, but place incorrect answers in a "thought bubble" to discuss.) The brainstorming can be a teacher-directed activity if students need extra support.

5. (T) Teaches Letter Formation. Use house paper to teach lowercase letters.
   a. (T) models with the solid letter. The letter "n" starts at the ceiling and goes down to the floor. Then, come back up to the ceiling, curve around, and come down to the floor.
   b. Using the screen and green crayon, (T&S) trace the solid while saying, "n says /n/" (3x).
   c. (T&S) use their finger to trace the solid while saying, "n says /n/" (3x).
   d. (S) trace the dotted letter and complete the remainder of the row independently.
   e. (S) move to smaller house and repeat process if needed.
   f. Teach capital letters throughout the week using the same process. Capital letters go outside the house.

6. (T) Dictates target sound. (S) Practice in the sand or other medium.
   a. Practice writing the letter using a different medium, such as sand, shaving cream, finger paint, gel board, iPad app, air writing, etc.
   b. Do this while stating: n says /n/, 3 times.

7. (T) Connects with literature.
   a. Have students signal when they hear the /n/ sound for the first page or two.
   b. Read again for language comprehension.
   c. Continue to work on language comprehension with rich literature throughout the week.

8. (S) Use decodable readers to practice the concepts learned.
   a. (S) Highlight words with the new concept. Read those words.
   b. (S) Highlight Red Words. Read those words.
   c. (S) Start reading the decodable reader.
   d. (S) Continue reading throughout the week.
   e. (S) Read a clean copy on Friday.
9. (T&S) Mark the Phoneme/Grapheme (P/G) chart by highlighting the target sound.

 ## Word Dictation

Materials Needed:
fingertapping hand, dictation paper, pencil

Create any syllables using the new concept and previously taught concepts. Practice daily. Use the Flip Chart to follow the steps for word dictation.

Day 1:	1. fan	2. bun	3. man	4. nod	5. pin
Day 2:	1. fin	2. not	3. ran	4. nap	5. bin
Day 3:	1. can	2. nut	3. fun	4. nip	5. Don
Days 4-5:	Review prior words. Optional additional words: ban, con, Dan, din, in, Jan, kin, nab, nag, Nan, nob, nun, on, pan, pun, run, tan, tin				

Below is a sample script:

1. (T) States word: *mom*. Uses it in a sentence: My *mom* is a wonderful lady. (Pounds) *mom*. (T) Models fingertapping if needed: /m/ /ŏ/ /m/. (Pounds) *mom*.
2. (S) State while pounding: *mom*. (Fingertap) /m/ /ŏ/ /m/. (Pound) *mom*. Write the letters known for the sounds.
3. (T) When yours looks like mine, rewrite the word.
4. (S) Rewrite.
5. Repeat the process for each word.
6. (S) Read the list of words multiple times to build automaticity.

 ## Sentence Dictation

Red Words are underlined. Students can fingertap the green words. Use the Flip Chart to follow the steps for sentence dictation.

1. The man had a nut from the bin.
2. Dan and Jim had fun in the cab.
3. The gal ran to the tub.
4. Mom and Dad had fun on the run.
5. The bin has a nut in it.
6. He hid the bun in the pan.
7. A pin was on the man.

8. Jan is kin to him.
9. The cat had a nap on the rug.
10. The pan is not hot.
11. Nan had a nut.
12. Jan can fan the hot pan.
13. Can Jan fan the cat?
14. Can the pup nip Don?
15. Don is not mad at Jan.

- Below is a sample script for sentence dictation.

> 1. (T): Listen to the sentence. *Tad had a cat.*
> 2. (T): Listen while I pound the syllables. *Tad had a cat.*
> 3. (T): Pound it with me. (T&S): *Tad had a cat.*
> 4. (T): You pound the sentence. (S): *Tad had a cat.*
> 5. (T): Watch me as I point to the lines while stating the sentence. *Tad had a cat.*
> 6. (T): You point to the lines while stating the sentence.
> 7. (S): *Tad had a cat.*
> 8. (T): Now write the sentence. Fingertap if needed.

- Below is a sample script to check CUPS*.

> 1. (T): C stands for capitalization. Did you remember a capital letter at the beginning of your sentence? It's also a name. *Tad* would always be capitalized. If you forgot, fix it. If you remembered, put a tally mark above the capital letter. Add a mark in the box for C.
> 2. (T): U stands for understanding. Is your sentence neat? Reread it to yourself. Does it make sense? Could someone else understand it? If not, fix it. Add a mark in the box for U.
> 3. (T): P stands for punctuation. Did you remember a period at the end? If not, fix it. If you remembered, put a tally mark above the period. Add a mark in the box for P.
> 4. (T): S stands for spelling. Did you spell your words correctly? Check them. Now, check yours with mine (show the teacher's copy). Fix any words you spelled incorrectly. Put a tally mark above the words you spelled correctly. Add a mark in the box for S.
> 5. (T): Rewrite your sentence with all of the corrections.
> 6. (T): Check for CUPS again. Put another mark in the boxes.
> 7. (T): Let's read the sentences.
> 8. (S) Read the sentences for fluency and automaticity.
>
> **Please note:** Once students understand how to use CUPS, transition to letting them check their sentence independently before showing the teacher's copy.

Weekly Red Words

Materials Needed:
screen, red crayon, red word paper

Introduce on Tuesday, and practice daily. Use the Flip Chart for steps.

New:	Review:	New Read-Only:	Review Read-Only:
he, has	the, was, is, a, and, to, for, go, I, like, of, will, get, no, want, with, said, you, put, see, stop, from, off	ouch	orange, white, brown, stop, red, yellow, bus, blue, eek, sun

Steps for Teaching a New Red Word:

1. (T) States the word. (*he*)
2. (T&S) Use tokens to determine how many sounds are in the word. (/h/ /ē/; 2)
3. (T&S) Discuss how we would expect to spell each sound as the teacher writes the grapheme(s) correctly. Identify what is unexpected or irregular about the spelling of the word. It could also be expected, but the concept hasn't been taught yet.
4. (T&S) Discuss the etymology of the word, if appropriate (lexical words). Visit www.etymonline.com for more information on the word.
5. (T) Defines the word, and writes a sentence using the word.
6. (T) Writes the word on Red Word paper with the screen underneath, using red crayon.
7. (S) Write the word on Red Word paper with the screen underneath, using red crayon. (S) Show the word to the teacher.
   (**NOTE:** The teacher should have students chunk the word if it has more than four letters.)
8. (T&S) Stand up, holding the Red Word in the nondominant hand. Armtap word while naming each letter. Then "underline" the word by sweeping left to right while stating the word, 3x. (**NOTE:** Left-handed students will place their left hand on their right wrist. They tap to their right shoulder. Underline from wrist to shoulder. Right-handed students place their right hand on their left shoulder. They tap to their left wrist. Underline shoulder to wrist.)
9. (T&S) Trace crayon bumps with the pointer finger while naming the letters, 3x.
10. (T&S) Place the screen over the paper and trace the word with the pointer finger while naming the letters, 3x.
11. (S) Turn paper over. With red crayon, write the word without the screen one time, and hold up the word for the teacher to check. (S) Write the word two more times.

12. (S) Write an original sentence in pencil and underline the Red Word with a red crayon. (**NOTE:** The sentence can also be dictated by the teacher while the student writes or dictated by the student while the teacher writes it.)

13. Repeat the steps for *has*. (/h/ /ă/ /z/; 3)

Review Ideas for Red Words:

- Sculpt the word using red Play-Doh or clay. Have students spell the word as they smash each letter.
- Print flashcards from IOG, and practice reading.
- Armtap the word to review.
- Cross-clap the word to review.
- Do Spelling Aerobics.

Fluency, Vocabulary, and Comprehension

- Incorporate fluency into your literacy lessons daily/weekly (minimum 30 min/ week) by using Rapid Word Charts, IMSE Decodable Readers, words and sentences, Acadience Reading K-6 or DIBELS 8th Edition, repeated reading, and other activities.
- Incorporate vocabulary into your literacy lessons daily/weekly (minimum 50 min/week) by choosing 3-5 appropriate tier two words (can pull from rich literature or decodable readers). Teach the words through explicit, direct instruction using student-friendly definitions, word webs, vocabulary charts, illustrations, and other activities.
- Incorporate oral language comprehension into your literacy lessons daily/weekly (approximately 100 min/week). Comprehension instruction should be explicit, direct instruction that includes teacher modeling, guided practice, and independent practice. Plan ahead to build on students' background knowledge, language structures, verbal reasoning, and literacy knowledge.

Extension Activity Ideas

- Continue to add to the multi-sensory ABC book. Have students glue Nerds (or another object) in the shape of the target letter.
- Have students compare and contrast Nerds and Nestlé Crunch using a Venn Diagram.
- Make a paper nest. Have students glue pictures of words that begin with the /n/ sound on the nest.
- Divide students into teams of 3 and have them lie on the ground to form the target letter. Take pictures to hang around the classroom.
- Create the target letter out of green Play-Doh or clay.
- Have students use a bingo dauber to find the target letter on a page with various letters.
- Have students go on a "sound hunt" around the room or outside to find objects that begin with the target sound.
- Coding activity: Have students underline and label the letters in words or syllables with a "v" for vowels and a "c" for consonants. For example, when using the word *mom*, each letter should be underlined with the labels "cvc" underneath the word. This activity will help prepare students for decoding multisyllabic words later in the sequence.
- Visit IMSE's Orton-Gillingham's Pinterest page for more ideas.

Weekly Lesson Reminders

- Any of the above extension activities
- Practice writing the target letter (capital and lowercase) using a screen, green crayon, and house paper.
- Practice writing the target letter using another medium (sand, paint, shaving cream, pudding, iPad app, etc.).
- Practice writing the target letter using age-appropriate paper and pencil.
- Daily practice with writing the weekly Red Word(s)
- Kilpatrick's "One-Minute Activities" for daily phonological awareness practice
- Zgonc's phonological awareness activities
- Listen to rich literature to work on oral language comprehension.
- Target letter practice sheets from IMSE's practice books and handwriting books
- Practice test on Thursday and test on Friday

Review for Concepts m–n

After teaching the first 18 concepts, the following words and sentences may be utilized for review. Teachers can dictate a different list (A, B, C, or D) and three sentences each day of the review. Teachers can spend up to a week on review *if needed*. If a review is not needed, this page can be skipped or partially utilized. Students can use IMSE workbooks or age-appropriate paper for recording their answers.

List A	List B	List C	List D
1. ban	1. bin	1. fat	1. rap
2. gum	2. jot	2. pin	2. kit
3. kid	3. rat	3. Kim	3. fob
4. nap	4. cut	4. jug	4. hit
5. jog	5. jam	5. rot	5. can
6. rod	6. fun	6. bag	6. Jim
7. fib	7. cob	7. lid	7. but
8. gap	8. tip	8. nut	8. pat
9. dig	9. kid	9. ram	9. gut
10. bad	10. fig	10. dip	10. nip

Sentences:

1. The kit is for Mom.
2. The cap got a big rip.
3. Will the cat and dog jog?
4. The mop is on the mat.
5. Did Dot hit the log?
6. The pan is not hot.
7. Did the cub tug on the bag?
8. Mom had to jog in the fog.
9. The jug had a lid on it.
10. I like fig jam.
11. Dan and Jim had fun in the cab.
12. The rig was in a big rut.

Notes:

_____

_____

_____

_____

_____

_____

_____

_____

_____

_____

_____

_____

_____

_____

_____

_____

_____

_____

_____

_____

Ee as in edge

Card Pack #19 Decodable Reader #11	
Object Ideas:	**Literature Ideas:**
edge (of table), echo, eggplant	▪ *Elmer (the Patchwork Elephant)* by David McKee ▪ *The Elf on the Shelf: A Christmas Tradition* by Carol V. Aebersold and Chanda A. Bell ▪ *Green Eggs and Ham* by Dr. Seuss ▪ *Everett Anderson's Goodbye* by Lucille Clifton ▪ *I Am Every Good Thing* by Derrick Barnes

Notes

- Use the Comprehensive Flip Chart for the steps on how to teach each part of IMSE's Lesson Plan.
- Ee /ĕ/ is a voiced vowel sound. To produce vowel sounds, articulators hold a shape but do not obstruct air. Refer to the Vowel Valley on sound production.
- Make a vowel stick or tent.
- Teach the visual cue: push lips back with thumb/index finger.

Phonological Awareness:

Materials Needed:
tokens, sound boxes, one-minute activities, or Zgonc PA book

Use the PAST assessment to determine a starting point for instruction. Incorporate daily phonological awareness activities by using Zgonc's tiered activities and/or Kilpatrick's One-Minute Activities in *Equipped for Reading Success*.

Phonemic awareness warm-up: Use tokens (or letter tiles once concepts have been taught) and sound boxes to do a quick phonemic awareness activity that ties in with the new concept, if appropriate.

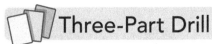 **Three-Part Drill**

Materials Needed:
review cards, sand, blending board, vowel tents or sticks

Do this at least 3x per week. Use the Flip Chart for steps. Include the new concept after Day 1.

- Include the Vowel Intensive with "a," "e," "i," "o," and "u."
- Include "e" once it has been taught.

V	VC	CVC
a	ag, ap, ab	lat, cad, zan
e	et, en, eb	zeg, ren, med
i	ig, ib, im	lin, hib, fid
o	ob, ot, oz	rom, hob, cog
u	un, ud, ub	sup, pum, dut

- Below is a sample script now that students know more than one way to spell a concept. Remember to use all of the review concepts.

1. **Visual:**
   (T) Tell me the sounds you know for these letters.
   (S) /m/, /l/, etc.
   Alternative:
   (T) Tell me the names and sounds you know for these letters.
   (S) m says /m/, l says /l/, etc.

2. **Auditory/Kinesthetic:**
   (T) You know two ways to spell this. (S) split trays. (T) Eyes on me.
   Spell /k/. Repeat.
   (S) /k/ c says /k/; k says /k/

3. **Blending:**
   (T) Tell me the sound for each letter as I point. Then blend the sounds together to read the word or syllable. Give me a thumbs up if it is a real word.
   (S) /mmm/ /ŏŏŏ/ /mmm/ *mom* (thumbs up)
   Alternative:
   (T) Watch me first. /mmm/ /ŏŏŏ/ /mmm/ *mom*
   (T) Do it with me. (T&S) /mmm/ /ŏŏŏ/ /mmm/ *mom*
   (T) Your turn. (S) /mmm/ /ŏŏŏ/ /mmm/ *mom* (thumbs up)

   *Vowel Intensive:** Model the visual cue while calling out the sound. Students will do the visual cue as they repeat the sound. Students will then hold up the vowel tent while stating the letter name and sound.
   - (T): Eyes on me. The sound is /ă/. Repeat.
   - (S): /ă/ a says /ă/

Teaching a New Concept

Materials Needed:
concept card, screen, green crayon, object, sand, decodable readers, literature, P/G chart

Introduce on Monday, and practice daily.

1. (T) Reads alliteration sentence. (S) Identify the target sound.

   a. Ed enjoyed echoing on the edge of the cliff.

   (T) Read the following sentence in which /ĕ/ is in the medial position. (S) Identify the target sound.

   b. Beth met a hen in the pen.

2. (T) Shows the new concept card.

   a. (T) Tells students the letter name and sound. Have (S) repeat, 3 times (e says /ĕ/).

   b. (T) Tells students that "e" is a vowel.

   c. (T) Tells students it is a voiced sound.

   d. (T) Asks students where they find "e" in the alphabet.

   e. (T) Uses mirrors to discuss the mouth, tongue, and teeth placement.

3. (T) Shows an object.

   a. (T) Allows students to manipulate the object and discuss prior knowledge. Reminds (S) that the object has the target sound spelled with the target letter.

4. (S) Brainstorm.

   a. Brainstorm words that have the target sound. (Accept all answers, but place incorrect answers in a "thought bubble" to discuss.) The brainstorming can be a teacher-directed activity if students need extra support. (**Note:** For short vowels, students can brainstorm word families or rhyming words containing the vowel sound.)

5. (T) Teaches Letter Formation. Use house paper to teach lowercase letters.

   a. (T) models with the solid letter. The letter "e" starts in the middle of the house then goes towards the wall. Come back around and bump the ceiling. Bump the floor, and stop.

   b. Using the screen and green crayon, (T&S) trace the solid while saying, "e says /ĕ/" (3x).

   c. (T&S) use their finger to trace the solid while saying, "e says /ĕ/" (3x).

   d. (S) trace the dotted letter and complete the remainder of the row independently.

   e. (S) move to smaller house and repeat process if needed.

   f. Teach capital letters throughout the week using the same process. Capital letters go outside the house.

6. (T) Dictates target sound. (S) Practice in the sand or other medium.

   a. Practice writing the letter using a different medium, such as sand, shaving cream, finger paint, gel board, iPad app, air writing, etc.

   b. Do this while stating: e says /ĕ/, 3 times.

7. (T) Connects with literature.

   a. Have students signal when they hear the /ĕ/ sound for the first page or two.

  b. Read again for language comprehension.

  c. Continue to work on language comprehension with rich literature throughout the week.

8. (S) Use decodable readers to practice the concepts learned.

  a. (S) Highlight words with the new concept. Read those words.

  b. (S) Highlight Red Words. Read those words.

  c. (S) Start reading the decodable reader.

  d. (S) Continue reading throughout the week.

  e. (S) Read a clean copy on Friday.

9. (T&S) Mark the Phoneme/Grapheme (P/G) chart by highlighting the target sound.

Word Dictation

Materials Needed:
fingertapping hand, dictation paper, pencil

Create any syllables using the new concept and previously taught concepts. Practice daily. Use the Flip Chart to follow the steps for word dictation.

Day 1:	1. led	2. get	3. Deb	4. met	5. ten
Day 2:	1. men	2. hen	3. beg	4. pen	5. Jed
Day 3:	1. bet	2. leg	3. net	4. Jen	5. pet
Days 4-5:	Review prior words. Optional additional words: den, hem, Ken, Peg				

Below is a sample script:

1. (T) States word: *mom.* Uses it in a sentence: My *mom* is a wonderful lady. (Pounds) *mom.* (T) Models fingertapping if needed: /m/ /ŏ/ /m/. (Pounds) *mom.*

2. (S) State while pounding: *mom.* (Fingertap) /m/ /ŏ/ /m/. (Pound) *mom.* Write the letters known for the sounds.

3. (T) When yours looks like mine, rewrite the word.

4. (S) Rewrite.

5. Repeat the process for each word.

6. (S) Read the list of words multiple times to build automaticity.

Sentence Dictation

Red Words are underlined. Students can fingertap the green words. Use the Flip Chart to follow the steps for sentence dictation.

1. Ken <u>is</u> ten.

2. Jim hid <u>the</u> fat pig in <u>the</u> pen.

3. <u>The</u> pin <u>was</u> on <u>the</u> hem.

4. Jed <u>and</u> Jen hid <u>the</u> net.

5. Mom led <u>me to the</u> mat.

6. The men ran in the pen.
7. Have Ken pet the rat.
8. The pig is in the big pen.
9. The pet can beg.
10. Peg met ten men at the net.
11. Ken bet Peg in the den.
12. Ben can beg Deb to get a pet.

▪ Below is a sample script for sentence dictation.

> 1. (T): Listen to the sentence. *Tad had a cat.*
> 2. (T): Listen while I pound the syllables. *Tad had a cat.*
> 3. (T): Pound it with me. (T&S): *Tad had a cat.*
> 4. (T): You pound the sentence. (S): *Tad had a cat.*
> 5. (T): Watch me as I point to the lines while stating the sentence. *Tad had a cat.*
> 6. (T): You point to the lines while stating the sentence.
> 7. (S): *Tad had a cat.*
> 8. (T): Now write the sentence. Fingertap if needed.

▪ Below is a sample script to check CUPS*.

> 1. (T): C stands for capitalization. Did you remember a capital letter at the beginning of your sentence? It's also a name. *Tad* would always be capitalized. If you forgot, fix it. If you remembered, put a tally mark above the capital letter. Add a mark in the box for C.
> 2. (T): U stands for understanding. Is your sentence neat? Reread it to yourself. Does it make sense? Could someone else understand it? If not, fix it. Add a mark in the box for U.
> 3. (T): P stands for punctuation. Did you remember a period at the end? If not, fix it. If you remembered, put a tally mark above the period. Add a mark in the box for P.
> 4. (T): S stands for spelling. Did you spell your words correctly? Check them. Now, check yours with mine (show the teacher's copy). Fix any words you spelled incorrectly. Put a tally mark above the words you spelled correctly. Add a mark in the box for S.
> 5. (T): Rewrite your sentence with all of the corrections.
> 6. (T): Check for CUPS again. Put another mark in the boxes.
> 7. (T): Let's read the sentences.
> 8. (S) Read the sentences for fluency and automaticity.
>
> **Please note:** Once students understand how to use CUPS, transition to letting them check their sentence independently before showing the teacher's copy.

Weekly Red Words

Materials Needed:
screen, red crayon, red word paper

Introduce on Tuesday, and practice daily. Use the Flip Chart for steps.

New:	Review:	New Read-Only:	Review Read-Only:
have, me	the, was, is, a, and, to, for, go, I, like, of, will, no, want, with, said, you, put, see, stop, from, off, he, has	pink	orange, white, brown, stop, yellow, bus, blue, eek, sun, ouch

Steps for Teaching a New Red Word:

1. (T) States the word. (*have*)
2. (T&S) Use tokens to determine how many sounds are in the word. (/h/ /ă/ /v/; 3)
3. (T&S) Discuss how we would expect to spell each sound as the teacher writes the grapheme(s) correctly. Identify what is unexpected or irregular about the spelling of the word. It could also be expected, but the concept hasn't been taught yet.
4. (T&S) Discuss the etymology of the word, if appropriate (lexical words). Visit www.etymonline.com for more information on the word.
5. (T) Defines the word, and writes a sentence using the word.
6. (T) Writes the word on Red Word paper with the screen underneath, using red crayon.
7. (S) Write the word on Red Word paper with the screen underneath, using red crayon. (S) Show the word to the teacher. (**NOTE:** The teacher should have students chunk the word if it has more than four letters.)
8. (T&S) Stand up, holding the Red Word in the nondominant hand. Armtap word while naming each letter. Then "underline" the word by sweeping left to right while stating the word, 3x. (**NOTE:** Left-handed students will place their left hand on their right wrist. They tap to their right shoulder. Underline from wrist to shoulder. Right-handed students place their right hand on their left shoulder. They tap to their left wrist. Underline shoulder to wrist.)
9. (T&S) Trace crayon bumps with the pointer finger while naming the letters, 3x.
10. (T&S) Place the screen over the paper and trace the word with the pointer finger while naming the letters, 3x.
11. (S) Turn paper over. With red crayon, write the word without the screen one time, and hold up the word for the teacher to check. (S) Write the word two more times.

12. (S) Write an original sentence in pencil and underline the Red Word with a red crayon. (**NOTE:** The sentence can also be dictated by the teacher while the student writes or dictated by the student while the teacher writes it.)

13. Repeat the steps for *me*. (/m/ /ē/; 2)

Review Ideas for Red Words:

▪ Sculpt the word using red Play-Doh or clay. Have students spell the word as they smash each letter.

▪ Print flashcards from IOG, and practice reading.

▪ Armtap the word to review.

▪ Cross-clap the word to review.

Fluency, Vocabulary, and Comprehension

▪ Incorporate fluency into your literacy lessons daily/weekly (minimum 30 min/week) by using Rapid Word Charts, IMSE Decodable Readers, words and sentences, Acadience Reading K-6 or DIBELS 8th Edition, repeated reading, and other activities.

▪ Incorporate vocabulary into your literacy lessons daily/weekly (minimum 50 min/week) by choosing 3-5 appropriate tier two words (can pull from rich literature or decodable readers). Teach the words through explicit, direct instruction using student-friendly definitions, word webs, vocabulary charts, illustrations, and other activities.

▪ Incorporate oral language comprehension into your literacy lessons daily/weekly (approximately 100 min/week). Comprehension instruction should be explicit, direct instruction that includes teacher modeling, guided practice, and independent practice. Plan ahead to build on students' background knowledge, language structures, verbal reasoning, and literacy knowledge.

Extension Activity Ideas

- Continue to add to the multi-sensory ABC book. Have students glue elbow macaroni (or another object) in the shape of the target letter.
- Have students compare and contrast an egg and an eggplant using a Venn Diagram.
- Make a paper table. Have students glue pictures of words that begin with the /ĕ/ sound around the edge of the table.
- Divide students into teams of 3 and have them lie on the ground to form the target letter. Take pictures to hang around the classroom.
- Create the target letter out of green Play-Doh or clay.
- Have students use a bingo dauber to find the target letter on a page with various letters.
- Have students go on a "sound hunt" around the room or outside to find objects that begin with the target sound.
- Coding activity: Have students underline and label the letters in words or syllables with a "v" for vowels and a "c" for consonants. For example, when using the word *mom*, each letter should be underlined with the labels "cvc" underneath the word. This activity will help prepare students for decoding multisyllabic words later in the sequence.
- Visit IMSE's Orton-Gillingham's Pinterest page for more ideas.

Weekly Lesson Reminders

- Any of the above extension activities
- Practice writing the target letter (capital and lowercase) using a screen, green crayon, and house paper.
- Practice writing the target letter using another medium (sand, paint, shaving cream, pudding, iPad app, etc.).
- Practice writing the target letter using age-appropriate paper and pencil.
- Daily practice with writing the weekly Red Word(s)
- Kilpatrick's "One-Minute Activities" for daily phonological awareness practice
- Zgonc's phonological awareness activities
- Listen to rich literature to work on oral language comprehension.
- Target letter practice sheets from IMSE's practice books and handwriting books
- Practice test on Thursday and test on Friday

Ss as in sun

Card Pack #20 Decodable Reader #12	
Object Ideas:	**Literature Ideas:**
sun, sea, sand, sunflower, soap, sock, seal, seasons, sticker, spaghetti, senses, Silly Putty, star, squeeze, sprint, SpongeBob, swamp, science, social studies, soup	▪ Flat Stanley series by Jeff Brown ▪ *Stellaluna* by Janell Cannon ▪ *Silly Sally* by Audrey Wood ▪ *Snowy Day* by Ezra Jack Keats ▪ *Snowmen at Night* by Caralyn Buehner ▪ *The Tiny Seed* by Eric Carle ▪ *Sulwe* by Lupita Nyong'o ▪ *Super Satya Saves the Day* by Raakhee Mirchandani ▪ *Strega Nona* by Tomie dePaola ▪ *Saturday* by Oge Mora

Notes

- Use the Comprehensive Flip Chart for the steps on how to teach each part of IMSE's Lesson Plan.
- Ss /s/ is an unvoiced, fricative consonant sound. The lips are pulled back, and the tip of the tongue is behind the teeth but not quite touching them.
- Keep "s" in the initial position at first. If /s/ is at the end of a one-syllable word with one short vowel, it is usually spelled "-ss."
- After the "Sammy" rule is learned, the "s" can go in either position to model syllables such as "hys" in "hysterical."

Phonological Awareness:

Materials Needed:
tokens, sound boxes, one-minute activities, or Zgonc PA book

Use the PAST assessment to determine a starting point for instruction. Incorporate daily phonological awareness activities by using Zgonc's tiered activities and/or Kilpatrick's One-Minute Activities in *Equipped for Reading Success*.

Phonemic awareness warm-up: Use tokens (or letter tiles once concepts have been taught) and sound boxes to do a quick phonemic awareness activity that ties in with the new concept, if appropriate.

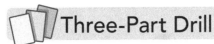

Three-Part Drill

Materials Needed:
review cards, sand, blending board, vowel tents or sticks

Do this at least 3x per week. Use the Flip Chart for steps. Include the new concept after Day 1.

- Include the Vowel Intensive with "a," "e," "i," "o," and "u."

V	VC	CVC
a	ag, ap, ab	lat, cad, zan
e	et, en, eb	zeg, ren, med
i	ig, ib, im	lin, hib, fid
o	ob, ot, oz	rom, hob, cog
u	un, ud, ub	sup, pum, dut

- Below is a sample script now that students know more than one way to spell a concept. Remember to use all of the review concepts.

1. **Visual:**
   (T) Tell me the sounds you know for these letters.
   (S) /m/, /l/, etc.
   Alternative:
   (T) Tell me the names and sounds you know for these letters.
   (S) m says /m/, l says /l/, etc.

2. **Auditory/Kinesthetic:**
   (T) You know two ways to spell this. (S) split trays. (T) Eyes on me.
   Spell /k/. Repeat.
   (S) /k/ c says /k/; k says /k/

3. **Blending:**
   (T) Tell me the sound for each letter as I point. Then blend the sounds together to read the word or syllable. Give me a thumbs up if it is a real word.
   (S) /mmm/ /ŏŏŏ/ /mmm/ *mom* (thumbs up)
   Alternative:
   (T) Watch me first. /mmm/ /ŏŏŏ/ /mmm/ *mom*
   (T) Do it with me. (T&S) /mmm/ /ŏŏŏ/ /mmm/ *mom*
   (T) Your turn. (S) /mmm/ /ŏŏŏ/ /mmm/ *mom* (thumbs up)

   *Vowel Intensive: Model the visual cue while calling out the sound. Students will do the visual cue as they repeat the sound. Students will then hold up the vowel tent while stating the letter name and sound.
   - (T): Eyes on me. The sound is /ă/. Repeat.
   - (S): /ă/ a says /ă/

Teaching a New Concept

Materials Needed:
concept card, screen, green crayon, object, sand, decodable readers, literature, P/G chart

Introduce on Monday, and practice daily.

1. (T) Reads alliteration sentences. (S) Identify the target sound.
   a. Susie sells seashells by the seashore.
   b. Steve says silly sayings.

2. (T) Shows the new concept card.
   a. (T) Tells students the letter name and sound. Have (S) repeat, 3 times (s says /s/).
   b. (T) Tells students that "s" is a consonant.
   c. (T) Tells students it is an unvoiced sound.
   d. (T) Asks students where they find "s" in the alphabet.
   e. (T) Uses mirrors to discuss the mouth, tongue, and teeth placement.

3. (T) Shows an object.
   a. (T) Allows students to manipulate the object and discuss prior knowledge. Reminds (S) that the object has the target sound spelled with the target letter.

4. (S) Brainstorm.
   a. Brainstorm words that have the target sound. (Accept all answers, but place incorrect answers in a "thought bubble" to discuss.) The brainstorming can be a teacher-directed activity if students need extra support.

5. (T) Teaches Letter Formation. Use house paper to teach lowercase letters.
   a. (T) models with the solid letter. The letter "s" starts right below the ceiling then comes up and bumps the ceiling. Wrap around to bump the floor and stop.
   b. Using the screen and green crayon, (T&S) trace the solid while saying, "s says /s/" (3x).
   c. (T&S) use their finger to trace the solid while saying, "s says /s/" (3x).
   d. (S) trace the dotted letter and complete the remainder of the row independently.
   e. (S) move to smaller house and repeat process if needed.
   f. Teach capital letters throughout the week using the same process. Capital letters go outside the house.

6. (T) Dictates target sound. (S) Practice in the sand or other medium.
   a. Practice writing the letter using a different medium, such as sand, shaving cream, finger paint, gel board, iPad app, air writing, etc.
   b. Do this while stating: s says /s/, 3 times.

7. (T) Connects with literature.
   a. Have students signal when they hear the /s/ sound for the first page or two.
   b. Read again for language comprehension.
   c. Continue to work on language comprehension with rich literature throughout the week.

8. (S) Use decodable readers to practice the concepts learned.
   a. (S) Highlight words with the new concept. Read those words.
   b. (S) Highlight Red Words. Read those words.
   c. (S) Start reading the decodable reader.
   d. (S) Continue reading throughout the week.
   e. (S) Read a clean copy on Friday.
9. (T&S) Mark the Phoneme/Grapheme (P/G) chart by highlighting the target sound.

Word Dictation

Materials Needed:
fingertapping hand, dictation paper, pencil

Create any syllables using the new concept and previously taught concepts. Practice daily. Use the Flip Chart to follow the steps for word dictation.

Day 1:	1. sub	2. sit	3. sip	4. sob	5. sat
Day 2:	1. sag	2. sum	3. Sam	4. sop	5. sap
Day 3:	1. Sal	2. sad	3. sun	4. sod	5. set
Days 4-5:	Review prior words. Optional additional words: Sid, sin, sog

Below is a sample script:

1. (T) States word: *mom.* Uses it in a sentence: My *mom* is a wonderful lady. (Pounds) *mom.* (T) Models fingertapping if needed: /m/ /ŏ/ /m/. (Pounds) *mom.*
2. (S) State while pounding: *mom.* (Fingertap) /m/ /ŏ/ /m/. (Pound) *mom.* Write the letters known for the sounds.
3. (T) When yours looks like mine, rewrite the word.
4. (S) Rewrite.
5. Repeat the process for each word.
6. (S) Read the list of words multiple times to build automaticity.

Sentence Dictation

Red Words are underlined. Students can fingertap the green words. Use the Flip Chart to follow the steps for sentence dictation.

1. Sal sat in the sun.
2. The dog sat on the lap of the kid.
3. Kim had fun in the sun and got a tan.
4. The sad hen sat on the log.
5. The sad hen sat on the log in the pen.
6. Sam was sad as he sat in his hot tub.
7. Jed hid the sod in the pit.

8. Sam got ten men to hum.

9. Sid is a sad man.

10. Ken set the net on the rug.

11. Deb can sit in the sun and sip.

12. Did Sam sip from the jug?

- Below is a sample script for sentence dictation.

> 1. (T): Listen to the sentence. *Tad had a cat.*
>
> 2. (T): Listen while I pound the syllables. *Tad had a cat.*
>
> 3. (T): Pound it with me. (T&S): *Tad had a cat.*
>
> 4. (T): You pound the sentence. (S): *Tad had a cat.*
>
> 5. (T): Watch me as I point to the lines while stating the sentence. *Tad had a cat.*
>
> 6. (T): You point to the lines while stating the sentence.
>
> 7. (S): *Tad had a cat.*
>
> 8. (T): Now write the sentence. Fingertap if needed.

- Below is a sample script to check CUPS*.

> 1. (T): C stands for capitalization. Did you remember a capital letter at the beginning of your sentence? It's also a name. *Tad* would always be capitalized. If you forgot, fix it. If you remembered, put a tally mark above the capital letter. Add a mark in the box for C.
>
> 2. (T): U stands for understanding. Is your sentence neat? Reread it to yourself. Does it make sense? Could someone else understand it? If not, fix it. Add a mark in the box for U.
>
> 3. (T): P stands for punctuation. Did you remember a period at the end? If not, fix it. If you remembered, put a tally mark above the period. Add a mark in the box for P.
>
> 4. (T): S stands for spelling. Did you spell your words correctly? Check them. Now, check yours with mine (show the teacher's copy). Fix any words you spelled incorrectly. Put a tally mark above the words you spelled correctly. Add a mark in the box for S.
>
> 5. (T): Rewrite your sentence with all of the corrections.
>
> 6. (T): Check for CUPS again. Put another mark in the boxes.
>
> 7. (T): Let's read the sentences.
>
> 8. (S) Read the sentences for fluency and automaticity.
>
> *Please note: Once students understand how to use CUPS, transition to letting them check their sentence independently before showing the teacher's copy.

Weekly Red Words

Materials Needed:
screen, red crayon, red word paper

Introduce on Tuesday, and practice daily. Use the Flip Chart for steps.

New:	Review:	New Read-Only:	Review Read-Only:
his, as	the, was, is, a, and, to, for, go, I, like, of, will, no, want, with, said, you, put, see, stop, from, off, he, has, have, me	green	orange, white, brown, stop, yellow, blue, eek, ouch, pink

Steps for Teaching a New Red Word:

1. (T) States the word. (*his*)
2. (T&S) Use tokens to determine how many sounds are in the word. (/h/ /ĭ/ /z/; 3)
3. (T&S) Discuss how we would expect to spell each sound as the teacher writes the grapheme(s) correctly. Identify what is unexpected or irregular about the spelling of the word. It could also be expected, but the concept hasn't been taught yet.
4. (T&S) Discuss the etymology of the word, if appropriate (lexical words). Visit www.etymonline.com for more information on the word.
5. (T) Defines the word, and writes a sentence using the word.
6. (T) Writes the word on Red Word paper with the screen underneath, using red crayon.
7. (S) Write the word on Red Word paper with the screen underneath, using red crayon. (S) Show the word to the teacher.
   (**NOTE:** The teacher should have students chunk the word if it has more than four letters.)
8. (T&S) Stand up, holding the Red Word in the nondominant hand. Armtap word while naming each letter. Then "underline" the word by sweeping left to right while stating the word, 3x. (**NOTE:** Left-handed students will place their left hand on their right wrist. They tap to their right shoulder. Underline from wrist to shoulder. Right-handed students place their right hand on their left shoulder. They tap to their left wrist. Underline shoulder to wrist.)
9. (T&S) Trace crayon bumps with the pointer finger while naming the letters, 3x.
10. (T&S) Place the screen over the paper and trace the word with the pointer finger while naming the letters, 3x.
11. (S) Turn paper over. With red crayon, write the word without the screen one time, and hold up the word for the teacher to check. (S) Write the word two more times.

12. (S) Write an original sentence in pencil and underline the Red Word with a red crayon. (**NOTE:** The sentence can also be dictated by the teacher while the student writes or dictated by the student while the teacher writes it.)

13. Repeat the steps for *as*. (/ă/ /z/; 2)

Review Ideas for Red Words:

- Sculpt the word using red Play-Doh or clay. Have students spell the word as they smash each letter.
- Print flashcards from IOG, and practice reading.
- Armtap the word to review.
- Cross-clap the word to review.
- Do Spelling Aerobics.

Fluency, Vocabulary, and Comprehension

- Incorporate fluency into your literacy lessons daily/weekly (minimum 30 min/week) by using Rapid Word Charts, IMSE Decodable Readers, words and sentences, Acadience Reading K-6 or DIBELS 8th Edition, repeated reading, and other activities.

- Incorporate vocabulary into your literacy lessons daily/weekly (minimum 50 min/week) by choosing 3-5 appropriate tier two words (can pull from rich literature or decodable readers). Teach the words through explicit, direct instruction using student-friendly definitions, word webs, vocabulary charts, illustrations, and other activities.

- Incorporate oral language comprehension into your literacy lessons daily/weekly (approximately 100 min/week). Comprehension instruction should be explicit, direct instruction that includes teacher modeling, guided practice, and independent practice. Plan ahead to build on students' background knowledge, language structures, verbal reasoning, and literacy knowledge.

Extension Activity Ideas

- Continue to add to the multi-sensory ABC book. Have students glue sunflower seeds (or another object) in the shape of the target letter.
- Have students compare and contrast the sea and sand using a Venn Diagram.
- Make a paper sunflower. Have students glue pictures of words that begin with the /s/ sound on the sunflower.
- Have students get into teams of 3 and lie on the ground to form the target letter. Take pictures to hang around the classroom.
- Create the target letter out of green Play-Doh or clay.
- Have students use a bingo dauber to find the target letter on a page with various letters.
- Have students go on a "sound hunt" around the room or outside to find objects that begin with the target sound.
- Coding activity: Have students underline and label the letters in words or syllables with a "v" for vowels and a "c" for consonants. For example, when using the word mom, each letter should be underlined with the labels "cvc" underneath the word. This activity will help prepare students for decoding multisyllabic words later in the sequence.
- Visit IMSE's Orton-Gillingham's Pinterest page for more ideas.

Weekly Lesson Reminders

- Any of the above extension activities
- Practice writing the target letter (capital and lowercase) using a screen, green crayon, and house paper.
- Practice writing the target letter using another medium (sand, paint, shaving cream, pudding, iPad app, etc.).
- Practice writing the target letter using age-appropriate paper and pencil.
- Daily practice with writing the weekly Red Word(s)
- Kilpatrick's "One-Minute Activities" for daily phonological awareness practice
- Zgonc's phonological awareness activities
- Listen to rich literature to work on oral language comprehension.
- Target letter practice sheets from IMSE's practice books and handwriting books
- Practice test on Thursday and test on Friday

Ww  as in wagon

© IMSE 2022

Card Pack #21 Decodable Reader #13	
Object Ideas:	**Literature Ideas:**
wiggle, wag, watermelon, wall, wagon, watch, worm, weather, web, wish, west, wax, window	<ul><li>*Diary of a Wimpy Kid* by Jeff Kinney</li><li>*Diary of a Worm* by Doreen Cronin</li><li>*There's a Wocket in My Pocket!* by Dr. Seuss</li><li>*Charlotte's Web* by E. B. White</li><li>*The Wednesday Surprise* by Eve Bunting</li><li>*The Water Princess* by Susan Verde</li><li>*We March* by Shane W. Evans</li><li>*Winnie-the-Pooh* by A. A. Milne</li><li>*Wonder* by R. J. Palacio</li><li>*Where Are You From?* by Yamile Saied Méndez</li><li>*The Water Protectors* by Carole Lindstrom</li><li>*Worm Loves Worm* by J. J. Austrian</li></ul>

Notes

- Use the Comprehensive Flip Chart for the steps on how to teach each part of IMSE's Lesson Plan.
- Ww /w/ is a voiced, consonant sound categorized as a glide. The lips pucker together. Glides have vowel-like qualities and are followed by a vowel.
- Place "w" in the initial position on the blending board. If it's placed in the final position, it will combine with the preceding vowel to make a different sound.

Phonological Awareness:

Materials Needed:
tokens, sound boxes, one-minute activities, or Zgonc PA book

Use the PAST assessment to determine a starting point for instruction. Incorporate daily phonological awareness activities by using Zgonc's tiered activities and/or Kilpatrick's One-Minute Activities in *Equipped for Reading Success*.

Phonemic awareness warm-up: Use tokens (or letter tiles once concepts have been taught) and sound boxes to do a quick phonemic awareness activity that ties in with the new concept, if appropriate.

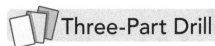 **Three-Part Drill**

Materials Needed:
review cards, sand, blending board, vowel tents or sticks

Do this at least 3x per week. Use the Flip Chart for steps. Include the new concept after Day 1.

- Include the Vowel Intensive with "a," "e," "i," "o," and "u."

V	VC	CVC
a	ag, ap, ab	lat, cad, zan
e	et, en, eb	zeg, ren, med
i	ig, ib, im	lin, hib, fid
o	ob, ot, oz	rom, hob, cog
u	un, ud, ub	sup, pum, dut

- Below is a sample script now that students know more than one way to spell a concept. Remember to use all of the review concepts.

1. **Visual:**
   (T) Tell me the sounds you know for these letters.
   (S) /m/, /l/, etc.
   Alternative:
   (T) Tell me the names and sounds you know for these letters.
   (S) m says /m/, l says /l/, etc.

2. **Auditory/Kinesthetic:**
   (T) You know two ways to spell this. (S) split trays. (T) Eyes on me.
   Spell /k/. Repeat.
   (S) /k/ c says /k/; k says /k/

3. **Blending:**
   (T) Tell me the sound for each letter as I point. Then blend the sounds together to read the word or syllable. Give me a thumbs up if it is a real word.
   (S) /mmm/ /ŏŏŏ/ /mmm/ *mom* (thumbs up)
   Alternative:
   (T) Watch me first. /mmm/ /ŏŏŏ/ /mmm/ *mom*
   (T) Do it with me. (T&S) /mmm/ /ŏŏŏ/ /mmm/ *mom*
   (T) Your turn. (S) /mmm/ /ŏŏŏ/ /mmm/ *mom* (thumbs up)

*Vowel Intensive: Model the visual cue while calling out the sound. Students will do the visual cue as they repeat the sound. Students will then hold up the vowel tent while stating the letter name and sound.
- (T): Eyes on me. The sound is /ă/. Repeat.
- (S): /ă/ a says /ă/

Teaching a New Concept

Materials Needed:
concept card, screen, green crayon, object, sand, decodable readers, literature, P/G chart

Introduce on Monday, and practice daily.

1. (T) Reads alliteration sentences. (S) Identify the target sound.
   a. Willie wandered with wagons.
   b. Wild walruses were wet with water.
2. (T) Shows the new concept card.
   a. (T) Tells students the letter name and sound. Have (S) repeat, 3 times (w says /w/).
   b. (T) Tells students that "w" is a consonant.
   c. (T) Tells students it is a voiced sound.
   d. (T) Asks students where they find "w" in the alphabet.
   e. (T) Uses mirrors to discuss the mouth, tongue, and teeth placement.
3. (T) Shows an object.
   a. (T) Allows students to manipulate the object and discuss prior knowledge. Reminds (S) that the object has the target sound spelled with the target letter.
4. (S) Brainstorm.
   a. Brainstorm words that have the target sound. (Accept all answers, but place incorrect answers in a "thought bubble" to discuss.) The brainstorming can be a teacher-directed activity if students need extra support.
5. (T) Teaches Letter Formation. Use house paper to teach lowercase letters.
   a. (T) models with the solid letter. The letter "w" starts at the ceiling and slants down to the floor. Then, go back up to the ceiling, slant back down to the floor, and go back up to the ceiling once again.
   b. Using the screen and green crayon, (T&S) trace the solid while saying, "w says /w/" (3x).
   c. (T&S) use their finger to trace the solid while saying, "w says /w/" (3x).
   d. (S) trace the dotted letter and complete the remainder of the row independently.
   e. (S) move to smaller house and repeat process if needed.
   f. Teach capital letters throughout the week using the same process. Capital letters go outside the house.
6. (T) Dictates target sound. (S) Practice in the sand or other medium.
   a. Practice writing the letter using a different medium, such as sand, shaving cream, finger paint, gel board, iPad app, air writing, etc.
   b. Do this while stating: w says /w/, 3 times.
7. (T) Connects with literature.
   a. Have students signal when they hear the /w/ sound for the first page or two.
   b. Read again for language comprehension.
   c. Continue to work on language comprehension with rich literature throughout the week.

8. (S) Use decodable readers to practice the concepts learned.

    a. (S) Highlight words with the new concept. Read those words.

    b. (S) Highlight Red Words. Read those words.

    c. (S) Start reading the decodable reader.

    d. (S) Continue reading throughout the week.

    e. (S) Read a clean copy on Friday.

9. (T&S) Mark the Phoneme/Grapheme (P/G) chart by highlighting the target sound.

 ## Word Dictation

Materials Needed:
fingertapping hand, dictation paper, pencil

Create any syllables using the new concept and previously taught concepts. Practice daily. Use the Flip Chart to follow the steps for word dictation.

Day 1:	1. wet	2. web	3. sub	4. win	5. wig
Day 2:	1. win	2. wag	3. wit	4. met	5. wed
Day 3:	1. wed	2. pet	3. wig	4. wet	5. web
Days 4-5:	Review prior words.				

Below is a sample script:

> 1. (T) States word: *mom*. Uses it in a sentence: My *mom* is a wonderful lady. (Pounds) *mom*. (T) Models fingertapping if needed: /m/ /ŏ/ /m/. (Pounds) *mom*.
> 2. (S) State while pounding: *mom*. (Fingertap) /m/ /ŏ/ /m/. (Pound) *mom*. Write the letters known for the sounds.
> 3. (T) When yours looks like mine, rewrite the word.
> 4. (S) Rewrite.
> 5. Repeat the process for each word.
> 6. (S) Read the list of words multiple times to build automaticity.

 ## Sentence Dictation

Red Words are underlined. Students can fingertap the green words. Use the Flip Chart to follow the steps for sentence dictation.

1. Pam wed Ken.

2. A web is at the top of a mop.

3. Did Kim get the wig?

4. Will he win it?

5. My wig was wet.

6. The rat ran into the web.

7. The cat is wet and sad.

8. The pig got wet in the pen.

9. The web is not hot but is big.

10. A wet web was on the hut.

- Below is a sample script for sentence dictation.

> 1. (T): Listen to the sentence. *Tad had a cat.*
> 2. (T): Listen while I pound the syllables. *Tad had a cat.*
> 3. (T): Pound it with me. (T&S): *Tad had a cat.*
> 4. (T): You pound the sentence. (S): *Tad had a cat.*
> 5. (T): Watch me as I point to the lines while stating the sentence. *Tad had a cat.*
> 6. (T): You point to the lines while stating the sentence.
> 7. (S): *Tad had a cat.*
> 8. (T): Now write the sentence. Fingertap if needed.

- Below is a sample script to check CUPS*.

> 1. (T): C stands for capitalization. Did you remember a capital letter at the beginning of your sentence? It's also a name. *Tad* would always be capitalized. If you forgot, fix it. If you remembered, put a tally mark above the capital letter. Add a mark in the box for C.
> 2. (T): U stands for understanding. Is your sentence neat? Reread it to yourself. Does it make sense? Could someone else understand it? If not, fix it. Add a mark in the box for U.
> 3. (T): P stands for punctuation. Did you remember a period at the end? If not, fix it. If you remembered, put a tally mark above the period. Add a mark in the box for P.
> 4. (T): S stands for spelling. Did you spell your words correctly? Check them. Now, check yours with mine (show the teacher's copy). Fix any words you spelled incorrectly. Put a tally mark above the words you spelled correctly. Add a mark in the box for S.
> 5. (T): Rewrite your sentence with all of the corrections.
> 6. (T): Check for CUPS again. Put another mark in the boxes.
> 7. (T): Let's read the sentences.
> 8. (S) Read the sentences for fluency and automaticity.
>
> ***Please note:** Once students understand how to use CUPS, transition to letting them check their sentence independently before showing the teacher's copy.

Weekly Red Words

Materials Needed:
screen, red crayon, red word paper

Introduce on Tuesday, and practice daily. Use the Flip Chart for steps.

New:	Review:	New Read-Only:	Review Read-Only:
my, into	the, was, is, a, and, to, for, go, I, like, of, will, no, want, with, said, you, put, see, stop, from, off, he, has, have, me, his, as		orange, white, brown, stop, yellow, blue, eek, ouch, pink, green

Steps for Teaching a New Red Word:

1. (T) States the word. (*my*)

2. (T&S) Use tokens to determine how many sounds are in the word. (/m/ /ī/; 2)

3. (T&S) Discuss how we would expect to spell each sound as the teacher writes the grapheme(s) correctly. Identify what is unexpected or irregular about the spelling of the word. It could also be expected, but the concept hasn't been taught yet.

4. (T&S) Discuss the etymology of the word, if appropriate (lexical words). Visit www.etymonline.com for more information on the word.

5. (T) Defines the word, and writes a sentence using the word.

6. (T) Writes the word on Red Word paper with the screen underneath, using red crayon.

7. (S) Write the word on Red Word paper with the screen underneath, using red crayon. (S) Show the word to the teacher.
   (**NOTE:** The teacher should have students chunk the word if it has more than four letters.)

8. (T&S) Stand up, holding the Red Word in the nondominant hand. Armtap word while naming each letter. Then "underline" the word by sweeping left to right while stating the word, 3x. (**NOTE:** Left-handed students will place their left hand on their right wrist. They tap to their right shoulder. Underline from wrist to shoulder. Right-handed students place their right hand on their left shoulder. They tap to their left wrist. Underline shoulder to wrist.)

9. (T&S) Trace crayon bumps with the pointer finger while naming the letters, 3x.

10. (T&S) Place the screen over the paper and trace the word with the pointer finger while naming the letters, 3x.

11. (S) Turn paper over. With red crayon, write the word without the screen one time, and hold up the word for the teacher to check. (S) Write the word two more times.

12. (S) Write an original sentence in pencil and underline the Red Word with a red crayon. (**NOTE:** The sentence can also be dictated by the teacher while the student writes or dictated by the student while the teacher writes it.)

13. Repeat the steps for *into*. (/ĭ/ /n/ /t/ / o͞o /; 4)

Review Ideas for Red Words:

▪ Sculpt the word using red Play-Doh or clay. Have students spell the word as they smash each letter.

▪ Print flashcards from IOG, and practice reading.

▪ Armtap the word to review.

▪ Cross-clap the word to review.

▪ Do Spelling Aerobics.

Fluency, Vocabulary, and Comprehension

▪ Incorporate fluency into your literacy lessons daily/weekly (minimum 30 min/week) by using Rapid Word Charts, IMSE Decodable Readers, words and sentences, Acadience Reading K-6 or DIBELS 8th Edition, repeated reading, and other activities.

▪ Incorporate vocabulary into your literacy lessons daily/weekly (minimum 50 min/week) by choosing 3-5 appropriate tier two words (can pull from rich literature or decodable readers). Teach the words through explicit, direct instruction using student-friendly definitions, word webs, vocabulary charts, illustrations, and other activities.

▪ Incorporate oral language comprehension into your literacy lessons daily/weekly (approximately 100 min/week). Comprehension instruction should be explicit, direct instruction that includes teacher modeling, guided practice, and independent practice. Plan ahead to build on students' background knowledge, language structures, verbal reasoning, and literacy knowledge.

Extension Activity Ideas

- Continue to add to the multi-sensory ABC book. Have students glue watermelon seeds (or another object) in the shape of the target letter.
- Have students compare and contrast water and watermelon using a Venn Diagram.
- Make a paper wagon. Have students glue pictures of words that begin with the /w/ sound on the wagon.
- Have students get into teams of 3 and lie on the ground to form the target letter. Take pictures to hang around the classroom.
- Create the target letter out of green Play-Doh or clay.
- Have students use a bingo dauber to find the target letter on a page with various letters.
- Have students go on a "sound hunt" around the room or outside to find objects that begin with the target sound.
- Coding activity: Have students underline and label the letters in words or syllables with a "v" for vowels and a "c" for consonants. For example, when using the word *mom*, each letter should be underlined with the labels "cvc" underneath the word. This activity will help prepare students for decoding multisyllabic words later in the sequence.
- Visit IMSE's Orton-Gillingham's Pinterest page for more ideas.

Weekly Lesson Reminders

- Any of the above extension activities
- Practice writing the target letter (capital and lowercase) using a screen, green crayon, and house paper.
- Practice writing the target letter using another medium (sand, paint, shaving cream, pudding, iPad app, etc.).
- Practice writing the target letter using age-appropriate paper and pencil.
- Daily practice with writing the weekly Red Word(s)
- Kilpatrick's "One-Minute Activities" for daily phonological awareness practice
- Zgonc's phonological awareness activities
- Listen to rich literature to work on oral language comprehension.
- Target letter practice sheets from IMSE's practice books and handwriting books
- Practice test on Thursday and test on Friday

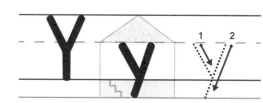

Yy as in yo-yo

Card Pack #22 Decodable Reader #14

Object Ideas:	Literature Ideas:
yarn, yellow, yo-yo, yak, yogurt, yardstick, yell, yam, yeast	<ul><li>*Yo! Yes?* by Chris Raschka</li><li>*Yertle the Turtle* by Dr. Seuss</li><li>*Extra Yarn* by Mac Barnett</li><li>*Yawn* by Sally Symes</li><li>*The Big Yawn* by Keith Faulkner</li><li>*Yes Day!* by Amy Krouse Rosenthal</li><li>*I Dare You Not to Yawn* by Helene Boudreau</li><li>*Yoko* by Rosemary Wells</li><li>*Little Blue and Little Yellow* by Leo Lionni</li></ul>

Notes

- Use the Comprehensive Flip Chart for the steps on how to teach each part of IMSE's Lesson Plan.
- Yy /y/ is a voiced, consonant sound categorized as a glide. The tongue is pulled back on the back roof of the mouth. Glides have vowel-like qualities and are followed by a vowel.
- In this lesson, "y" is a consonant. It has to be in the initial position in order to make the /y/ sound.
- This is a short lesson because there aren't many words that can be used for dictation. You could teach another new concept this week.

Phonological Awareness:

Materials Needed:
tokens, sound boxes, one-minute activities, or Zgonc PA book

Use the PAST assessment to determine a starting point for instruction. Incorporate daily phonological awareness activities by using Zgonc's tiered activities and/or Kilpatrick's One-Minute Activities in *Equipped for Reading Success.*

Phonemic awareness warm-up: Use tokens (or letter tiles once concepts have been taught) and sound boxes to do a quick phonemic awareness activity that ties in with the new concept, if appropriate.

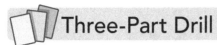

Three-Part Drill

Materials Needed:
review cards, sand, blending board, vowel tents or sticks

Do this at least 3x per week. Use the Flip Chart for steps. Include the new concept after Day 1.

- Include the Vowel Intensive with "a," "e," "i," "o," and "u."

V	VC	CVC
a	ag, ap, ab	lat, cad, zan
e	et, en, eb	zeg, ren, med
i	ig, ib, im	lin, hib, fid
o	ob, ot, oz	rom, hob, cog
u	un, ud, ub	sup, pum, dut

- Below is a sample script now that students know more than one way to spell a concept. Remember to use all of the review concepts.

1. **Visual:**
   (T) Tell me the sounds you know for these letters.
   (S) /m/, /l/, etc.
   Alternative:
   (T) Tell me the names and sounds you know for these letters.
   (S) m says /m/, l says /l/, etc.

2. **Auditory/Kinesthetic:**
   (T) You know two ways to spell this. (S) split trays. (T) Eyes on me.
   Spell /k/. Repeat.
   (S) /k/ c says /k/; k says /k/

3. **Blending:**
   (T) Tell me the sound for each letter as I point. Then blend the sounds together to read the word or syllable. Give me a thumbs up if it is a real word.
   (S) /mmm/ /ŏŏŏ/ /mmm/ *mom* (thumbs up)
   Alternative:
   (T) Watch me first. /mmm/ /ŏŏŏ/ /mmm/ *mom*
   (T) Do it with me. (T&S) /mmm/ /ŏŏŏ/ /mmm/ *mom*
   (T) Your turn. (S) /mmm/ /ŏŏŏ/ /mmm/ *mom* (thumbs up)

   *Vowel Intensive: Model the visual cue while calling out the sound. Students will do the visual cue as they repeat the sound. Students will then hold up the vowel tent while stating the letter name and sound.
   - (T): Eyes on me. The sound is /ă/. Repeat.
   - (S): /ă/ a says /ă/

Teaching a New Concept

Materials Needed:
concept card, screen, green crayon, object, sand, decodable readers, literature, P/G chart

Introduce on Monday, and practice daily.

1. (T) Reads alliteration sentences. (S) Identify the target sound.
   a. Yucky Yolanda yelled at the yo-yo.
   b. The yak yawned with yellow yarn in the yard.

2. (T) Shows the new concept card.
   a. (T) Tells students the letter name and sound. Have (S) repeat, 3 times (y says /y/).
   b. (T) Tells students that "y" is a consonant.
   c. (T) Tells students it is a voiced sound.
   d. (T) Asks students where they find "y" in the alphabet.
   e. (T) Uses mirrors to discuss the mouth, tongue, and teeth placement.

3. (T) Shows an object.
   a. (T) Allows students to manipulate the object and discuss prior knowledge. Reminds (S) that the object has the target sound spelled with the target letter.

4. (S) Brainstorm.
   a. Brainstorm words that have the target sound. (Accept all answers, but place incorrect answers in a "thought bubble" to discuss.) The brainstorming can be a teacher-directed activity if students need extra support.

5. (T) Teaches Letter Formation. Use house paper to teach lowercase letters.
   a. (T) models with the solid letter. The letter "y" starts at the ceiling and slants down to the floor. Then, go back up to the other side of the ceiling, slant back down to the floor, and end in the basement.
   b. Using the screen and green crayon, (T&S) trace the solid while saying, "y says /y/" (3x).
   c. (T&S) use their finger to trace the solid while saying, "y says /y/" (3x).
   d. (S) trace the dotted letter and complete the remainder of the row independently.
   e. (S) move to smaller house and repeat process if needed.
   f. Teach capital letters throughout the week using the same process. Capital letters go outside the house.

6. (T) Dictates target sound. (S) Practice in the sand or other medium.
   a. Practice writing the letter using a different medium, such as sand, shaving cream, finger paint, gel board, iPad app, air writing, etc.
   b. Do this while stating: y says /y/, 3 times.

7. (T) Connects with literature.
   a. Have students signal when they hear the /y/ sound for the first page or two.
   b. Read again for language comprehension.
   c. Continue to work on language comprehension with rich literature throughout the week.

8. (S) Use decodable readers to practice the concepts learned.
   a. (S) Highlight words with the new concept. Read those words.
   b. (S) Highlight Red Words. Read those words.
   c. (S) Start reading the decodable reader.
   d. (S) Continue reading throughout the week.
   e. (S) Read a clean copy on Friday.
9. (T&S) Mark the Phoneme/Grapheme (P/G) chart by highlighting the target sound.

 ## Word Dictation

Materials Needed:
fingertapping hand, dictation paper, pencil

Create any syllables using the new concept and previously taught concepts. Practice daily. Use the Flip Chart to follow the steps for word dictation.

Day 1:	1. yam	2. yes	3. tin	4. yon	5. web
Day 2:	1. yap	2. yet	3. leg	4. yam	5. fin
Day 3:	1. yen	2. set	3. yip	4. nut	5. yes
Days 4-5:	Review prior words.				

Below is a sample script:

> 1. (T) States word: *mom*. Uses it in a sentence: My *mom* is a wonderful lady. (Pounds) *mom*. (T) Models fingertapping if needed: /m/ /ŏ/ /m/. (Pounds) *mom*.
> 2. (S) State while pounding: *mom*. (Fingertap) /m/ /ŏ/ /m/. (Pound) *mom*. Write the letters known for the sounds.
> 3. (T) When yours looks like mine, rewrite the word.
> 4. (S) Rewrite.
> 5. Repeat the process for each word.
> 6. (S) Read the list of words multiple times to build automaticity.

 ## Sentence Dictation

Red Words are underlined. Students can fingertap the green words. Use the Flip Chart to follow the steps for sentence dictation.

1. See, the yam was hot!
2. Jed had a yen to jog.
3. Mom said yes!
4. The dog and cat can yap.
5. Yes, the new dog did yap at Mom.
6. Did the yam get hot now?
7. Bob and Tim yen to run.

8. The lad had a hot yam.
9. Pam had a ham and a yam.
10. Sal can yap at Kim.

- Below is a sample script for sentence dictation.

> 1. (T): Listen to the sentence. *Tad had a cat.*
> 2. (T): Listen while I pound the syllables. *Tad had a cat.*
> 3. (T): Pound it with me. (T&S): *Tad had a cat.*
> 4. (T): You pound the sentence. (S): *Tad had a cat.*
> 5. (T): Watch me as I point to the lines while stating the sentence. *Tad had a cat.*
> 6. (T): You point to the lines while stating the sentence.
> 7. (S): *Tad had a cat.*
> 8. (T): Now write the sentence. Fingertap if needed.

- Below is a sample script to check CUPS*.

> 1. (T): C stands for capitalization. Did you remember a capital letter at the beginning of your sentence? It's also a name. *Tad* would always be capitalized. If you forgot, fix it. If you remembered, put a tally mark above the capital letter. Add a mark in the box for C.
> 2. (T): U stands for understanding. Is your sentence neat? Reread it to yourself. Does it make sense? Could someone else understand it? If not, fix it. Add a mark in the box for U.
> 3. (T): P stands for punctuation. Did you remember a period at the end? If not, fix it. If you remembered, put a tally mark above the period. Add a mark in the box for P.
> 4. (T): S stands for spelling. Did you spell your words correctly? Check them. Now, check yours with mine (show the teacher's copy). Fix any words you spelled incorrectly. Put a tally mark above the words you spelled correctly. Add a mark in the box for S.
> 5. (T): Rewrite your sentence with all of the corrections.
> 6. (T): Check for CUPS again. Put another mark in the boxes.
> 7. (T): Let's read the sentences.
> 8. (S) Read the sentences for fluency and automaticity.
>
> **Please note:** Once students understand how to use CUPS, transition to letting them check their sentence independently before showing the teacher's copy.

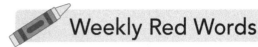

Weekly Red Words

Materials Needed:
screen, red crayon, red word paper

Introduce on Tuesday, and practice daily. Use the Flip Chart for steps.

New:	Review:	New Read-Only:	Review Read-Only:
now, new	the, was, is, a, and, to, for, go, I, like, of, will, no, want, with, said, you, put, see, stop, from, off, he, has, have, me, his, as, my, into		orange, white, brown, stop, yellow, blue, eek, ouch, pink, green

Steps for Teaching a New Red Word:

1. (T) States the word. (*now*)
2. (T&S) Use tokens to determine how many sounds are in the word. (/n/ /ou/; 2)
3. (T&S) Discuss how we would expect to spell each sound as the teacher writes the grapheme(s) correctly. Identify what is unexpected or irregular about the spelling of the word. It could also be expected, but the concept hasn't been taught yet.
4. (T&S) Discuss the etymology of the word, if appropriate (lexical words). Visit www.etymonline.com for more information on the word.
5. (T) Defines the word, and writes a sentence using the word.
6. (T) Writes the word on Red Word paper with the screen underneath, using red crayon.
7. (S) Write the word on Red Word paper with the screen underneath, using red crayon. (S) Show the word to the teacher.
   (**NOTE:** The teacher should have students chunk the word if it has more than four letters.)
8. (T&S) Stand up, holding the Red Word in the nondominant hand. Armtap word while naming each letter. Then "underline" the word by sweeping left to right while stating the word, 3x. (**NOTE:** Left-handed students will place their left hand on their right wrist. They tap to their right shoulder. Underline from wrist to shoulder. Right-handed students place their right hand on their left shoulder. They tap to their left wrist. Underline shoulder to wrist.)
9. (T&S) Trace crayon bumps with the pointer finger while naming the letters, 3x.
10. (T&S) Place the screen over the paper and trace the word with the pointer finger while naming the letters, 3x.
11. (S) Turn paper over. With red crayon, write the word without the screen one time, and hold up the word for the teacher to check. (S) Write the word two more times.
12. (S) Write an original sentence in pencil and underline the Red Word with a red crayon.

(**NOTE:** The sentence can also be dictated by the teacher while the student writes or dictated by the student while the teacher writes it.)

13. Repeat the steps for *new*. (/n/ / $\overline{oo}$ /; 2)

Review Ideas for Red Words:

- Sculpt the word using red Play-Doh or clay. Have students spell the word as they smash each letter.
- Print flashcards from IOG, and practice reading.
- Armtap the word to review.
- Cross-clap the word to review.
- Do Spelling Aerobics.

Fluency, Vocabulary, and Comprehension

- Incorporate fluency into your literacy lessons daily/weekly (minimum 30 min/week) by using Rapid Word Charts, IMSE Decodable Readers, words and sentences, Acadience Reading K-6 or DIBELS 8th Edition, repeated reading, and other activities.
- Incorporate vocabulary into your literacy lessons daily/weekly (minimum 50 min/week) by choosing 3-5 appropriate tier two words (can pull from rich literature or decodable readers). Teach the words through explicit, direct instruction using student-friendly definitions, word webs, vocabulary charts, illustrations, and other activities.
- Incorporate oral language comprehension into your literacy lessons daily/weekly (approximately 100 min/week). Comprehension instruction should be explicit, direct instruction that includes teacher modeling, guided practice, and independent practice. Plan ahead to build on students' background knowledge, language structures, verbal reasoning, and literacy knowledge.

Extension Activity Ideas

- Continue to add to the multi-sensory ABC book. Have students glue yarn (or another object) in the shape of the target letter.
- Have students compare and contrast a yam and yogurt using a Venn Diagram.
- Make a yellow blob. Have students glue pictures of words that begin with the /y/ sound on the yellow blob.
- Divide students into teams of 3 and have them lie on the ground to form the target letter. Take pictures to hang around the classroom.
- Create the target letter out of green Play-Doh or clay.
- Have students use a bingo dauber to find the target letter on a page with various letters.
- Have students go on a "sound hunt" around the room or outside to find objects that begin with the target sound.
- Coding activity: Have students underline and label the letters in words or syllables with a "v" for vowels and a "c" for consonants. For example, when using the word mom, each letter should be underlined with the labels "cvc" underneath the word. This activity will help prepare students for decoding multisyllabic words later in the sequence.
- Visit IMSE's Orton-Gillingham's Pinterest page for more ideas.

Weekly Lesson Reminders

- Any of the above extension activities
- Practice writing the target letter (capital and lowercase) using a screen, green crayon, and house paper.
- Practice writing the target letter using another medium (sand, paint, shaving cream, pudding, iPad app, etc.).
- Practice writing the target letter using age-appropriate paper and pencil.
- Daily practice with writing the weekly Red Word(s)
- Kilpatrick's "One-Minute Activities" for daily phonological awareness practice
- Zgonc's phonological awareness activities
- Listen to rich literature to work on oral language comprehension.
- Target letter practice sheets from IMSE's practice books and handwriting books
- Practice test on Thursday and test on Friday

Vv as in violin

Card Pack #23 Decodable Reader #15	
Object Ideas:	**Literature Ideas:**
violin, vegetable, valentine, vase, vest, volleyball, volcano	▪ *The Velveteen Rabbit* by Margery Williams ▪ *The Very Busy Spider* by Eric Carle ▪ *The Very Hungry Caterpillar* by Eric Carle ▪ *The Viper* by Lisa Thiesing ▪ *What in the World Is a Violin?* by Mary Elizabeth Salzmann ▪ *Growing Vegetable Soup* by Lois Ehlert ▪ *The Vegetables We Eat* by Gail Gibbons ▪ *I Want to Be a Vet* by Dan Liebman ▪ *¡Vamos! Let's Go to the Market* by Raúl the Third

Notes

- Use the Comprehensive Flip Chart for the steps on how to teach each part of IMSE's Lesson Plan.
- Vv /v/ is a voiced, fricative consonant sound. The teeth are on the bottom lip.
- Keep "v" in the initial position on the blending board. English words do not end with "v." (The word *rev* is included for word dictation. It has been "clipped" from the word *revolution*.)

Phonological Awareness:

Materials Needed:
tokens, sound boxes, one-minute activities, or Zgonc PA book

Use the PAST assessment to determine a starting point for instruction. Incorporate daily phonological awareness activities by using Zgonc's tiered activities and/or Kilpatrick's One-Minute Activities in *Equipped for Reading Success.*

Phonemic awareness warm-up: Use tokens (or letter tiles once concepts have been taught) and sound boxes to do a quick phonemic awareness activity that ties in with the new concept, if appropriate.

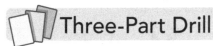
Three-Part Drill

Materials Needed:
review cards, sand, blending board, vowel tents or sticks

Do this at least 3x per week. Use the Flip Chart for steps. Include the new concept after Day 1.

- Include the Vowel Intensive with "a," "e," "i," "o," and "u."

V	VC	CVC
a	ag, ap, ab	lat, cad, zan
e	et, en, eb	zeg, ren, med
i	ig, ib, im	lin, hib, fid
o	ob, ot, oz	rom, hob, cog
u	un, ud, ub	sup, pum, dut

- Below is a sample script now that students know more than one way to spell a concept. Remember to use all of the review concepts.

1. **Visual:**
   (T) Tell me the sounds you know for these letters.
   (S) /m/, /l/, etc.
   Alternative:
   (T) Tell me the names and sounds you know for these letters.
   (S) m says /m/, l says /l/, etc.

2. **Auditory/Kinesthetic:**
   (T) You know two ways to spell this. (S) split trays. (T) Eyes on me.
   Spell /k/. Repeat.
   (S) /k/ c says /k/; k says /k/

3. **Blending:**
   (T) Tell me the sound for each letter as I point. Then blend the sounds together to read the word or syllable. Give me a thumbs up if it is a real word.
   (S) /mmm/ /ŏŏŏ/ /mmm/ *mom* (thumbs up)
   Alternative:
   (T) Watch me first. /mmm/ /ŏŏŏ/ /mmm/ *mom*
   (T) Do it with me. (T&S) /mmm/ /ŏŏŏ/ /mmm/ *mom*
   (T) Your turn. (S) /mmm/ /ŏŏŏ/ /mmm/ *mom* (thumbs up)

   *Vowel Intensive: Model the visual cue while calling out the sound. Students will do the visual cue as they repeat the sound. Students will then hold up the vowel tent while stating the letter name and sound.
   - (T): Eyes on me. The sound is /ă/. Repeat.
   - (S): /ă/ a says /ă/

Teaching a New Concept

Materials Needed:
concept card, screen, green crayon, object, sand, decodable readers, literature, P/G chart

Introduce on Monday, and practice daily.

1. (T) Reads alliteration sentences. (S) Identify the target sound.
   a. Viola visited valiant visitors and violins.
   b. Victor vacated the volcano.
2. (T) Shows the new concept card.
   a. (T) Tells students the letter name and sound. Have (S) repeat, 3 times (v says /v/).
   b. (T) Tells students that "v" is a consonant.
   c. (T) Tells students it is a voiced sound.
   d. (T) Asks students where they find "v" in the alphabet.
   e. (T) Uses mirrors to discuss the mouth, tongue, and teeth placement.
3. (T) Shows an object.
   a. (T) Allows students to manipulate the object and discuss prior knowledge. Reminds (S) that the object has the target sound spelled with the target letter.
4. (S) Brainstorm.
   a. Brainstorm words that have the target sound. (Accept all answers, but place incorrect answers in a "thought bubble" to discuss.) The brainstorming can be a teacher-directed activity if students need extra support.
5. (T) Teaches Letter Formation. Use house paper to teach lowercase letters.
   a. (T) models with the solid letter. The letter "v" starts at the ceiling and slants down to the floor. Then, go back up to the ceiling and stop.
   b. Using the screen and green crayon, (T&S) trace the solid while saying, "v says /v/" (3x).
   c. (T&S) use their finger to trace the solid while saying, "v says /v/" (3x).
   d. (S) trace the dotted letter and complete the remainder of the row independently.
   e. (S) move to smaller house and repeat process if needed.
   f. Teach capital letters throughout the week using the same process. Capital letters go outside the house.
6. (T) Dictates target sound. (S) Practice in the sand or other medium.
   a. Practice writing the letter using a different medium, such as sand, shaving cream, finger paint, gel board, iPad app, air writing, etc.
   b. Do this while stating: v says /v/, 3 times.
7. (T) Connects with literature.
   a. Have students signal when they hear the /v/ sound for the first page or two.
   b. Read again for language comprehension.
   c. Continue to work on language comprehension with rich literature throughout the week.

8. (S) Use decodable readers to practice the concepts learned.

   a. (S) Highlight words with the new concept. Read those words.

   b. (S) Highlight Red Words. Read those words.

   c. (S) Start reading the decodable reader.

   d. (S) Continue reading throughout the week.

   e. (S) Read a clean copy on Friday.

9. (T&S) Mark the Phoneme/Grapheme (P/G) chart by highlighting the target sound.

Word Dictation

Materials Needed:
fingertapping hand, dictation paper, pencil

Create any syllables using the new concept and previously taught concepts. Practice daily. Use the Flip Chart to follow the steps for word dictation.

Day 1:	1. rev	2. van	3. men	4. vet	5. sun
Day 2:	1. Val	2. beg	3. vim	4. yes	5. vat
Day 3:	1. van	2. Val	3. yet	4. vet	5. nap
Days 4-5:	Review prior words.				

Below is a sample script:

> 1. (T) States word: *mom*. Uses it in a sentence: My *mom* is a wonderful lady. (Pounds) *mom*. (T) Models fingertapping if needed: /m/ /ŏ/ /m/. (Pounds) *mom*.
> 2. (S) State while pounding: *mom*. (Fingertap) /m/ /ŏ/ /m/. (Pound) *mom*. Write the letters known for the sounds.
> 3. (T) When yours looks like mine, rewrite the word.
> 4. (S) Rewrite.
> 5. Repeat the process for each word.
> 6. (S) Read the list of words multiple times to build automaticity.

Sentence Dictation

Red Words are underlined. Students can fingertap the green words. Use the Flip Chart to follow the steps for sentence dictation.

1. The cat sat on the van.
2. The pug was at the vet.
3. The van had a pig in it.
4. The vat had ten men in it.
5. Val is a vet.
6. Give Val the pug.
7. The vat has a hot ham in it.

8. Ted hid <u>a</u> log in <u>the</u> van.
9. Bob can jog <u>with</u> vim.
10. <u>You</u> can <u>put</u> <u>the</u> mat in <u>the</u> van.

- Below is a sample script for sentence dictation.

> 1. (T): Listen to the sentence. *Tad had a cat.*
> 2. (T): Listen while I pound the syllables. *Tad had a cat.*
> 3. (T): Pound it with me. (T&S): *Tad had a cat.*
> 4. (T): You pound the sentence. (S): *Tad had a cat.*
> 5. (T): Watch me as I point to the lines while stating the sentence. *Tad had a cat.*
> 6. (T): You point to the lines while stating the sentence.
> 7. (S): *Tad had a cat.*
> 8. (T): Now write the sentence. Fingertap if needed.

- Below is a sample script to check CUPS*.

> 1. (T): C stands for capitalization. Did you remember a capital letter at the beginning of your sentence? It's also a name. *Tad* would always be capitalized. If you forgot, fix it. If you remembered, put a tally mark above the capital letter. Add a mark in the box for C.
> 2. (T): U stands for understanding. Is your sentence neat? Reread it to yourself. Does it make sense? Could someone else understand it? If not, fix it. Add a mark in the box for U.
> 3. (T): P stands for punctuation. Did you remember a period at the end? If not, fix it. If you remembered, put a tally mark above the period. Add a mark in the box for P.
> 4. (T): S stands for spelling. Did you spell your words correctly? Check them. Now, check yours with mine (show the teacher's copy). Fix any words you spelled incorrectly. Put a tally mark above the words you spelled correctly. Add a mark in the box for S.
> 5. (T): Rewrite your sentence with all of the corrections.
> 6. (T): Check for CUPS again. Put another mark in the boxes.
> 7. (T): Let's read the sentences.
> 8. (S) Read the sentences for fluency and automaticity.
>
> ***Please note:** Once students understand how to use CUPS, transition to letting them check their sentence independently before showing the teacher's copy.

Weekly Red Words

Materials Needed:
screen, red crayon, red word paper

Introduce on Tuesday, and practice daily. Use the Flip Chart for steps.

New:	Review:	New Read-Only:	Review Read-Only:
give	the, was, is, a, and, to, for, go, I, like, of, will, no, want, with, said, you, put, see, stop, from, off, he, has, have, me, his, as, my, into, now, new	black	orange, white, brown, stop, yellow, blue, eek, ouch, pink, green

Steps for Teaching a New Red Word:

1. (T) States the word. (*give*)

2. (T&S) Use tokens to determine how many sounds are in the word. (/g/ /ĭ/ /v/; 3)

3. (T&S) Discuss how we would expect to spell each sound as the teacher writes the grapheme(s) correctly. Identify what is unexpected or irregular about the spelling of the word. It could also be expected, but the concept hasn't been taught yet.

4. (T&S) Discuss the etymology of the word, if appropriate (lexical words). Visit www.etymonline.com for more information on the word.

5. (T) Defines the word, and writes a sentence using the word.

6. (T) Writes the word on Red Word paper with the screen underneath, using red crayon.

7. (S) Write the word on Red Word paper with the screen underneath, using red crayon. (S) Show the word to the teacher.
   (**NOTE:** The teacher should have students chunk the word if it has more than four letters.)

8. (T&S) Stand up, holding the Red Word in the nondominant hand. Armtap word while naming each letter. Then "underline" the word by sweeping left to right while stating the word, 3x. (**NOTE:** Left-handed students will place their left hand on their right wrist. They tap to their right shoulder. Underline from wrist to shoulder. Right-handed students place their right hand on their left shoulder. They tap to their left wrist. Underline shoulder to wrist.)

9. (T&S) Trace crayon bumps with the pointer finger while naming the letters, 3x.

10. (T&S) Place the screen over the paper and trace the word with the pointer finger while naming the letters, 3x.

11. (S) Turn paper over. With red crayon, write the word without the screen one time, and hold up the word for the teacher to check. (S) Write the word two more times.

12. (S) Write an original sentence in pencil and underline the Red Word with a red crayon. (**NOTE:** The sentence can also be dictated by the teacher while the student writes or dictated by the student while the teacher writes it.)

Review Ideas for Red Words:

- Sculpt the word using red Play-Doh or clay. Have students spell the word as they smash each letter.
- Print flashcards from IOG, and practice reading.
- Armtap the word to review.
- Cross-clap the word to review.
- Do Spelling Aerobics.

Fluency, Vocabulary, and Comprehension

- Incorporate fluency into your literacy lessons daily/weekly (minimum 30 min/week) by using Rapid Word Charts, IMSE Decodable Readers, words and sentences, Acadience Reading K-6 or DIBELS 8th Edition, repeated reading, and other activities.
- Incorporate vocabulary into your literacy lessons daily/weekly (minimum 50 min/week) by choosing 3-5 appropriate tier two words (can pull from rich literature or decodable readers). Teach the words through explicit, direct instruction using student-friendly definitions, word webs, vocabulary charts, illustrations, and other activities.
- Incorporate oral language comprehension into your literacy lessons daily/weekly (approximately 100 min/week). Comprehension instruction should be explicit, direct instruction that includes teacher modeling, guided practice, and independent practice. Plan ahead to build on students' background knowledge, language structures, verbal reasoning, and literacy knowledge.

Extension Activity Ideas

- Continue to add to the multi-sensory ABC book. Have students glue velvet (or another object) in the shape of the target letter.
- Make a paper valentine. Have students glue pictures of words that begin with the /v/ sound on the valentine.
- Divide students into teams of 3 and have them lie on the ground to form the target letter. Take pictures to hang around the classroom.
- Create the target letter out of green Play-Doh or clay.
- Have students use a bingo dauber to find the target letter on a page with various letters.
- Have students go on a "sound hunt" around the room or outside to find objects that begin with the target sound.
- Coding activity: Have students underline and label the letters in words or syllables with a "v" for vowels and a "c" for consonants. For example, when using the word *mom*, each letter should be underlined with the labels "cvc" underneath the word. This activity will help prepare students for decoding multisyllabic words later in the sequence.
- Visit IMSE's Orton-Gillingham's Pinterest page for more ideas.

Weekly Lesson Reminders

- Any of the above extension activities
- Practice writing the target letter (capital and lowercase) using a screen, green crayon, and house paper.
- Practice writing the target letter using another medium (sand, paint, shaving cream, pudding, iPad app, etc.).
- Practice writing the target letter using age-appropriate paper and pencil.
- Daily practice with writing the weekly Red Word(s)
- Kilpatrick's "One-Minute Activities" for daily phonological awareness practice
- Zgonc's phonological awareness activities
- Listen to rich literature to work on oral language comprehension.
- Target letter practice sheets from IMSE's practice books and handwriting books
- Practice test on Thursday and test on Friday

Xx as in box

Card Pack #24 Decodable Reader #16	
Object Ideas:	**Literature Ideas:**
box, ax, fox, saxophone, wax, ox	▪ *Fox in Socks* by Dr. Seuss ▪ *Fantastic Mr. Fox* by Roald Dahl ▪ *The Lorax* by Dr. Seuss ▪ *Flossie and the Fox* by Patricia McKissack ▪ *Hello, Red Fox* by Eric Carle ▪ *Christina Katerina and the Box* by Patricia Lee Gauch ▪ *The Crayon Box That Talked* by Shane DeRolf ▪ *The Adventures of Taxi Dog* by Debra and Sal Barracca ▪ *Max's ABC* by Rosemary Wells ▪ *Fox on the Job* by James Marshall ▪ *Hattie and the Fox* by Mem Fox

Notes

- Use the Comprehensive Flip Chart for the steps on how to teach each part of IMSE's Lesson Plan.
- Xx /ks/ is a combination of two unvoiced consonant sounds. When students are counting phonemes in words, remember that "x" has two phonemes. Therefore, in a CVC word ending in "x," such as *box*, there are four phonemes (/b/ /ŏ/ /k/ /s/).
- Keep the "x" in the final position, as that is the only place where "x" says /ks/.

Phonological Awareness:

Materials Needed:
tokens, sound boxes, one-minute activities, or Zgonc PA book

Use the PAST assessment to determine a starting point for instruction. Incorporate daily phonological awareness activities by using Zgonc's tiered activities and/or Kilpatrick's One-Minute Activities in *Equipped for Reading Success*.

Phonemic awareness warm-up: Use tokens (or letter tiles once concepts have been taught) and sound boxes to do a quick phonemic awareness activity that ties in with the new concept, if appropriate.

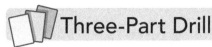

Three-Part Drill

Materials Needed:
review cards, sand, blending board, vowel tents or sticks

Do this at least 3x per week. Use the Flip Chart for steps. Include the new concept after Day 1.

- Include the Vowel Intensive with "a," "e," "i," "o," and "u."

V	VC	CVC
a	ag, ap, ab	lat, cad, zan
e	et, en, eb	zeg, ren, med
i	ig, ib, im	lin, hib, fid
o	ob, ot, oz	rom, hob, cog
u	un, ud, ub	sup, pum, dut

- Below is a sample script now that students know more than one way to spell a concept. Remember to use all of the review concepts.

1. **Visual:**
   (T) Tell me the sounds you know for these letters.
   (S) /m/, /l/, etc.
   Alternative:
   (T) Tell me the names and sounds you know for these letters.
   (S) m says /m/, l says /l/, etc.

2. **Auditory/Kinesthetic:**
   (T) You know two ways to spell this. (S) split trays. (T) Eyes on me.
   Spell /k/. Repeat.
   (S) /k/ c says /k/; k says /k/

3. **Blending:**
   (T) Tell me the sound for each letter as I point. Then blend the sounds together to read the word or syllable. Give me a thumbs up if it is a real word.
   (S) /mmm/ /ŏŏŏ/ /mmm/ *mom* (thumbs up)
   Alternative:
   (T) Watch me first. /mmm/ /ŏŏŏ/ /mmm/ *mom*
   (T) Do it with me. (T&S) /mmm/ /ŏŏŏ/ /mmm/ *mom*
   (T) Your turn. (S) /mmm/ /ŏŏŏ/ /mmm/ *mom* (thumbs up)

Vowel Intensive: Model the visual cue while calling out the sound. Students will do the visual cue as they repeat the sound. Students will then hold up the vowel tent while stating the letter name and sound.

- (T): Eyes on me. The sound is /ă/. Repeat.
- (S): /ă/ a says /ă/

Teaching a New Concept

Materials Needed:
concept card, screen, green crayon, object, sand, decodable readers, literature, P/G chart

Introduce on Monday, and practice daily.

1. (T) Reads alliteration sentences. (S) Identify the target sounds.
   a. Listen to these words: fox, Max, fix, ax, ox, six, vex. What sounds do you hear at the end of each word?

2. (T) Shows the new concept card.
   a. (T) Tells students the letter name and sounds. Have (S) repeat, 3 times (x says /ks/).
   b. (T) Tells students that "x" is a consonant.
   c. (T) Tells students it makes unvoiced sounds.
   d. (T) Asks students where they find "x" in the alphabet.
   e. (T) Uses mirrors to discuss the mouth, tongue, and teeth placement.

3. (T) Shows an object.
   a. (T) Allows students to manipulate the object and discuss prior knowledge. Reminds (S) that the object has the target sounds spelled with the target letter.

4. (S) Brainstorm.
   a. Brainstorm words that have the target sounds. (Accept all answers, but place incorrect answers in a "thought bubble" to discuss.) The brainstorming can be a teacher-directed activity if students need extra support.

5. (T) Teaches Letter Formation. Use house paper to teach lowercase letters.
   a. (T) models with the solid letter. The letter "x" starts at the ceiling and slants down to the floor. Then, go back up to the other side of the ceiling and slant back down to the floor.
   b. Using the screen and green crayon, (T&S) trace the solid while saying, "x says /ks/" (3x).
   c. (T&S) use their finger to trace the solid while saying, "x says /ks/" (3x).
   d. (S) trace the dotted letter and complete the remainder of the row independently.
   e. (S) move to smaller house and repeat process if needed.
   f. Teach capital letters throughout the week using the same process. Capital letters go outside the house.

6. (T) Dictates target sounds. (S) Practice in the sand or other medium.
   a. Practice writing the letter using a different medium, such as sand, shaving cream, finger paint, gel board, iPad app, air writing, etc.
   b. Do this while stating: x says /ks/, 3 times.

7. (T) Connects with literature.
   a. Have students signal when they hear /ks/ for the first page or two.
   b. Read again for language comprehension.
   c. Continue to work on language comprehension with rich literature throughout the week.

8. (S) Use decodable readers to practice the concepts learned.
   a. (S) Highlight words with the new concept. Read those words.
   b. (S) Highlight Red Words. Read those words.
   c. (S) Start reading the decodable reader.
   d. (S) Continue reading throughout the week.
   e. (S) Read a clean copy on Friday.
9. (T&S) Mark the Phoneme/Grapheme (P/G) chart by highlighting the target concept.

 ## Word Dictation

Materials Needed:
fingertapping hand, dictation paper, pencil

Create any syllables using the new concept and previously taught concepts. Practice daily. Use the Flip Chart to follow the steps for word dictation.

Day 1:	1. mix	2. ax	3. six	4. tux	5. wax
Day 2:	1. fix	2. Max	3. ox	4. sax	5. fax
Day 3:	1. lax	2. nix	3. box	4. Rex	5. tax
Days 4-5:	Review prior words.				

Below is a sample script:

1. (T) States word: *mom*. Uses it in a sentence: My *mom* is a wonderful lady. (Pounds) *mom*. (T) Models fingertapping if needed: /m/ /ŏ/ /m/. (Pounds) *mom*.
2. (S) State while pounding: *mom*. (Fingertap) /m/ /ŏ/ /m/. (Pound) *mom*. Write the letters known for the sounds.
3. (T) When yours looks like mine, rewrite the word.
4. (S) Rewrite.
5. Repeat the process for each word.
6. (S) Read the list of words multiple times to build automaticity.

 ## Sentence Dictation

Red Words are underlined. Students can fingertap the green words. Use the Flip Chart to follow the steps for sentence dictation.

1. Max did fix <u>the</u> wet map.
2. <u>The</u> ax cut <u>the</u> log.
3. <u>The</u> man got <u>a</u> tux.
4. Jim did not cut <u>the</u> tax.
5. <u>Was</u> a fox <u>or</u> an ox in <u>the</u> den?
6. <u>The</u> fox hid <u>by the</u> log <u>and</u> sat.
7. Mix <u>the</u> wax in <u>the</u> pot.

8. Pat can wax <u>the</u> van.
9. Can <u>you</u> fix <u>the</u> box?
10. <u>The</u> ox <u>is</u> at <u>the</u> vet.
11. Six men <u>will</u> run.

- Below is a sample script for sentence dictation.

> 1. (T): Listen to the sentence. *Tad had a cat.*
> 2. (T): Listen while I pound the syllables. *Tad had a cat.*
> 3. (T): Pound it with me. (T&S): *Tad had a cat.*
> 4. (T): You pound the sentence. (S): *Tad had a cat.*
> 5. (T): Watch me as I point to the lines while stating the sentence. *Tad had a cat.*
> 6. (T): You point to the lines while stating the sentence.
> 7. (S): *Tad had a cat.*
> 8. (T): Now write the sentence. Fingertap if needed.

- Below is a sample script to check CUPS*.

> 1. (T): C stands for capitalization. Did you remember a capital letter at the beginning of your sentence? It's also a name. *Tad* would always be capitalized. If you forgot, fix it. If you remembered, put a tally mark above the capital letter. Add a mark in the box for C.
> 2. (T): U stands for understanding. Is your sentence neat? Reread it to yourself. Does it make sense? Could someone else understand it? If not, fix it. Add a mark in the box for U.
> 3. (T): P stands for punctuation. Did you remember a period at the end? If not, fix it. If you remembered, put a tally mark above the period. Add a mark in the box for P.
> 4. (T): S stands for spelling. Did you spell your words correctly? Check them. Now, check yours with mine (show the teacher's copy). Fix any words you spelled incorrectly. Put a tally mark above the words you spelled correctly. Add a mark in the box for S.
> 5. (T): Rewrite your sentence with all of the corrections.
> 6. (T): Check for CUPS again. Put another mark in the boxes.
> 7. (T): Let's read the sentences.
> 8. (S) Read the sentences for fluency and automaticity.
>
> ***Please note:** Once students understand how to use CUPS, transition to letting them check their sentence independently before showing the teacher's copy.

 Weekly Red Words

Materials Needed:
screen, red crayon, red word paper

Introduce on Tuesday, and practice daily. Use the Flip Chart for steps.

New:	Review:	New Read-Only:	Review Read-Only:
or, by	the, was, is, a, and, to, for, go, I, like, of, will, no, want, with, said, you, put, see, stop, from, off, he, has, have, me, his, as, my, into, now, new, give	look	orange, white, brown, stop, yellow, blue, eek, ouch, pink, green, black

Steps for Teaching a New Red Word:

1. (T) States the word. (*or*)
2. (T&S) Use tokens to determine how many sounds are in the word. (/or/; 1)
3. (T&S) Discuss how we would expect to spell each sound as the teacher writes the grapheme(s) correctly. Identify what is unexpected or irregular about the spelling of the word. It could also be expected, but the concept hasn't been taught yet.
4. (T&S) Discuss the etymology of the word, if appropriate (lexical words). Visit www.etymonline.com for more information on the word.
5. (T) Defines the word, and writes a sentence using the word.
6. (T) Writes the word on Red Word paper with the screen underneath, using red crayon.
7. (S) Write the word on Red Word paper with the screen underneath, using red crayon. (S) Show the word to the teacher. (**NOTE:** The teacher should have students chunk the word if it has more than four letters.)
8. (T&S) Stand up, holding the Red Word in the nondominant hand. Armtap word while naming each letter. Then "underline" the word by sweeping left to right while stating the word, 3x. (**NOTE:** Left-handed students will place their left hand on their right wrist. They tap to their right shoulder. Underline from wrist to shoulder. Right-handed students place their right hand on their left shoulder. They tap to their left wrist. Underline shoulder to wrist.)
9. (T&S) Trace crayon bumps with the pointer finger while naming the letters, 3x.
10. (T&S) Place the screen over the paper and trace the word with the pointer finger while naming the letters, 3x.

11. (S) Turn paper over. With red crayon, write the word without the screen one time, and hold up the word for the teacher to check. (S) Write the word two more times.

12. (S) Write an original sentence in pencil and underline the Red Word with a red crayon. (**NOTE:** The sentence can also be dictated by the teacher while the student writes or dictated by the student while the teacher writes it.)

13. Repeat the steps for *by*. (/b/ /ī/; 2)

Review Ideas for Red Words:

▪ Sculpt the word using red Play-Doh or clay. Have students spell the word as they smash each letter.

▪ Print flashcards from IOG, and practice reading.

▪ Armtap the word to review.

▪ Cross-clap the word to review.

▪ Do Spelling Aerobics.

Fluency, Vocabulary, and Comprehension

▪ Incorporate fluency into your literacy lessons daily/weekly (minimum 30 min/week) by using Rapid Word Charts, IMSE Decodable Readers, words and sentences, Acadience Reading K-6 or DIBELS 8th Edition, repeated reading, and other activities.

▪ Incorporate vocabulary into your literacy lessons daily/weekly (minimum 50 min/week) by choosing 3-5 appropriate tier two words (can pull from rich literature or decodable readers). Teach the words through explicit, direct instruction using student-friendly definitions, word webs, vocabulary charts, illustrations, and other activities.

▪ Incorporate oral language comprehension into your literacy lessons daily/weekly (approximately 100 min/week). Comprehension instruction should be explicit, direct instruction that includes teacher modeling, guided practice, and independent practice. Plan ahead to build on students' background knowledge, language structures, verbal reasoning, and literacy knowledge.

Extension Activity Ideas

- Continue to add to the multi-sensory ABC book. Have students glue little foxes (or another object) in the shape of the target letter.
- Fill a box with objects that have the /ks/ sounds.
- Make a paper fox. Have students glue pictures of words that end with the /ks/ sounds on the fox.
- Divide students into teams of 3 and have them lie on the ground to form the target letter. Take pictures to hang around the classroom.
- Create the target letter out of green Play-Doh or clay.
- Have students use a bingo dauber to find the target letter on a page with various letters.
- Have students go on a "sound hunt" around the room or outside to find objects that end with the target sounds.
- Coding activity: Have students underline and label the letters in words or syllables with a "v" for vowels and a "c" for consonants. For example, when using the word *mom*, each letter should be underlined with the labels "cvc" underneath the word. This activity will help prepare students for decoding multisyllabic words later in the sequence.
- Visit IMSE's Orton-Gillingham's Pinterest page for more ideas.

Weekly Lesson Reminders

- Any of the above extension activities
- Practice writing the target letter (capital and lowercase) using a screen, green crayon, and house paper.
- Practice writing the target letter using another medium (sand, paint, shaving cream, pudding, iPad app, etc.).
- Practice writing the target letter using age-appropriate paper and pencil.
- Daily practice with writing the weekly Red Word(s)
- Kilpatrick's "One-Minute Activities" for daily phonological awareness practice
- Zgonc's phonological awareness activities
- Listen to rich literature to work on oral language comprehension.
- Target letter practice sheets from IMSE's practice books and handwriting books
- Practice test on Thursday and test on Friday

Zz as in zebra

Object Ideas:	Literature Ideas:
zipper, zoo, zebra, Zumba	▪ *Zero the Hero* by Joan Holub ▪ *Zack's Alligator* by Shirley Mozelle ▪ *Put Me in the Zoo* by Robert Lopshire ▪ *Zin! Zin! Zin! A Violin* by Lloyd Moss ▪ *Izzy Gizmo* by Pip Jones ▪ Hank Zipzer series by Henry Winkler and Lin Oliver

Notes

- Use the Comprehensive Flip Chart for the steps on how to teach each part of IMSE's Lesson Plan.
- Zz /z/ is a voiced, fricative consonant sound. The lips are pulled back, and the tip of the tongue is behind the teeth but not quite touching them.
- Keep "z" in the initial position at first. If /z/ is at the end of a one-syllable word with one short vowel, it is spelled "-zz." After open and closed syllables have been taught, "z" can be moved to the final position to support syllables such as "Az" in "Aztec."

Phonological Awareness:

Materials Needed:
tokens, sound boxes, one-minute activities, or Zgonc PA book

Use the PAST assessment to determine a starting point for instruction. Incorporate daily phonological awareness activities by using Zgonc's tiered activities and/or Kilpatrick's One-Minute Activities in *Equipped for Reading Success*.

Phonemic awareness warm-up: Use tokens (or letter tiles once concepts have been taught) and sound boxes to do a quick phonemic awareness activity that ties in with the new concept, if appropriate.

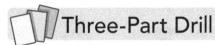

Three-Part Drill

Materials Needed:
review cards, sand, blending board, vowel tents or sticks

Do this at least 3x per week. Use the Flip Chart for steps. Include the new concept after Day 1.

- Include the Vowel Intensive with "a," "e," "i," "o," and "u."

V	VC	CVC
a	ag, ap, ab	lat, cad, zan
e	et, en, eb	zeg, ren, med
i	ig, ib, im	lin, hib, fid
o	ob, ot, oz	rom, hob, cog
u	un, ud, ub	sup, pum, dut

- Below is a sample script now that students know more than one way to spell a concept. Remember to use all of the review concepts.

1. **Visual:**
   (T) Tell me the sounds you know for these letters.
   (S) /m/, /l/, etc.
   Alternative:
   (T) Tell me the names and sounds you know for these letters.
   (S) m says /m/, l says /l/, etc.

2. **Auditory/Kinesthetic:**
   (T) You know two ways to spell this. (S) split trays. (T) Eyes on me.
   Spell /k/. Repeat.
   (S) /k/ c says /k/; k says /k/

3. **Blending:**
   (T) Tell me the sound for each letter as I point. Then blend the sounds together to read the word or syllable. Give me a thumbs up if it is a real word.
   (S) /mmm/ /ŏŏŏ/ /mmm/ *mom* (thumbs up)
   Alternative:
   (T) Watch me first. /mmm/ /ŏŏŏ/ /mmm/ *mom*
   (T) Do it with me. (T&S) /mmm/ /ŏŏŏ/ /mmm/ *mom*
   (T) Your turn. (S) /mmm/ /ŏŏŏ/ /mmm/ *mom* (thumbs up)

*Vowel Intensive: Model the visual cue while calling out the sound. Students will do the visual cue as they repeat the sound. Students will then hold up the vowel tent while stating the letter name and sound.

- (T): Eyes on me. The sound is /ă/. Repeat.
- (S): /ă/ a says /ă/

Teaching a New Concept

Materials Needed:
concept card, screen, green crayon, object, sand, decodable readers, literature, P/G chart

Introduce on Monday, and practice daily.

1. (T) Reads alliteration sentences. (S) Identify the target sound.
   a. Zesty Zeus zaps zippers.
   b. Zoey zigzags.
2. (T) Shows the new concept card.
   a. (T) Tells students the letter name and sound. Have (S) repeat, 3 times (z says /z/).
   b. (T) Tells students that "z" is a consonant.
   c. (T) Tells students it is a voiced sound.
   d. (T) Asks students where they find "z" in the alphabet.
   e. (T) Uses mirrors to discuss the mouth, tongue, and teeth placement.
3. (T) Shows an object.
   a. (T) Allows students to manipulate the object and discuss prior knowledge. Reminds (S) that the object has the target sound spelled with the target letter.
4. (S) Brainstorm.
   a. Brainstorm words that have the target sound. (Accept all answers, but place incorrect answers in a "thought bubble" to discuss.) The brainstorming can be a teacher-directed activity if students need extra support.
5. (T) Teaches Letter Formation. Use house paper to teach lowercase letters.
   a. (T) models with the solid letter. The letter "z" goes across the ceiling, slants down to the floor, and then goes across the floor.
   b. Using the screen and green crayon, (T&S) trace the solid while saying, "z says /z/" (3x).
   c. (T&S) use their finger to trace the solid while saying, "z says /z/" (3x).
   d. (S) trace the dotted letter and complete the remainder of the row independently.
   e. (S) move to smaller house and repeat process if needed.
   f. Teach capital letters throughout the week using the same process. Capital letters go outside the house.
6. (T) Dictates target sound. (S) Practice in the sand or other medium.
   a. Practice writing the letter using a different medium, such as sand, shaving cream, finger paint, gel board, iPad app, air writing, etc.
   b. Do this while stating: z says /z/, 3 times.
7. (T) Connects with literature.
   a. Have students signal when they hear the /z/ sound for the first page or two.
   b. Read again for language comprehension.
   c. Continue to work on language comprehension with rich literature throughout the week.

8. (S) Use decodable readers to practice the concepts learned.
   a. (S) Highlight words with the new concept. Read those words.
   b. (S) Highlight Red Words. Read those words.
   c. (S) Start reading the decodable reader.
   d. (S) Continue reading throughout the week.
   e. (S) Read a clean copy on Friday.
9. (T&S) Mark the Phoneme/Grapheme (P/G) chart by highlighting the target sound.

 ## Word Dictation

Materials Needed:
fingertapping hand, dictation paper, pencil

Create any syllables using the new concept and previously taught concepts. Practice daily. Use the Flip Chart to follow the steps for word dictation.

Day 1:	1. zag	2. wax	3. zip	4. zap	5. yam
Day 2:	1. zig	2. zit	3. vet	4. zag	5. wig
Day 3:	1. zap	2. box	3. zip	4. sob	5. zig
Days 4-5:	Review prior words.				

Below is a sample script:

1. (T) States word: *mom*. Uses it in a sentence: My *mom* is a wonderful lady. (Pounds) *mom*. (T) Models fingertapping if needed: /m/ /ŏ/ /m/. (Pounds) *mom*.
2. (S) State while pounding: *mom*. (Fingertap) /m/ /ŏ/ /m/. (Pound) *mom*. Write the letters known for the sounds.
3. (T) When yours looks like mine, rewrite the word.
4. (S) Rewrite.
5. Repeat the process for each word.
6. (S) Read the list of words multiple times to build automaticity.

 ## Sentence Dictation

Red Words are underlined. Students can fingertap the green words. Use the Flip Chart to follow the steps for sentence dictation.

1. Rob will zip to the bin.
2. A hen did zig and zag to the pen.
3. Pat will zig and zag on the run.
4. Will the hog zip to the top?
5. A bug went zip in the fog.
6. Did the bug zap you?
7. Mom had a zit.
8. Ben did not zip.

- Below is a sample script for sentence dictation.

> 1. (T): Listen to the sentence. *Tad had a cat.*
> 2. (T): Listen while I pound the syllables. *Tad had a cat.*
> 3. (T): Pound it with me. (T&S): *Tad had a cat.*
> 4. (T): You pound the sentence. (S): *Tad had a cat.*
> 5. (T): Watch me as I point to the lines while stating the sentence. *Tad had a cat.*
> 6. (T): You point to the lines while stating the sentence.
> 7. (S): *Tad had a cat.*
> 8. (T): Now write the sentence. Fingertap if needed.

- Below is a sample script to check CUPS*.

> 1. (T): C stands for capitalization. Did you remember a capital letter at the beginning of your sentence? It's also a name. *Tad* would always be capitalized. If you forgot, fix it. If you remembered, put a tally mark above the capital letter. Add a mark in the box for C.
> 2. (T): U stands for understanding. Is your sentence neat? Reread it to yourself. Does it make sense? Could someone else understand it? If not, fix it. Add a mark in the box for U.
> 3. (T): P stands for punctuation. Did you remember a period at the end? If not, fix it. If you remembered, put a tally mark above the period. Add a mark in the box for P.
> 4. (T): S stands for spelling. Did you spell your words correctly? Check them. Now, check yours with mine (show the teacher's copy). Fix any words you spelled incorrectly. Put a tally mark above the words you spelled correctly. Add a mark in the box for S.
> 5. (T): Rewrite your sentence with all of the corrections.
> 6. (T): Check for CUPS again. Put another mark in the boxes.
> 7. (T): Let's read the sentences.
> 8. (S) Read the sentences for fluency and automaticity.
>
> **Please note:** Once students understand how to use CUPS, transition to letting them check their sentence independently before showing the teacher's copy.

Weekly Red Words

Materials Needed:
screen, red crayon, red word paper

Introduce on Tuesday, and practice daily. Use the Flip Chart for steps.

New:	Review:	New Read-Only:	Review Read-Only:
went	the, was, is, a, and, to, for, go, I, like, of, will, no, want, with, said, you, put, see, stop, from, off, he, has, have, me, his, as, my, into, now, new, give, or, by		orange, white, brown, stop, yellow, blue, eek, ouch, pink, green, black, look

Steps for Teaching a New Red Word:

1. (T) States the word. (*went*)
2. (T&S) Use tokens to determine how many sounds are in the word. (/w/ /ĕ/ /n/ /t/; 4)
3. (T&S) Discuss how we would expect to spell each sound as the teacher writes the grapheme(s) correctly. Identify what is unexpected or irregular about the spelling of the word. It could also be expected, but the concept hasn't been taught yet.
4. (T&S) Discuss the etymology of the word, if appropriate (lexical words). Visit www.etymonline.com for more information on the word.
5. (T) Defines the word, and writes a sentence using the word.
6. (T) Writes the word on Red Word paper with the screen underneath, using red crayon.
7. (S) Write the word on Red Word paper with the screen underneath, using red crayon. (S) Show the word to the teacher. (**NOTE:** The teacher should have students chunk the word if it has more than four letters.)
8. (T&S) Stand up, holding the Red Word in the nondominant hand. Armtap word while naming each letter. Then "underline" the word by sweeping left to right while stating the word, 3x. (**NOTE:** Left-handed students will place their left hand on their right wrist. They tap to their right shoulder. Underline from wrist to shoulder. Right-handed students place their right hand on their left shoulder. They tap to their left wrist. Underline shoulder to wrist.)
9. (T&S) Trace crayon bumps with the pointer finger while naming the letters, 3x.
10. (T&S) Place the screen over the paper and trace the word with the pointer finger while naming the letters, 3x.

11. (S) Turn paper over. With red crayon, write the word without the screen one time, and hold up the word for the teacher to check. (S) Write the word two more times.

12. (S) Write an original sentence in pencil and underline the Red Word with a red crayon. (**NOTE:** The sentence can also be dictated by the teacher while the student writes or dictated by the student while the teacher writes it.)

Review Ideas for Red Words:

- Sculpt the word using red Play-Doh or clay. Have students spell the word as they smash each letter.
- Print flashcards from IOG, and practice reading.
- Armtap the word to review.
- Cross-clap the word to review.
- Do Spelling Aerobics.

Fluency, Vocabulary, and Comprehension

- Incorporate fluency into your literacy lessons daily/weekly (minimum 30 min/week) by using Rapid Word Charts, IMSE Decodable Readers, words and sentences, Acadience Reading K-6 or DIBELS 8th Edition, repeated reading, and other activities.

- Incorporate vocabulary into your literacy lessons daily/weekly (minimum 50 min/week) by choosing 3-5 appropriate tier two words (can pull from rich literature or decodable readers). Teach the words through explicit, direct instruction using student-friendly definitions, word webs, vocabulary charts, illustrations, and other activities.

- Incorporate oral language comprehension into your literacy lessons daily/weekly (approximately 100 min/week). Comprehension instruction should be explicit, direct instruction that includes teacher modeling, guided practice, and independent practice. Plan ahead to build on students' background knowledge, language structures, verbal reasoning, and literacy knowledge.

Extension Activity Ideas

- Continue to add to the multi-sensory ABC book. Have students glue zigzags (or another object) in the shape of the target letter.
- Make a paper zebra. Have students glue pictures of words that begin with the /z/ sound on the zebra.
- Divide students into teams of 3 and have them lie on the ground to form the target letter. Take pictures to hang around the classroom.
- Create the target letter out of green Play-Doh or clay.
- Have students use a bingo dauber to find the target letter on a page with various letters.
- Have students go on a "sound hunt" around the room or outside to find objects that begin with the target sound.
- Coding activity: Have students underline and label the letters in words or syllables with a "v" for vowels and a "c" for consonants. For example, when using the word *mom*, each letter should be underlined with the labels "cvc" underneath the word. This activity will help prepare students for decoding multisyllabic words later in the sequence.
- Visit IMSE's Orton-Gillingham's Pinterest page for more ideas.

Weekly Lesson Reminders

- Any of the above extension activities
- Practice writing the target letter (capital and lowercase) using a screen, green crayon, and house paper.
- Practice writing the target letter using another medium (sand, paint, shaving cream, pudding, iPad app, etc.).
- Practice writing the target letter using age-appropriate paper and pencil.
- Daily practice with writing the weekly Red Word(s)
- Kilpatrick's "One-Minute Activities" for daily phonological awareness practice
- Zgonc's phonological awareness activities
- Listen to rich literature to work on oral language comprehension.
- Target letter practice sheets from IMSE's practice books and handwriting books
- Practice test on Thursday and test on Friday

qu as in queen

Card Pack #26   Decodable Reader #18

Object Ideas:	Literature Ideas:
quilt, queen, quarter, question mark, quail, quartz, quart, quote, quick, quiet, quack	▪ *The Patchwork Quilt* by Valerie Flournoy ▪ *The Wedding of Q and U* by Denise Dillon-Hreha ▪ *The Recess Queen* by Alexis O'Neill ▪ *Quinito, Day and Night* by Ina Cumpiano ▪ *Sweet Clara and the Freedom Quilt* by Deborah Hopkinson ▪ *The Queen's Feet* by Sarah Ellis ▪ *Quick, Quack, Quick!* by Marsha Arnold ▪ *The Quiltmaker's Gift* by Jeff Brumbeau ▪ *If I Were Queen of the World* by Fred Hiatt ▪ *Giggle, Giggle, Quack* by Doreen Cronin ▪ *Quack!* by Phyllis Root ▪ *Little Quack* by Lauren Thompson ▪ *The Queen With Bees in Her Hair* by Cheryl Harness

Notes

▪ Use the Comprehensive Flip Chart for the steps on how to teach each part of IMSE's Lesson Plan.

▪ Qu /kw/ is a voiced consonant unit. It contains two phonemes (/k/ and /w/). The word *quit* has 4 sounds (/k/ /w/ /ĭ/ /t/).

▪ "Qu" gets an extra visual of a heart around the grapheme line to indicate that "q" and "u" are a pair. Wherever "q" goes, "u" will follow.

▪ The heart around the grapheme line only goes with the word dictation, not sentence dictation.

▪ "Qu" goes in the initial position on the blending board. Avoid the "u" vowel card next to "qu" on the blending board.

▪ Remember there is a "qu" poem in the Masters.

▪ Google "q and u wedding" for cute videos.

Phonological Awareness:

Materials Needed:
tokens, sound boxes, one-minute activities, or Zgonc PA book

Use the PAST assessment to determine a starting point for instruction. Incorporate daily phonological awareness activities by using Zgonc's tiered activities and/or Kilpatrick's One-Minute Activities in *Equipped for Reading Success.*

Phonemic awareness warm-up: Use tokens (or letter tiles once concepts have been taught) and sound boxes to do a quick phonemic awareness activity that ties in with the new concept, if appropriate.

Three-Part Drill

Materials Needed:
review cards, sand, blending board, vowel tents or sticks

Do this at least 3x per week. Use the Flip Chart for steps. Include the new concept after Day 1.

- Include the Vowel Intensive with "a," "e," "i," "o," and "u."

V	VC	CVC
a	ag, ap, ab	lat, cad, zan
e	et, en, eb	zeg, ren, med
i	ig, ib, im	lin, hib, fid
o	ob, ot, oz	rom, hob, cog
u	un, ud, ub	sup, pum, dut

- Below is a sample script now that students know more than one way to spell a sound. Remember to use all of the review concepts.

1. **Visual:**
   (T) Tell me the sounds you know for these letters.
   (S) /m/, /l/, etc.
   Alternative:
   (T) Tell me the names and sounds you know for these letters.
   (S) m says /m/, l says /l/, etc.

2. **Auditory/Kinesthetic:**
   (T) You know two ways to spell this. (S) split trays. (T) Eyes on me.
   Spell /k/. Repeat.
   (S) /k/ c says /k/; k says /k/

3. **Blending:**

(T) Tell me the sound for each letter as I point. Then blend the sounds together to read the word or syllable. Give me a thumbs up if it is a real word.

(S) /mmm/ /ŏŏŏ/ /mmm/ *mom* (thumbs up)

Alternative:

(T) Watch me first. /mmm/ /ŏŏŏ/ /mmm/ *mom*

(T) Do it with me. (T&S) /mmm/ /ŏŏŏ/ /mmm/ *mom*

(T) Your turn. (S) /mmm/ /ŏŏŏ/ /mmm/ *mom* (thumbs up)

*Vowel Intensive: Model the visual cue while calling out the sound. Students will do the visual cue as they repeat the sound. Students will then hold up the vowel tent while stating the letter name and sound.

- (T): Eyes on me. The sound is /ă/. Repeat.

- (S): /ă/ a says /ă/

Teaching a New Concept

Materials Needed:
concept card, screen, green crayon, object, sand, decodable readers, literature, P/G chart

Introduce on Monday, and practice daily.

1. (T) Reads alliteration sentences. (S) Identify the target sounds.
   a. Quincy quietly quilted quickly.
   b. Quinn is quite quirky.
2. (T) Shows the new concept card.
   a. (T) Tells students the letter names and sounds. Have (S) repeat, 3 times (qu says /kw/).
   b. (T) Tells students that "qu" is a consonant unit.
   c. (T) Tells students it is a voiced unit.
   d. (T) Asks students where they find "q" in the alphabet.
   e. (T) Uses mirrors to discuss the mouth, tongue, and teeth placement.
3. (T) Shows an object.
   a. (T) Allows students to manipulate the object and discuss prior knowledge. Reminds (S) that the object has the target sounds spelled with the target letters.
4. (S) Brainstorm.
   a. Brainstorm words that have the target sounds. (Accept all answers, but place incorrect answers in a "thought bubble" to discuss.) The brainstorming can be a teacher-directed activity if students need extra support.
5. (T) Teaches Letter Formation. Use house paper to teach lowercase letters.
   a. (T) models with the solid letter. The letter "q" starts below the ceiling and goes around, touches the floor, and comes back to the ceiling. Then come down through the house and into the basement. Curve around. The letter "u" starts at the ceiling, touches the floor, comes back up to the ceiling, and back down to the floor.

    b. Using the screen and green crayon, (T&S) trace the solid while saying, "qu says /kw/" (3x).

    c. (T&S) use their finger to trace the solid while saying, "qu says /kw/" (3x).

    d. (S) trace the dotted letter and complete the remainder of the row independently.

    e. (S) move to smaller house and repeat process if needed.

    f. Teach capital letters throughout the week using the same process. Capital letters go outside the house.

6. (T) Dictates target sounds. (S) Practice in the sand or other medium.

    a. Practice writing the letters using a different medium, such as sand, shaving cream, finger paint, gel board, iPad app, air writing, etc.

    b. Do this while stating: qu says /kw/, 3 times.

7. (T) Connects with literature.

    a. Have students signal when they hear /kw/ for the first page or two.

    b. Read again for language comprehension.

    c. Continue to work on language comprehension with rich literature throughout the week.

8. (S) Use decodable readers to practice the concepts learned.

    a. (S) Highlight words with the new concept. Read those words.

    b. (S) Highlight Red Words. Read those words.

    c. (S) Start reading the decodable reader.

    d. (S) Continue reading throughout the week.

    e. (S) Read a clean copy on Friday.

9. (T&S) Mark the Phoneme/Grapheme (P/G) chart by highlighting the target concept.

 ## Word Dictation

Materials Needed:
fingertapping hand, dictation paper, pencil

Create any syllables using the new concept and previously taught concepts. Practice daily. Use the Flip Chart to follow the steps for word dictation.

Day 1:	1. quit	2. quiz	3. mix	4. wag	5. quig
Day 2:	1. quip	2. quag	3. van	4. quit	5. sad
Day 3:	1. quiz	2. yes	3. quip	4. box	5. quag
Days 4-5:	Review prior words.				

Below is a sample script:

> 1. (T) States word: *mom*. Uses it in a sentence: My *mom* is a wonderful lady. (Pounds) *mom*. (T) Models fingertapping if needed: /m/ /ŏ/ /m/. (Pounds) *mom*.
>
> 2. (S) State while pounding: *mom*. (Fingertap) /m/ /ŏ/ /m/. (Pound) *mom*. Write the letters known for the sounds.
>
> 3. (T) When yours looks like mine, rewrite the word.

4. (S) Rewrite.

5. Repeat the process for each word.

6. (S) Read the list of words multiple times to build automaticity.

Sentence Dictation

Red Words are underlined. Students can fingertap the green words. Use the Flip Chart to follow the steps for sentence dictation.

1. Bob had a fun quip.
2. The pup quit the run.
3. The pup quit the run and sat in the sun.
4. Jed quit the quip.
5. Sam said yes to the quiz.
6. Are Dan and Don set to quit the job?
7. The quag was wet and dim.
8. Did Sam get the vet to quit?
9. The quiz was fun!
10. Dan, do you want to quit the job?

- Below is a sample script for sentence dictation.

  1. (T): Listen to the sentence. *Tad had a cat.*
  2. (T): Listen while I pound the syllables. *Tad had a cat.*
  3. (T): Pound it with me. (T&S): *Tad had a cat.*
  4. (T): You pound the sentence. (S): *Tad had a cat.*
  5. (T): Watch me as I point to the lines while stating the sentence. *Tad had a cat.*
  6. (T): You point to the lines while stating the sentence.
  7. (S): *Tad had a cat.*
  8. (T): Now write the sentence. Fingertap if needed.

- Below is a sample script to check CUPS*.

  1. (T): C stands for capitalization. Did you remember a capital letter at the beginning of your sentence? It's also a name. *Tad* would always be capitalized. If you forgot, fix it. If you remembered, put a tally mark above the capital letter. Add a mark in the box for C.
  2. (T): U stands for understanding. Is your sentence neat? Reread it to yourself. Does it make sense? Could someone else understand it? If not, fix it. Add a mark in the box for U.
  3. (T): P stands for punctuation. Did you remember a period at the end? If not, fix it. If you remembered, put a tally mark above the period. Add a mark in the box for P.

4. (T): S stands for spelling. Did you spell your words correctly? Check them. Now, check yours with mine (show the teacher's copy). Fix any words you spelled incorrectly. Put a tally mark above the words you spelled correctly. Add a mark in the box for S.

5. (T): Rewrite your sentence with all of the corrections.

6. (T): Check for CUPS again. Put another mark in the boxes.

7. (T): Let's read the sentences.

8. (S) Read the sentences for fluency and automaticity.

*Please note: Once students understand how to use CUPS, transition to letting them check their sentence independently before showing the teacher's copy.

Weekly Red Words

Materials Needed:
screen, red crayon, red word paper

Introduce on Tuesday, and practice daily. Use the Flip Chart for steps.

New:	Review:	New Read-Only:	Review Read-Only:
do, are	the, was, is, a, and, to, for, go, I, like, of, will, no, want, with, said, you, put, see, stop, from, off, he, has, have, me, his, as, my, into, now, new, give, or, by, went	good	orange, white, brown, stop, yellow, blue, eek, ouch, pink, green, black, look

Steps for Teaching a New Red Word:

1. (T) States the word. (*do*)

2. (T&S) Use tokens to determine how many sounds are in the word. (/d/ / $\overline{oo}$ /; 2)

3. (T&S) Discuss how we would expect to spell each sound as the teacher writes the grapheme(s) correctly. Identify what is unexpected or irregular about the spelling of the word. It could also be expected, but the concept hasn't been taught yet.

4. (T&S) Discuss the etymology of the word, if appropriate (lexical words). Visit www.etymonline.com for more information on the word.

5. (T) Defines the word, and writes a sentence using the word.

6. (T) Writes the word on Red Word paper with the screen underneath, using red crayon.

7. (S) Write the word on Red Word paper with the screen underneath, using red crayon. (S) Show the word to the teacher.
   (**NOTE:** The teacher should have students chunk the word if it has more than four letters.)

8. (T&S) Stand up, holding the Red Word in the nondominant hand. Armtap word while naming each letter. Then "underline" the word by sweeping left to right while stating the word, 3x. (**NOTE:** Left-handed students will place their left hand on their right wrist. They tap to their right shoulder. Underline from wrist to shoulder. Right-handed students place their right hand on their left shoulder. They tap to their left wrist. Underline shoulder to wrist.)

9. (T&S) Trace crayon bumps with the pointer finger while naming the letters, 3x.

10. (T&S) Place the screen over the paper and trace the word with the pointer finger while naming the letters, 3x.

11. (S) Turn paper over. With red crayon, write the word without the screen one time, and hold up the word for the teacher to check. (S) Write the word two more times.

12. (S) Write an original sentence in pencil and underline the Red Word with a red crayon. (**NOTE:** The sentence can also be dictated by the teacher while the student writes or dictated by the student while the teacher writes it.)

13. Repeat the steps for *are*. (/ar/; 1)

Review Ideas for Red Words:

- Sculpt the word using red Play-Doh or clay. Have students spell the word as they smash each letter.
- Print flashcards from IOG, and practice reading.
- Armtap the word to review.
- Cross-clap the word to review.
- Do Spelling Aerobics.

 # Fluency, Vocabulary, and Comprehension

- Incorporate fluency into your literacy lessons daily/weekly (minimum 30 min/week) by using Rapid Word Charts, IMSE Decodable Readers, words and sentences, Acadience Reading K-6 or DIBELS 8th Edition, repeated reading, and other activities.
- Incorporate vocabulary into your literacy lessons daily/weekly (minimum 50 min/week) by choosing 3-5 appropriate tier two words (can pull from rich literature or decodable readers). Teach the words through explicit, direct instruction using student-friendly definitions, word webs, vocabulary charts, illustrations, and other activities.
- Incorporate oral language comprehension into your literacy lessons daily/weekly (approximately 100 min/week). Comprehension instruction should be explicit, direct instruction that includes teacher modeling, guided practice, and independent practice. Plan ahead to build on students' background knowledge, language structures, verbal reasoning, and literacy knowledge.

Extension Activity Ideas

- Continue to add to the multi-sensory ABC book. Have students glue queens (or another object) in the shape of the target grapheme.
- Make a paper queen. Have students glue pictures of words that begin with the /kw/ sounds on the queen.
- Divide students into teams of 6 and have them lie on the ground to form the letters "qu." Take pictures to hang around the classroom.
- Create the target letters out of green Play-Doh or clay.
- Have a "q" and "u" wedding ceremony. Invite parents, administrators, etc. Have wedding cupcakes. Have students play the role of a letter. One student can be "q," and another student can be "u." Additional students can play the role of the four remaining vowels, acting as bridesmaids or groomsmen. The rest of the students can be assigned the part of other letters and act as the wedding guests. Have someone serve as the officiant (teacher could do this).
- Have the class make a paper "quilt" in which each square is a different letter students have learned.
- Have students use a bingo dauber to find the target grapheme on a page with various letters.
- Have students go on a "sound hunt" around the room or outside to find objects that begin with the target sounds.
- Coding activity: Have students underline and label the letters in words or syllables with a "v" for vowels and a "c" for consonants. For example, when using the word *mom*, each letter should be underlined with the labels "cvc" underneath the word. This activity will help prepare students for decoding multisyllabic words later in the sequence.
- Visit IMSE's Orton-Gillingham's Pinterest page for more ideas.

Weekly Lesson Reminders

- Any of the above extension activities
- Practice writing the target grapheme (capital and lowercase) using a screen, green crayon, and house paper. (In this case, students will practice the combinations "Qu" and "qu.")
- Practice writing the target grapheme using another medium (sand, paint, shaving cream, pudding, iPad app, etc.).
- Practice writing the target grapheme using age-appropriate paper and pencil.
- Daily practice with writing the weekly Red Word(s)
- Kilpatrick's "One-Minute Activities" for daily phonological awareness practice
- Zgonc's phonological awareness activities
- Listen to rich literature to work on oral language comprehension.
- Target grapheme practice sheets from IMSE's practice books and handwriting books
- Practice test on Thursday and test on Friday

Long Vowels: a, e, i, o, u

(as in me, no, hi, mu/sic, ra/ven)

Card Pack #2, 4, 10, 14, 19	Decodable Reader #19
Object Ideas:	**Literature Ideas:**
house with door	• *Aesop's Fables* • *No, David!* by David Shannon • *Go, Dog. Go!* by P. D. Eastman • Olivia series by Ian Falconer • *Lon Po Po: A Red-Riding Hood Story From China* by Ed Young • *Abiyoyo* by Pete Seeger

 Notes

- Use the Comprehensive Flip Chart for the steps on how to teach each part of IMSE's Lesson Plan.
- Pull out the 5 vowels: cards 2, 4, 10, 14, and 19.
- Long, single vowels are voiced sounds.
- After this is taught, students state both sounds they know for the vowels during the Visual portion of the Three-Part Drill. Students should state the short sound first and then state the long sound. The teacher can provide the visual cue of a bent left arm (to represent a closed door) and then an extended left arm (to represent an open door).
- In the Auditory/Kinesthetic part of the drill, students only know one way to spell each of the long vowels.
- In the Blending part of the drill, practice an open syllable (long vowel sound) by occasionally removing the final consonant.
- Students do not need to do letter formation since this was taught previously.
- The Vowel Intensive is only for *short* vowel sounds; do not include long vowels in that drill.
- Take note of the sounds of /o͞o/ and /yo͞o/.
- Start with /yo͞o/. Then teach /o͞o/ as students begin to encounter words with that sound. When the "u" card comes up in the Visual Drill, students say: /ŭ/ /yo͞o/ /o͞o/.
- For kindergarten students, teaching syllabication with multisyllabic words is not necessary at this point. For older students, you can combine this lesson with Concept Lesson 35 (Closed and Open Syllables).

Phonological Awareness:

Materials Needed:
tokens, sound boxes, one-minute activities, or Zgonc PA book

Use the PAST assessment to determine a starting point for instruction. Incorporate daily phonological awareness activities by using Zgonc's tiered activities and/or Kilpatrick's One-Minute Activities in *Equipped for Reading Success*.

Phonemic awareness warm-up: Use tokens (or letter tiles once concepts have been taught) and sound boxes to do a quick phonemic awareness activity that ties in with the new concept, if appropriate.

 Three-Part Drill

Materials Needed:
review cards, sand, blending board, vowel tents or sticks

Do this at least 3x per week. Use the Flip Chart for steps. Include the new concept after Day 1.

- Include the Vowel Intensive with "a," "e," "i," "o," and "u."

V	VC	CVC
a	ag, ap, ab	lat, cad, zan
e	et, en, eb	zeg, ren, med
i	ig, ib, im	lin, hib, fid
o	ob, ot, oz	rom, hob, cog
u	un, ud, ub	sup, pum, dut

- Below is a sample script now that students know more than one way to spell a sound. Remember to use all of the review concepts.

1. **Visual:**
   (T) Tell me the sounds you know for these letters.
   (S) /m/, /l/, etc.
   Alternative:
   (T) Tell me the names and sounds you know for these letters.
   (S) m says /m/, l says /l/, etc.

2. **Auditory/Kinesthetic:**
   (T) You know two ways to spell this. (S) split trays. (T) Eyes on me.
   Spell /k/. Repeat.
   (S) /k/ c says /k/; k says /k/

3. **Blending:**
   (T) Tell me the sound for each letter as I point. Then blend the sounds together to read the word or syllable. Give me a thumbs up if it is a real word.
   (S) /mmm/ /ŏŏŏ/ /mmm/ *mom* (thumbs up)
   Alternative:
   (T) Watch me first. /mmm/ /ŏŏŏ/ /mmm/ *mom*
   (T) Do it with me. (T&S) /mmm/ /ŏŏŏ/ /mmm/ *mom*
   (T) Your turn. (S) /mmm/ /ŏŏŏ/ /mmm/ *mom* (thumbs up)

   *Vowel Intensive:** Model the visual cue while calling out the sound. Students will do the visual cue as they repeat the sound. Students will then hold up the vowel tent while stating the letter name and sound.
   - (T): Eyes on me. The sound is /ă/. Repeat.
   - (S): /ă/ a says /ă/

Teaching a New Concept

Materials Needed:
concept card, screen, green crayon, object, sand, decodable readers, literature, P/G chart

Introduce on Monday, and practice daily.

1. (T) Shows the new concept card(s).
   a. (T) Shows all 5 vowel cards.
      i. Remind students of the sounds they know for these letters. Review each of the short vowels while doing the hand gestures.
      ii. Inform students that today they are going to learn another sound for these letters. Sometimes these letters say their name. Sometimes "a" just says /ā/, "e" says /ē/, "i" says /ī/, "o" says /ō/, and "u" says /yo͞o/. Have students repeat each of the long vowel sounds as the teacher shows the cards.
      iii. Tell students that they need to learn when to make the short sound and when to make the long sound (where the vowel just says its name).
   b. (T) Reminds students that vowels are voiced sounds.
   c. (T) Reminds students where to find the vowels in the alphabet.
   d. (T) Uses mirrors to discuss the mouth, tongue, and teeth placement.

2. (T) Shows an object.
   a. Show a house (IOG) with the word *bed* written on it. The "d" should be on the door. Have students read the word on the house. Ask if the door is open or closed (closed). Tell students that the consonant "d" is closing in the vowel. This is called a closed syllable.

   b. Now open the door. The consonant is gone and the vowel is free to say its own name (extend your left arm). Now the word says *be*. Is the door open or closed? (open) Tell students that this is an open syllable.

3. (S) Brainstorm.
   a. Continue to brainstorm words together using paper houses (made from IOG or copied from the *Masters*).

4. (T) Teaches Letter Formation, *if needed*. Students could begin to learn cursive.
   a. Use the steps for teaching letter formation on the Flip Chart.
   b. Use house paper to teach lowercase letters.
   c. Teach capital letters throughout the week. Capital letters go outside the house.

5. (T) Dictates target sound(s). (S) Practice in the sand or other medium.
   a. Practice writing the letter using a different medium, such as sand, shaving cream, finger paint, gel board, iPad app, air writing, etc.
   b. Do this while stating the target sound(s) one at a time: /ā/, "a" says /ā/; /ē/, "e" says /ē/; /ī/, "i" says /ī/; /ō/, "o" says /ō/; and /yo͞o/, "u" says /yo͞o/.

6. (T) Connects with literature.
   a. Have students signal when they hear the long vowel sound for the first page or two.
   b. Read again for language comprehension.
   c. Continue to work on language comprehension with rich literature throughout the week.

7. (S) Use decodable readers to practice the concepts learned.
   a. (S) Highlight words with the new concept. Read those words.
   b. (S) Highlight Red Words. Read those words.
   c. (S) Start reading the decodable reader.
   d. (S) Continue reading throughout the week.
   e. (S) Read a clean copy on Friday.

8. (T&S) Mark the Phoneme/Grapheme (P/G) chart by highlighting the target sounds.

 ## Word Dictation

Materials Needed:
fingertapping hand, dictation paper, pencil

Create any syllables using the new concept and previously taught concepts. Practice daily. Use the Flip Chart to follow the steps for word dictation.

Day 1:	1. he	2. bā (as in baby)	3. hi	4. go	5. pū (as in pupil)
Day 2:	1. no	2. pā (as in paper)	3. mū (as in music)	4. I	5. me
Day 3:	1. be	2. so	3. lā (as in lazy)	4. fī (as in final)	5. we
Days 4-5:	Review prior words. Optional additional words: dō (as in donut), rā (as in raven), rō (as in robot)				

Below is a sample script:

1. (T) States word: *mom*. Uses it in a sentence: My *mom* is a wonderful lady. (Pounds) *mom*. (T) Models fingertapping if needed: /m/ /ŏ/ /m/. (Pounds) *mom*.
2. (S) State while pounding: *mom*. (Fingertap) /m/ /ŏ/ /m/. (Pound) *mom*. Write the letters known for the sounds.
3. (T) When yours looks like mine, rewrite the word.
4. (S) Rewrite.
5. Repeat the process for each word.
6. (S) Read the list of words multiple times to build automaticity.

Sentence Dictation

Red Words are underlined. Students can fingertap the green words. Use the Flip Chart to follow the steps for sentence dictation.

1. I said hi to Bob.
2. We had to go to the pen to get the pig.
3. He said yes.
4. Kim will go with me.
5. Did they go to the den?
6. Ben said no to the dog.
7. Dad said no to the dog you want.
8. The lid is so hot.
9. Jim did see me.
10. Did he see any wax?
11. Ben said hi to the six men.
12. Did he go to bed?
13. I had to go to the vet.
14. So, did Tim go to win the dog?
15. They said to go to bed!

- Below is a sample script for sentence dictation.

1. (T): Listen to the sentence. *Tad had a cat.*
2. (T): Listen while I pound the syllables. *Tad had a cat.*
3. (T): Pound it with me. (T&S): *Tad had a cat.*
4. (T): You pound the sentence. (S): *Tad had a cat.*
5. (T): Watch me as I point to the lines while stating the sentence. *Tad had a cat.*
6. (T): You point to the lines while stating the sentence.
7. (S): *Tad had a cat.*
8. (T): Now write the sentence. Fingertap if needed.

- Below is a sample script to check CUPS*.

1. (T): C stands for capitalization. Did you remember a capital letter at the beginning of your sentence? It's also a name. *Tad* would always be capitalized. If you forgot, fix it. If you remembered, put a tally mark above the capital letter. Add a mark in the box for C.

2. (T): U stands for understanding. Is your sentence neat? Reread it to yourself. Does it make sense? Could someone else understand it? If not, fix it. Add a mark in the box for U.

3. (T): P stands for punctuation. Did you remember a period at the end? If not, fix it. If you remembered, put a tally mark above the period. Add a mark in the box for P.

4. (T): S stands for spelling. Did you spell your words correctly? Check them. Now, check yours with mine (show the teacher's copy). Fix any words you spelled incorrectly. Put a tally mark above the words you spelled correctly. Add a mark in the box for S.

5. (T): Rewrite your sentence with all of the corrections.

6. (T): Check for CUPS again. Put another mark in the boxes.

7. (T): Let's read the sentences.

8. (S) Read the sentences for fluency and automaticity.

***Please note:** Once students understand how to use CUPS, transition to letting them check their sentence independently before showing the teacher's copy.

Weekly Red Words

Materials Needed:
screen, red crayon, red word paper

Introduce on Tuesday, and practice daily. Use the Flip Chart for steps.

New:	Review:	New Read-Only:	Review Read-Only:
they, any	the, was, is, a, and, to, for, like, of, will, want, with, said, you, put, see, stop, from, off, has, have, his, as, my, into, now, new, give, or, by, went, do, are	fish	orange, white, brown, stop, yellow, blue, eek, ouch, pink, green, black, look, good

Steps for Teaching a New Red Word:

1. (T) States the word. (*they*)
2. (T&S) Use tokens to determine how many sounds are in the word. (/TH/ /ā/; 2)
3. (T&S) Discuss how we would expect to spell each sound as the teacher writes the grapheme(s) correctly. Identify what is unexpected or irregular about the spelling of the word. It could also be expected, but the concept hasn't been taught yet.
4. (T&S) Discuss the etymology of the word, if appropriate (lexical words). Visit www.etymonline.com for more information on the word.
5. (T) Defines the word, and writes a sentence using the word.
6. (T) Writes the word on Red Word paper with the screen underneath, using red crayon.
7. (S) Write the word on Red Word paper with the screen underneath, using red crayon. (S) Show the word to the teacher.
   (**NOTE:** The teacher should have students chunk the word if it has more than four letters.)
8. (T&S) Stand up, holding the Red Word in the nondominant hand. Armtap word while naming each letter. Then "underline" the word by sweeping left to right while stating the word, 3x. (**NOTE:** Left-handed students will place their left hand on their right wrist. They tap to their right shoulder. Underline from wrist to shoulder. Right-handed students place their right hand on their left shoulder. They tap to their left wrist. Underline shoulder to wrist.)
9. (T&S) Trace crayon bumps with the pointer finger while naming the letters, 3x.
10. (T&S) Place the screen over the paper and trace the word with the pointer finger while naming the letters, 3x.
11. (S) Turn paper over. With red crayon, write the word without the screen one time, and hold up the word for the teacher to check. (S) Write the word two more times.
12. (S) Write an original sentence in pencil and underline the Red Word with a red crayon. (**NOTE:** The sentence can also be dictated by the teacher while the student writes or dictated by the student while the teacher writes it.)
13. Repeat the steps for *any*. (/ĕ/ /n/ /ē/; 3)

Review Ideas for Red Words:

- Sculpt the word using red Play-Doh or clay. Have students spell the word as they smash each letter.
- Print flashcards from IOG, and practice reading.
- Armtap the word to review.
- Cross-clap the word to review.
- Do Spelling Aerobics.

Fluency, Vocabulary, and Comprehension

- Incorporate fluency into your literacy lessons daily/weekly (minimum 30 min/week) by using Rapid Word Charts, IMSE Decodable Readers, words and sentences, Acadience Reading K-6 or DIBELS 8th Edition, repeated reading, and other activities.
- Incorporate vocabulary into your literacy lessons daily/weekly (minimum 50 min/week) by choosing 3-5 appropriate tier two words (can pull from rich literature or decodable readers). Teach the words through explicit, direct instruction using student-friendly definitions, word webs, vocabulary charts, illustrations, and other activities.
- Incorporate oral language comprehension into your literacy lessons daily/weekly (approximately 100 min/week). Comprehension instruction should be explicit, direct instruction that includes teacher modeling, guided practice, and independent practice. Plan ahead to build on students' background knowledge, language structures, verbal reasoning, and literacy knowledge.

Extension Activity Ideas

- Create multiple "houses" for students' Interactive Notebooks.
- Coding activity: Have students underline and label the letters in words or syllables with a "v" for vowels and a "c" for consonants. For example, when using the word *mom*, each letter should be underlined with the labels "cvc" underneath the word. This activity will help prepare students for decoding multisyllabic words later in the sequence.
- Visit IMSE's Orton-Gillingham's Pinterest page for more ideas.

Weekly Lesson Reminders

- Daily practice with writing the weekly Red Word(s)
- Kilpatrick's "One-Minute Activities" for daily phonological awareness practice
- Zgonc's phonological awareness activities
- Listen to rich literature to work on oral language comprehension.
- Target letter practice sheets from IMSE's practice books
- Practice test on Thursday and test on Friday

Review for Concepts m–long vowels

After teaching the first 27 concepts, the following words and sentences may be utilized for review. Teachers can dictate a different list (A, B, C, or D) and three sentences each day of the review. Teachers can spend up to a week on review *if needed*. If a review is not needed, this page can be skipped or partially utilized. Students can use IMSE workbooks or age-appropriate paper for recording their answers.

List A	List B	List C	List D
1. led	1. wig	1. net	1. sub
2. yam	2. ox	2. Val	2. zag
3. zap	3. Deb	3. sob	3. pen
4. web	4. vet	4. tux	4. van
5. box	5. yes	5. men	5. win
6. he	6. sun	6. zig	6. yap
7. Max	7. zip	7. wet	7. tax
8. sit	8. quiz	8. hi	8. bet
9. quit	9. met	9. yet	9. quit
10. van	10. go	10. quip	10. be

Sentences:
1. The pig is in the big pen.
2. The lid is so hot.
3. The cat is wet and sad.
4. I said hi to Bob.
5. Ted hid a log in the van.
6. Did the bug zap you?
7. Ken set the net on the rug.
8. Can you fix the box?
9. I had to go to the vet.
10. The lad had a hot yam.
11. Kim will go with me.
12. Did Sam get the vet to quit?

Notes:

ch as in chair

Card Pack #27 Decodable Reader #20	
Object Ideas:	**Literature Ideas:**
chair, chocolate chip, chimpanzee, Cheetos, chain, chopsticks, musical chairs, chalk, cheese, ChapStick, Cheerios, chicken	<ul><li>*Chester's Way* by Kevin Henkes</li><li>*Peter's Chair* by Ezra Jack Keats</li><li>*Charlie and the Chocolate Factory* by Roald Dahl</li><li>Charlie Brown series by Charles M. Schulz</li><li>*The Chocolate Touch* by Patrick Skene Catling</li><li>*Chicka Chicka Boom Boom* by Bill Martin, Jr., and John Archambault</li><li>*The Stinky Cheese Man and Other Fairly Stupid Tales* by Jon Scieszka</li><li>*Chocolate Fever* by Robert Kimmel Smith</li><li>*Chocolate Me!* by Taye Diggs</li><li>*A Chair for My Mother* by Vera Williams</li></ul>

 Notes

- Use the Comprehensive Flip Chart for the steps on how to teach each part of IMSE's Lesson Plan.
- Di means two; graph means letters. A digraph is two letters that make one sound.
- In the P/G chart, the digraphs listed in the Consonant Digraphs column are only the consonant digraphs that make a *new* sound.
- Digraphs get an extra visual cue under the grapheme line. This is a wavy line that informs the student to be careful, as there are two letters that make this sound.
- The wavy grapheme line only goes with the word dictation, not sentence dictation.

- Keep "ch" in the initial position at first. There is a /ch/ rule that will be taught later.
- "Ch" is an affricate that is formed with the lips forward and the tongue pulled back on the roof of the mouth.

Phonological Awareness:

Materials Needed:
tokens, sound boxes, one-minute activities, or Zgonc PA book

Use the PAST assessment to determine a starting point for instruction. Incorporate daily phonological awareness activities by using Zgonc's tiered activities and/or Kilpatrick's One-Minute Activities in *Equipped for Reading Success*.

Phonemic awareness warm-up: Use tokens (or letter tiles once concepts have been taught) and sound boxes to do a quick phonemic awareness activity that ties in with the new concept, if appropriate.

Three-Part Drill

Materials Needed:
review cards, sand, blending board, vowel tents or sticks

Do this at least 3x per week. Use the Flip Chart for steps. Include the new concept after Day 1.

- Include the Vowel Intensive with "a," "e," "i," "o," and "u."

V	VC	CVC
a	ag, ap, ab	lat, cad, zan
e	et, en, eb	zeg, ren, med
i	ig, ib, im	lin, hib, fid
o	ob, ot, oz	rom, hob, cog
u	un, ud, ub	sup, pum, dut

- Below is a sample script now that students know more than one way to spell a concept. Remember to use all of the review concepts.

1. **Visual:**
   (T) Tell me the sounds you know for these letters.
   (S) /m/, /l/, etc.
   Alternative:
   (T) Tell me the names and sounds you know for these letters.
   (S) m says /m/, l says /l/, etc.
2. **Auditory/Kinesthetic:**
   (T) You know two ways to spell this. (S) split trays. (T) Eyes on me.
   Spell /k/. Repeat.
   (S) /k/ c says /k/; k says /k/

3. **Blending:**

(T) Tell me the sound for each letter as I point. Then blend the sounds together to read the word or syllable. Give me a thumbs up if it is a real word.

(S) /mmm/ /ŏŏŏ/ /mmm/ *mom* (thumbs up)

Alternative:

(T) Watch me first. /mmm/ /ŏŏŏ/ /mmm/ *mom*

(T) Do it with me. (T&S) /mmm/ /ŏŏŏ/ /mmm/ *mom*

(T) Your turn. (S) /mmm/ /ŏŏŏ/ /mmm/ *mom* (thumbs up)

*Vowel Intensive: Model the visual cue while calling out the sound. Students will do the visual cue as they repeat the sound. Students will then hold up the vowel tent while stating the letter name and sound.

- (T): Eyes on me. The sound is /ă/. Repeat.

- (S): /ă/ a says /ă/

Teaching a New Concept

Materials Needed:
concept card, screen, green crayon, object, sand, decodable readers, literature, P/G chart

Introduce on Monday, and practice daily.

1. (T) Reads alliteration sentences. (S) Identify the target sound.
    a. Chimps choose cheese and Cheetos.
    b. Charming Charlie chews chocolate chips.

2. (T) Shows the new concept card.
    a. (T) Tells students that "ch" is a digraph. A digraph is two letters that work together to make one sound. "Ch" says /ch/. Have students repeat, 3 times.
    b. (T) Tells students that it is an unvoiced sound.
    c. (T) Uses mirrors to discuss the mouth, tongue, and teeth placement.

3. (T) Shows an object.
    a. (T) Allows students to manipulate the object and discuss prior knowledge. Reminds (S) that the object has the target sound spelled with the target letters.

4. (S) Brainstorm.
    a. Brainstorm words that have the target sound. (Accept all answers, but place incorrect answers in a "thought bubble" to discuss.) The brainstorming can be a teacher-directed activity if students need extra support.

5. (T) Teaches Letter Formation, *if needed*. Students could begin to learn cursive.
    a. Use the steps for teaching letter formation on the Flip Chart.
    b. Use house paper to teach lowercase letters.
    c. Teach capital letters throughout the week. Capital letters go outside the house.

6. (T) Dictates target sound. (S) Practice in the sand or other medium.
    a. Practice writing the letters using a different medium, such as sand, shaving cream, finger paint, gel board, iPad app, air writing, etc.
    b. Do this while stating: ch says /ch/, 3 times.

7. (T) Connects with literature.

   a. Have students signal when they hear the target sound for the first page or two.

   b. Read again for language comprehension.

   c. Continue to work on language comprehension with rich literature throughout the week.

8. (S) Use decodable readers to practice the concepts learned.

   a. (S) Highlight words with the new concept. Read those words.

   b. (S) Highlight Red Words. Read those words.

   c. (S) Start reading the decodable reader.

   d. (S) Continue reading throughout the week.

   e. (S) Read a clean copy on Friday.

9. (T&S) Mark the Phoneme/Grapheme (P/G) chart by highlighting the target sound.

 ## Word Dictation

> **Materials Needed:**
> fingertapping hand, dictation paper, pencil

Create any syllables using the new concept and previously taught concepts. Practice daily. Use the Flip Chart to follow the steps for word dictation.

Day 1:	1. chip	2. chop	3. chat	4. chum	5. chin
Day 2:	1. chit	2. Chad	3. chin	4. chip	5. quiz
Day 3:	1. chap	2. chim	3. quit	4. chug	5. chip
Days 4-5:	Review prior words.				

Below is a sample script:

1. (T) States word: *mom*. Uses it in a sentence: My *mom* is a wonderful lady. (Pounds) *mom*. (T) Models fingertapping if needed: /m/ /ŏ/ /m/. (Pounds) *mom*.

2. (S) State while pounding: *mom*. (Fingertap) /m/ /ŏ/ /m/. (Pound) *mom*. Write the letters known for the sounds.

3. (T) When yours looks like mine, rewrite the word.

4. (S) Rewrite.

5. Repeat the process for each word.

6. (S) Read the list of words multiple times to build automaticity.

 ## Sentence Dictation

Red Words are underlined. Students can fingertap the green words. Use the Flip Chart to follow the steps for sentence dictation.

1. Chad did chug <u>from the</u> jug.

2. Tad <u>will</u> chop <u>the</u> log <u>and</u> sit.

3. Bob <u>is a</u> chum.

© IMSE 2022

4. Dot got the chip.
5. Pam had a chat with Chad.
6. Jim will chop the hot log.
7. Don will chug the jug and gag.
8. The chap had a cap.
9. Tim and Chad had a chip.
10. Did Tom and the chap chat?
11. Did the chap chop the log?

- Below is a sample script for sentence dictation.

> 1. (T): Listen to the sentence. *Tad had a cat.*
> 2. (T): Listen while I pound the syllables. *Tad had a cat.*
> 3. (T): Pound it with me. (T&S): *Tad had a cat.*
> 4. (T): You pound the sentence. (S): *Tad had a cat.*
> 5. (T): Watch me as I point to the lines while stating the sentence. *Tad had a cat.*
> 6. (T): You point to the lines while stating the sentence.
> 7. (S): *Tad had a cat.*
> 8. (T): Now write the sentence. Fingertap if needed.

- Below is a sample script to check CUPS*.

> 1. (T): C stands for capitalization. Did you remember a capital letter at the beginning of your sentence? It's also a name. *Tad* would always be capitalized. If you forgot, fix it. If you remembered, put a tally mark above the capital letter. Add a mark in the box for C.
> 2. (T): U stands for understanding. Is your sentence neat? Reread it to yourself. Does it make sense? Could someone else understand it? If not, fix it. Add a mark in the box for U.
> 3. (T): P stands for punctuation. Did you remember a period at the end? If not, fix it. If you remembered, put a tally mark above the period. Add a mark in the box for P.
> 4. (T): S stands for spelling. Did you spell your words correctly? Check them. Now, check yours with mine (show the teacher's copy). Fix any words you spelled incorrectly. Put a tally mark above the words you spelled correctly. Add a mark in the box for S.
> 5. (T): Rewrite your sentence with all of the corrections.
> 6. (T): Check for CUPS again. Put another mark in the boxes.
> 7. (T): Let's read the sentences.
> 8. (S) Read the sentences for fluency and automaticity.
>
> ***Please note:** Once students understand how to use CUPS, transition to letting them check their sentence independently before showing the teacher's copy.

Weekly Red Words

Materials Needed:
screen, red crayon, red word paper

Introduce on Tuesday, and practice daily. Use the Flip Chart for steps.

New:	Review:	New Read-Only:	Review Read-Only:
black, blue, brown, gray, green	the, was, is, a, and, to, for, like, of, will, want, with, said, you, put, see, stop, from, off, has, have, his, as, my, into, now, new, give, or, by, went, do, are, they, any	help	orange, white, stop, yellow, eek, ouch, pink, look, good, fish

Steps for Teaching a New Red Word:

1. (T) States the word. (*black*)

2. (T&S) Use tokens to determine how many sounds are in the word. (/b/ /l/ /ă/ /k/; 4)

3. (T&S) Discuss how we would expect to spell each sound as the teacher writes the grapheme(s) correctly. Identify what is unexpected or irregular about the spelling of the word. It could also be expected, but the concept hasn't been taught yet.

4. (T&S) Discuss the etymology of the word, if appropriate (lexical words). Visit www.etymonline.com for more information on the word.

5. (T) Defines the word, and writes a sentence using the word.

6. (T) Writes the word on Red Word paper with the screen underneath, using red crayon.

7. (S) Write the word on Red Word paper with the screen underneath, using red crayon. (S) Show the word to the teacher.
   (**NOTE:** The teacher should have students chunk the word if it has more than four letters.)

8. (T&S) Stand up, holding the Red Word in the nondominant hand. Armtap word while naming each letter. Then "underline" the word by sweeping left to right while stating the word, 3x. (**NOTE:** Left-handed students will place their left hand on their right wrist. They tap to their right shoulder. Underline from wrist to shoulder. Right-handed students place their right hand on their left shoulder. They tap to their left wrist. Underline shoulder to wrist.)

9. (T&S) Trace crayon bumps with the pointer finger while naming the letters, 3x.

10. (T&S) Place the screen over the paper and trace the word with the pointer finger while naming the letters, 3x.

11. (S) Turn paper over. With red crayon, write the word without the screen one time, and hold up the word for the teacher to check. (S) Write the word two more times.

12. (S) Write an original sentence in pencil and underline the Red Word with a red crayon. (**NOTE:** The sentence can also be dictated by the teacher while the student writes or dictated by the student while the teacher writes it.)

13. Repeat the steps for *blue* (/b/ /l/ / $\overline{oo}$ /; 3), *brown* (/b/ /r/ /ou/ /n/; 4), *gray* (/g/ /r/ /ā/; 3), *green* (/g/ /r/ /ē/ /n/; 4).

Review Ideas for Red Words:

- Sculpt the word using red Play-Doh or clay. Have students spell the word as they smash each letter.
- Print flashcards from IOG, and practice reading.
- Armtap the word to review.
- Cross-clap the word to review.
- Do Spelling Aerobics.

Fluency, Vocabulary, and Comprehension

- Incorporate fluency into your literacy lessons daily/weekly (minimum 30 min/week) by using Rapid Word Charts, IMSE Decodable Readers, words and sentences, Acadience Reading K-6 or DIBELS 8th Edition, repeated reading, and other activities.
- Incorporate vocabulary into your literacy lessons daily/weekly (minimum 50 min/week) by choosing 3-5 appropriate tier two words (can pull from rich literature or decodable readers). Teach the words through explicit, direct instruction using student-friendly definitions, word webs, vocabulary charts, illustrations, and other activities.
- Incorporate oral language comprehension into your literacy lessons daily/weekly (approximately 100 min/week). Comprehension instruction should be explicit, direct instruction that includes teacher modeling, guided practice, and independent practice. Plan ahead to build on students' background knowledge, language structures, verbal reasoning, and literacy knowledge.

Extension Activity Ideas

- Continue to add to the multi-sensory ABC book. Have students glue chocolate chips (or another object) in the shape of the target grapheme.
- Have students compare and contrast chocolate chips and potato chips using a Venn Diagram.
- Make a paper chicken. Have students glue pictures of words that begin with the /ch/ sound on the chicken.
- Have students go on a "sound hunt" around the room or outside to find objects that begin with the target sound.
- Coding activity: Have students underline and label the letters in words or syllables with a "v" for vowels and a "c" for consonants. For example, when using the word *mom*, each letter should be underlined with the labels "cvc" underneath the word. This activity will help prepare students for decoding multisyllabic words later in the sequence.
- Visit IMSE's Orton-Gillingham's Pinterest page for more ideas.

Weekly Lesson Reminders

- Any of the above extension activities
- Practice writing the target grapheme (capital and lowercase) using a screen, green crayon, and house paper.
- Practice writing the target grapheme using another medium (sand, paint, shaving cream, pudding, iPad app, etc.).
- Practice writing the target grapheme using age-appropriate paper and pencil.
- Daily practice with writing the weekly Red Word(s)
- Kilpatrick's "One-Minute Activities" for daily phonological awareness practice
- Zgonc's phonological awareness activities
- Listen to rich literature to work on oral language comprehension.
- Target grapheme practice sheets from IMSE's practice books and handwriting books
- Practice test on Thursday and test on Friday

sh as in shell

Card Pack #28 Decodable Reader #21	
Object Ideas:	**Literature Ideas:**
shaving cream, shadow, shell, shark, shape, shamrock, ship, shoe, sheep, shout, shore, shut, shake, shiver, share, shower, shampoo	▪ *Mrs. Wishy Washy's Farm* by Joy Cowley ▪ *Sharks* by Gail Gibbons ▪ *Mrs. McNosh and the Great Big Squash* by Sarah Weeks ▪ *Shiloh* by Phyllis Reynolds Naylor ▪ "Shake Your Sillies Out" song by The Learning Station ▪ *Sheep in a Jeep* by Nancy Shaw ▪ *Sheila Rae, the Brave* by Kevin Henkes ▪ *Ashanti to Zulu: African Traditions* by Margaret Musgrove ▪ *Shaq and the Beanstalk and Other Very Tall Tales* by Shaquille O'Neal ▪ *Salt in His Shoes: Michael Jordan in Pursuit of a Dream* by Deloris and Roslyn Jordan ▪ *Shaking Things Up: 14 Young Women Who Changed the World* by Susan Hood ▪ *Those Shoes* by Maribeth Boelts

 ## Notes

- Use the Comprehensive Flip Chart for the steps on how to teach each part of IMSE's Lesson Plan.
- Di means two; graph means letters. A digraph is two letters that make one sound.
- In the P/G chart, the digraphs listed in the Consonant Digraphs column are only the consonant digraphs that make a *new* sound.
- Digraphs get an extra visual cue under the grapheme line. This is a wavy line that informs the student to be careful, as there are two letters that make this sound.
- The wavy grapheme line only goes with the word dictation, not sentence dictation.

- "Sh" can go in either position. To balance out the piles on the blending board, you can place the "sh" card in the final consonant pile.
- "Sh" is a fricative that is formed with the lips forward and the sides of the tongue pulled back on the roof of the mouth.

Phonological Awareness:

Materials Needed:
tokens, sound boxes, one-minute activities, or Zgonc PA book

Use the PAST assessment to determine a starting point for instruction. Incorporate daily phonological awareness activities by using Zgonc's tiered activities and/or Kilpatrick's One-Minute Activities in *Equipped for Reading Success*.

Phonemic awareness warm-up: Use tokens (or letter tiles once concepts have been taught) and sound boxes to do a quick phonemic awareness activity that ties in with the new concept, if appropriate.

Three-Part Drill

Materials Needed:
review cards, sand, blending board, vowel tents or sticks

Do this at least 3x per week. Use the Flip Chart for steps. Include the new concept after Day 1.

- Include the Vowel Intensive with "a," "e," "i," "o," and "u."

V	VC	CVC
a	ag, ap, ab	lat, cad, zan
e	et, en, eb	zeg, ren, med
i	ig, ib, im	lin, hib, fid
o	ob, ot, oz	rom, hob, cog
u	un, ud, ub	sup, pum, dut

- Below is a sample script now that students know more than one way to spell a sound. Remember to use all of the review concepts.

1. **Visual:**
   (T) Tell me the sounds you know for these letters.
   (S) /m/, /l/, etc.
   Alternative:
   (T) Tell me the names and sounds you know for these letters.
   (S) m says /m/, l says /l/, etc.

2. **Auditory/Kinesthetic:**
   (T) You know two ways to spell this. (S) split trays. (T) Eyes on me.
   Spell /k/. Repeat.
   (S) /k/ c says /k/; k says /k/

3. **Blending:**
   (T) Tell me the sound for each letter as I point. Then blend the sounds together to read the word or syllable. Give me a thumbs up if it is a real word.
   (S) /mmm/ /ŏŏŏ/ /mmm/ *mom* (thumbs up)
   Alternative:
   (T) Watch me first. /mmm/ /ŏŏŏ/ /mmm/ *mom*
   (T) Do it with me. (T&S) /mmm/ /ŏŏŏ/ /mmm/ *mom*
   (T) Your turn. (S) /mmm/ /ŏŏŏ/ /mmm/ *mom* (thumbs up)

   Vowel Intensive: Model the visual cue while calling out the sound. Students will do the visual cue as they repeat the sound. Students will then hold up the vowel tent while stating the letter name and sound.
   ▪ (T): Eyes on me. The sound is /ă/. Repeat.
   ▪ (S): /ă/ a says /ă/

Teaching a New Concept

Materials Needed:
concept card, screen, green crayon, object, sand, decodable readers, literature, P/G chart

Introduce on Monday, and practice daily.

1. (T) Reads alliteration sentences. (S) Identify the target sound.
   a. She shined Shaq's shoes.
   b. Shy Sheila shushed Sheldon.

2. (T) Shows the new concept card.
   a. (T) Tells students that "sh" is a digraph. A digraph is two letters that work together to make one sound. "Sh" says /sh/. Have students repeat, 3 times.
   b. (T) Tells students that it is an unvoiced sound.
   c. (T) Uses mirrors to discuss the mouth, tongue, and teeth placement.

3. (T) Shows an object.
   a. (T) Allows students to manipulate the object and discuss prior knowledge. Reminds (S) that the object has the target sound spelled with the target letters.

4. (S) Brainstorm.
   a. Brainstorm words that have the target sound. (Accept all answers, but place incorrect answers in a "thought bubble" to discuss.) The brainstorming can be a teacher-directed activity if students need extra support.

5. (T) Teaches Letter Formation, *if needed*. Students could begin to learn cursive.
   a. Use the steps for teaching letter formation on the Flip Chart.
   b. Use house paper to teach lowercase letters.
   c. Teach capital letters throughout the week. Capital letters go outside the house.

6. (T) Dictates target sound. (S) Practice in the sand or other medium.
   a. Practice writing the letters using a different medium, such as sand, shaving cream, finger paint, gel board, iPad app, air writing, etc.
   b. Do this while stating: sh says /sh/, 3 times.

7. (T) Connects with literature.
   a. Have students signal when they hear the target sound for the first page or two.
   b. Read again for language comprehension.
   c. Continue to work on language comprehension with rich literature throughout the week.
8. (S) Use decodable readers to practice the concepts learned.
   a. (S) Highlight words with the new concept. Read those words.
   b. (S) Highlight Red Words. Read those words.
   c. (S) Start reading the decodable reader.
   d. (S) Continue reading throughout the week.
   e. (S) Read a clean copy on Friday.
9. (T&S) Mark the Phoneme/Grapheme (P/G) chart by highlighting the target sound.

 # Word Dictation

Materials Needed:
fingertapping hand, dictation paper, pencil

Create any syllables using the new concept and previously taught concepts. Practice daily. Use the Flip Chart to follow the steps for word dictation.

Day 1:	1. mash	2. shag	3. gush	4. dash	5. hush
Day 2:	1. cash	2. dish	3. Josh	4. she	5. wish
Day 3:	1. fish	2. lash	3. shed	4. ash	5. mesh
Days 4-5:	Review prior words. Optional additional words: bash, gash, gosh, hash, lush, mush, nosh, posh, rash, sash, sham, shin, ship, shop, shot, shun, shut				

Below is a sample script:

1. (T) States word: *mom*. Uses it in a sentence: My *mom* is a wonderful lady. (Pounds) *mom*. (T) Models fingertapping if needed: /m/ /ŏ/ /m/. (Pounds) *mom*.
2. (S) State while pounding: *mom*. (Fingertap) /m/ /ŏ/ /m/. (Pound) *mom*. Write the letters known for the sounds.
3. (T) When yours looks like mine, rewrite the word.
4. (S) Rewrite.
5. Repeat the process for each word.
6. (S) Read the list of words multiple times to build automaticity.

Sentence Dictation

Red Words are underlined. Students can fingertap the green words. Use the Flip Chart to follow the steps for sentence dictation.

1. Tad got a gash on his shin.
2. Chad and Bob got to fish on the ship.
3. Josh got a fish on a dish.
4. Did Kim get the dish at the shop?
5. A kid had ten orange fish.
6. Ship the dish to the shop.
7. Can Bob mash the ham in the pot?
8. Sam had a black rash.
9. Did Sal get the dish for the dog?
10. Is the cash in the shop?
11. Kim will nosh on the blue fish.
12. The mush was hot.
13. Sal hit his shin on the log.
14. The rash on his leg is red.
15. The posh shed has cash in it.

- Below is a sample script for sentence dictation.

> 1. (T): Listen to the sentence. *Tad had a cat.*
> 2. (T): Listen while I pound the syllables. *Tad had a cat.*
> 3. (T): Pound it with me. (T&S): *Tad had a cat.*
> 4. (T): You pound the sentence. (S): *Tad had a cat.*
> 5. (T): Watch me as I point to the lines while stating the sentence. *Tad had a cat.*
> 6. (T): You point to the lines while stating the sentence.
> 7. (S): *Tad had a cat.*
> 8. (T): Now write the sentence. Fingertap if needed.

- Below is a sample script to check CUPS*.

> 1. (T): C stands for capitalization. Did you remember a capital letter at the beginning of your sentence? It's also a name. *Tad* would always be capitalized. If you forgot, fix it. If you remembered, put a tally mark above the capital letter. Add a mark in the box for C.
> 2. (T): U stands for understanding. Is your sentence neat? Reread it to yourself. Does it make sense? Could someone else understand it? If not, fix it. Add a mark in the box for U.

3. (T): P stands for punctuation. Did you remember a period at the end? If not, fix it. If you remembered, put a tally mark above the period. Add a mark in the box for P.

4. (T): S stands for spelling. Did you spell your words correctly? Check them. Now, check yours with mine (show the teacher's copy). Fix any words you spelled incorrectly. Put a tally mark above the words you spelled correctly. Add a mark in the box for S.

5. (T): Rewrite your sentence with all of the corrections.

6. (T): Check for CUPS again. Put another mark in the boxes.

7. (T): Let's read the sentences.

8. (S) Read the sentences for fluency and automaticity.

***Please note:** Once students understand how to use CUPS, transition to letting them check their sentence independently before showing the teacher's copy.

Weekly Red Words

Materials Needed:
screen, red crayon, red word paper

Introduce on Tuesday, and practice daily. Use the Flip Chart for steps.

New:	Review:	New Read-Only:	Review Read-Only:
orange, pink, purple, white, yellow	the, was, is, a, and, to, for, like, of, will, want, with, said, you, put, see, stop, from, off, has, have, his, as, my, into, now, new, give, or, by, went, do, are, they, any, black, blue, brown, gray, green		stop, eek, ouch, look, good, help

Steps for Teaching a New Red Word:

1. (T) States the word. (*orange*)

2. (T&S) Use tokens to determine how many sounds are in the word. (/or/ /ĭ/ /n/ /j/; 4)
   NOTE: This word may be pronounced differently depending on dialect.

3. (T&S) Discuss how we would expect to spell each sound as the teacher writes the grapheme(s) correctly. Identify what is unexpected or irregular about the spelling of the word. It could also be expected, but the concept hasn't been taught yet.

4. (T&S) Discuss the etymology of the word, if appropriate (lexical words). Visit www. etymonline.com for more information on the word.

5. (T) Defines the word, and writes a sentence using the word.

6. (T) Writes the word on Red Word paper with the screen underneath, using red crayon.

7. (S) Write the word on Red Word paper with the screen underneath, using red crayon. (S) Show the word to the teacher.
(**NOTE:** The teacher should have students chunk the word if it has more than four letters.)

8. (T&S) Stand up, holding the Red Word in the nondominant hand. Armtap word while naming each letter. Then "underline" the word by sweeping left to right while stating the word, 3x. (**NOTE:** Left-handed students will place their left hand on their right wrist. They tap to their right shoulder. Underline from wrist to shoulder. Right-handed students place their right hand on their left shoulder. They tap to their left wrist. Underline shoulder to wrist.)

9. (T&S) Trace crayon bumps with the pointer finger while naming the letters, 3x.

10. (T&S) Place the screen over the paper and trace the word with the pointer finger while naming the letters, 3x.

11. (S) Turn paper over. With red crayon, write the word without the screen one time, and hold up the word for the teacher to check. (S) Write the word two more times.

12. (S) Write an original sentence in pencil and underline the Red Word with a red crayon. (**NOTE:** The sentence can also be dictated by the teacher while the student writes or dictated by the student while the teacher writes it.)

13. Repeat the steps for *pink* (/p/ /ĭ/ /ŋ/ /k/; 4), *purple* (/p/ /er/ /p/ /ə/ /l/; 5), *white* (/w/ /ī/ /t/; 3), *yellow* (/y/ /ĕ/ /l/ /ō/; 4).

Review Ideas for Red Words:

- Sculpt the word using red Play-Doh or clay. Have students spell the word as they smash each letter.
- Print flashcards from IOG, and practice reading.
- Armtap the word to review.
- Cross-clap the word to review.
- Do Spelling Aerobics.

Fluency, Vocabulary, and Comprehension

- Incorporate fluency into your literacy lessons daily/weekly (minimum 30 min/ week) by using Rapid Word Charts, IMSE Decodable Readers, words and sentences, Acadience Reading K-6 or DIBELS 8th Edition, repeated reading, and other activities.
- Incorporate vocabulary into your literacy lessons daily/weekly (minimum 50 min/week) by choosing 3-5 appropriate tier two words (can pull from rich literature or decodable readers). Teach the words through explicit, direct instruction using student-friendly definitions, word webs, vocabulary charts, illustrations, and other activities.

- Incorporate oral language comprehension into your literacy lessons daily/weekly (approximately 100 min/week). Comprehension instruction should be explicit, direct instruction that includes teacher modeling, guided practice, and independent practice. Plan ahead to build on students' background knowledge, language structures, verbal reasoning, and literacy knowledge.

Extension Activity Ideas

- Continue to add to the multi-sensory ABC book. Have students glue shells (or another object) in the shape of the target grapheme.
- Have students compare and contrast shaving cream and shampoo using a Venn Diagram.
- Make a paper shark. Have students glue pictures of words that begin with the /sh/ sound on the shark.
- Have students go on a "sound hunt" around the room or outside to find objects that begin with target sound.
- Coding activity: Have students underline and label the letters in words or syllables with a "v" for vowels and a "c" for consonants. For example, when using the word *mom*, each letter should be underlined with the labels "cvc" underneath the word. This activity will help prepare students for decoding multisyllabic words later in the sequence.
- Visit IMSE's Orton-Gillingham's Pinterest page for more ideas.

Weekly Lesson Reminders

- Any of the above extension activities
- Practice writing the target grapheme (capital and lowercase) using a screen, green crayon, and house paper.
- Practice writing the target grapheme using another medium (sand, paint, shaving cream, pudding, iPad app, etc.).
- Practice writing the target grapheme using age-appropriate paper and pencil.
- Daily practice with writing the weekly Red Word(s)
- Kilpatrick's "One-Minute Activities" for daily phonological awareness practice
- Zgonc's phonological awareness activities
- Listen to rich literature to work on oral language comprehension.
- Target grapheme practice sheets from IMSE's practice books and handwriting books
- Practice test on Thursday and test on Friday

th as in them (voiced)

Card Pack #29 Decodable Reader #22	
Object Ideas:	**Literature Ideas:**
mother, father, brother, feather	<ul><li>*That's Good! That's Bad!* by Margery Cuyler</li><li>*This Is the House That Jack Built* by Simms Taback</li><li>*Phantom Stallion #10: Red Feather Filly* by Terri Farley</li><li>*Of Thee I Sing: A Letter to My Daughters* by Barack Obama</li><li>*Those Shoes* by Maribeth Boelts</li></ul>

 ## Notes

- Use the Comprehensive Flip Chart for the steps on how to teach each part of IMSE's Lesson Plan.
- Di means two; graph means letters. A digraph is two letters that make one sound.
- In the P/G chart, the digraphs listed in the Consonant Digraphs column are only the consonant digraphs that make a *new* sound.
- Digraphs get an extra visual cue under the grapheme line. This is a wavy line that informs the student to be careful, as there are two letters that make this sound.
- The wavy grapheme line only goes with the word dictation, not sentence dictation.

- "Th" can go in either position on the blending board. There are 2 "th" cards. Place one in the initial position (can be voiced or unvoiced), and place the other one in the final position (unvoiced only). *The unvoiced sound will only be incorporated after it has been taught. (See Concept #31: unvoiced "th.")*
- Voiced "th" is not usually at the end of a syllable unless followed by a silent "e," as in *breathe.*
- Give the voiced "th" a visual hand gesture of the hand on the throat to indicate there is a vibration when making the sound.
- Voiced "th" is a fricative formed by sticking the tongue out between the teeth.

Phonological Awareness:

Materials Needed:
tokens, sound boxes, one-minute activities, or Zgonc PA book

Use the PAST assessment to determine a starting point for instruction. Incorporate daily phonological awareness activities by using Zgonc's tiered activities and/or Kilpatrick's One-Minute Activities in *Equipped for Reading Success*.

Phonemic awareness warm-up: Use tokens (or letter tiles once concepts have been taught) and sound boxes to do a quick phonemic awareness activity that ties in with the new concept, if appropriate.

Three-Part Drill

Materials Needed:
review cards, sand, blending board, vowel tents or sticks

Do this at least 3x per week. Use the Flip Chart for steps. Include the new concept after Day 1.

- Include the Vowel Intensive with "a," "e," "i," "o," and "u."

V	VC	CVC
a	ag, ap, ab	lat, cad, zan
e	et, en, eb	zeg, ren, med
i	ig, ib, im	lin, hib, fid
o	ob, ot, oz	rom, hob, cog
u	un, ud, ub	sup, pum, dut

- Below is a sample script now that students know more than one way to spell a sound. Remember to use all of the review concepts.

1. **Visual:**
   (T) Tell me the sounds you know for these letters.
   (S) /m/, /l/, etc.
   Alternative:
   (T) Tell me the names and sounds you know for these letters.
   (S) m says /m/, l says /l/, etc.

2. **Auditory/Kinesthetic:**
   (T) You know two ways to spell this. (S) split trays. (T) Eyes on me.
   Spell /k/. Repeat.
   (S) /k/ c says /k/; k says /k/

3. **Blending:**

(T) Tell me the sound for each letter as I point. Then blend the sounds together to read the word or syllable. Give me a thumbs up if it is a real word.

(S) /mmm/ /ŏŏŏ/ /mmm/ *mom* (thumbs up)

Alternative:

(T) Watch me first. /mmm/ /ŏŏŏ/ /mmm/ *mom*

(T) Do it with me. (T&S) /mmm/ /ŏŏŏ/ /mmm/ *mom*

(T) Your turn. (S) /mmm/ /ŏŏŏ/ /mmm/ *mom* (thumbs up)

*Vowel Intensive:** Model the visual cue while calling out the sound. Students will do the visual cue as they repeat the sound. Students will then hold up the vowel tent while stating the letter name and sound.

- (T): Eyes on me. The sound is /ă/. Repeat.
- (S): /ă/ a says /ă/

Teaching a New Concept

Materials Needed:
concept card, screen, green crayon, object, sand, decodable readers, literature, P/G chart

Introduce on Monday, and practice daily.

1. (T) Reads alliteration sentences. (S) Identify the target sound.
   a. Listen to these words: they, that, then, there, this, them. What sound do you hear?
2. (T) Shows the new concept card.
   a. (T) Tells students that "th" is a digraph. A digraph is two letters that work together to make one sound. "Th" says /TH/ (voiced). Have students repeat, 3 times.
   b. (T) Tells students that it is a voiced sound. Teach the visual gesture of a hand on the throat to feel the vibration in the vocal cords.
   c. (T) Uses mirrors to discuss the mouth, tongue, and teeth placement.
3. (T) Shows an object.
   a. (T) Allows students to manipulate the object and discuss prior knowledge. Reminds (S) that the object has the target sound spelled with the target letters.
4. (S) Brainstorm.
   a. Brainstorm words that have the target sound. (Accept all answers, but place incorrect answers in a "thought bubble" to discuss.) The brainstorming can be a teacher-directed activity if students need extra support.
5. (T) Teaches Letter Formation, *if needed*. Students could begin to learn cursive.
   a. Use the steps for teaching letter formation on the Flip Chart.
   b. Use house paper to teach lowercase letters.
   c. Teach capital letters throughout the week. Capital letters go outside the house.
6. (T) Dictates target sound. (S) Practice in the sand or other medium.
   a. Practice writing the letters using a different medium, such as sand, shaving cream, finger paint, gel board, iPad app, air writing, etc.
   b. Do this while stating: th says /TH/ (voiced), 3 times.

7. (T) Connects with literature.
   a. Have students signal when they hear the target sound for the first page or two.
   b. Read again for language comprehension.
   c. Continue to work on language comprehension with rich literature throughout the week.
8. (S) Use decodable readers to practice the concepts learned.
   a. (S) Highlight words with the new concept. Read those words.
   b. (S) Highlight Red Words. Read those words.
   c. (S) Start reading the decodable reader.
   d. (S) Continue reading throughout the week.
   e. (S) Read a clean copy on Friday.
9. (T&S) Mark the Phoneme/Grapheme (P/G) chart by highlighting the target sound.

 ## Word Dictation

Materials Needed:
fingertapping hand, dictation paper, pencil

Create any syllables using the new concept and previously taught concepts. Practice daily. Use the Flip Chart to follow the steps for word dictation.

Day 1:	1. them	2. that	3. she	4. this	5. cash
Day 2:	1. them	2. that	3. thus	4. wish	5. ship
Day 3:	1. than	2. dish	3. this	4. them	5. chop
Days 4-5:	Review prior words.				

Below is a sample script:

1. (T) States word: *mom*. Uses it in a sentence: My *mom* is a wonderful lady. (Pounds) *mom*. (T) Models fingertapping if needed: /m/ /ŏ/ /m/. (Pounds) *mom*.
2. (S) State while pounding: *mom*. (Fingertap) /m/ /ŏ/ /m/. (Pound) *mom*. Write the letters known for the sounds.
3. (T) When yours looks like mine, rewrite the word.
4. (S) Rewrite.
5. Repeat the process for each word.
6. (S) Read the list of words multiple times to build automaticity.

C ▢
U ▢
P ▢
S ▢

Sentence Dictation

Red Words are underlined. Students can fingertap the green words. Use the Flip Chart to follow the steps for sentence dictation.

1. This hog <u>is</u> red <u>and</u> hot.
2. That man <u>will</u> run <u>to the</u> pen.
3. This bed <u>is</u> in <u>the</u> shop.

4. Sam got them to shut the shop.
5. Did Pam cash this?
6. That one ship was in a jam.
7. That dish is hot.
8. This is not the shed that has cash.
9. Is that them on the ship?
10. Then Josh will jog on the ship.
11. Can Sid get them to shut the shop?
12. Did Kim get that purple top at this shop?

▪ Below is a sample script for sentence dictation.

> 1. (T): Listen to the sentence. *Tad had a cat.*
> 2. (T): Listen while I pound the syllables. *Tad had a cat.*
> 3. (T): Pound it with me. (T&S): *Tad had a cat.*
> 4. (T): You pound the sentence. (S): *Tad had a cat.*
> 5. (T): Watch me as I point to the lines while stating the sentence. *Tad had a cat.*
> 6. (T): You point to the lines while stating the sentence.
> 7. (S): *Tad had a cat.*
> 8. (T): Now write the sentence. Fingertap if needed.

▪ Below is a sample script to check CUPS*.

> 1. (T): C stands for capitalization. Did you remember a capital letter at the beginning of your sentence? It's also a name. *Tad* would always be capitalized. If you forgot, fix it. If you remembered, put a tally mark above the capital letter. Add a mark in the box for C.
> 2. (T): U stands for understanding. Is your sentence neat? Reread it to yourself. Does it make sense? Could someone else understand it? If not, fix it. Add a mark in the box for U.
> 3. (T): P stands for punctuation. Did you remember a period at the end? If not, fix it. If you remembered, put a tally mark above the period. Add a mark in the box for P.
> 4. (T): S stands for spelling. Did you spell your words correctly? Check them. Now, check yours with mine (show the teacher's copy). Fix any words you spelled incorrectly. Put a tally mark above the words you spelled correctly. Add a mark in the box for S.
> 5. (T): Rewrite your sentence with all of the corrections.
> 6. (T): Check for CUPS again. Put another mark in the boxes.
> 7. (T): Let's read the sentences.
> 8. (S) Read the sentences for fluency and automaticity.
>
> *Please note:** Once students understand how to use CUPS, transition to letting them check their sentence independently before showing the teacher's copy.

Weekly Red Words

Materials Needed:
screen, red crayon, red word paper

Introduce on Tuesday, and practice daily. Use the Flip Chart for steps.

New:	Review:	New Read-Only:	Review Read-Only:
one, two	the, was, is, a, and, to, for, like, of, will, want, with, said, you, put, see, stop, from, off, has, have, his, as, my, into, now, new, give, or, by, went, do, are, they, any, black, blue, brown, gray, green, orange, pink, purple, white, yellow	three, four, five, seven, eight, nine	stop, eek, ouch, look, good, help

Steps for Teaching a New Red Word:

1. (T) States the word. (*one*)

2. (T&S) Use tokens to determine how many sounds are in the word. (/w/ /ŭ/ /n/; 3)

3. (T&S) Discuss how we would expect to spell each sound as the teacher writes the grapheme(s) correctly. Identify what is unexpected or irregular about the spelling of the word. It could also be expected, but the concept hasn't been taught yet.

4. (T&S) Discuss the etymology of the word, if appropriate (lexical words). Visit www.etymonline.com for more information on the word.

5. (T) Defines the word, and writes a sentence using the word.

6. (T) Writes the word on Red Word paper with the screen underneath, using red crayon.

7. (S) Write the word on Red Word paper with the screen underneath, using red crayon. (S) Show the word to the teacher.
   (**NOTE:** The teacher should have students chunk the word if it has more than four letters.)

8. (T&S) Stand up, holding the Red Word in the nondominant hand. Armtap word while naming each letter. Then "underline" the word by sweeping left to right while stating the word, 3x. (**NOTE:** Left-handed students will place their left hand on their right wrist. They tap to their right shoulder. Underline from wrist to shoulder. Right-handed students place their right hand on their left shoulder. They tap to their left wrist. Underline shoulder to wrist.)

9. (T&S) Trace crayon bumps with the pointer finger while naming the letters, 3x.

10. (T&S) Place the screen over the paper and trace the word with the pointer finger while naming the letters, 3x.

11. (S) Turn paper over. With red crayon, write the word without the screen one time, and hold up the word for the teacher to check. (S) Write the word two more times.

12. (S) Write an original sentence in pencil and underline the Red Word with a red crayon. (**NOTE:** The sentence can also be dictated by the teacher while the student writes or dictated by the student while the teacher writes it.)

13. Repeat the steps for two. (/t/ / $\overline{oo}$ /; 2)

Review Ideas for Red Words:

- Sculpt the word using red Play-Doh or clay. Have students spell the word as they smash each letter.
- Print flashcards from IOG, and practice reading.
- Armtap the word to review.
- Cross-clap the word to review.
- Do Spelling Aerobics.

Fluency, Vocabulary, and Comprehension

- Incorporate fluency into your literacy lessons daily/weekly (minimum 30 min/week) by using Rapid Word Charts, IMSE Decodable Readers, words and sentences, Acadience Reading K-6 or DIBELS 8th Edition, repeated reading, and other activities.

- Incorporate vocabulary into your literacy lessons daily/weekly (minimum 50 min/week) by choosing 3-5 appropriate tier two words (can pull from rich literature or decodable readers). Teach the words through explicit, direct instruction using student-friendly definitions, word webs, vocabulary charts, illustrations, and other activities.

- Incorporate oral language comprehension into your literacy lessons daily/weekly (approximately 100 min/week). Comprehension instruction should be explicit, direct instruction that includes teacher modeling, guided practice, and independent practice. Plan ahead to build on students' background knowledge, language structures, verbal reasoning, and literacy knowledge.

Extension Activity Ideas

- Continue to add to the multi-sensory ABC book. Have students glue feathers (or another object) in the shape of the target grapheme.
- Make a paper feather. Have students glue pictures of words that begin with the voiced /TH/ sound on the feather.
- Have students go on a "sound hunt" around the room or outside to find objects that begin with the target sound.
- Coding activity: Have students underline and label the letters in words or syllables with a "v" for vowels and a "c" for consonants. For example, when using the word *mom*, each letter should be underlined with the labels "cvc" underneath the word. This activity will help prepare students for decoding multisyllabic words later in the sequence.
- Visit IMSE's Orton-Gillingham's Pinterest page for more ideas.

Weekly Lesson Reminders

- Any of the above extension activities
- Practice writing the target grapheme (capital and lowercase) using a screen, green crayon, and house paper.
- Practice writing the target grapheme using another medium (sand, paint, shaving cream, pudding, iPad app, etc.).
- Practice writing the target grapheme using age-appropriate paper and pencil.
- Daily practice with writing the weekly Red Word(s)
- Kilpatrick's "One-Minute Activities" for daily phonological awareness practice
- Zgonc's phonological awareness activities
- Listen to rich literature to work on oral language comprehension.
- Target grapheme practice sheets from IMSE's practice books and handwriting books
- Practice test on Thursday and test on Friday

th as in thumb (unvoiced)

Card Pack #29 Decodable Reader #23	
Object Ideas:	**Literature Ideas:**
thumb, math, bathtub, thunder, moth, thimble, myth, theater	▪ *Tom Thumb* by Richard Jesse Watson ▪ *Thunder Cake* by Patricia Polacco ▪ *Three Little Kittens* by Paul Galdone ▪ *King Bidgood's in the Bathtub* by Audrey Wood ▪ *Thump, Quack, Moo: A Whacky Adventure* by Doreen Cronin ▪ *Thank You, Mr. Falker* by Patricia Polacco ▪ *The Story of the H Brothers* by Sarah Wagner

 ## Notes

- Use the Comprehensive Flip Chart for the steps on how to teach each part of IMSE's Lesson Plan.
- Di means two; graph means letters. A digraph is two letters that make one sound.
- In the P/G chart, the digraphs listed in the Consonant Digraphs column are only the consonant digraphs that make a *new* sound.
- Digraphs get an extra visual cue under the grapheme line. This is a wavy line that informs the student to be careful, as there are two letters that make this sound.
- The wavy grapheme line only goes with the word dictation, not sentence dictation.

- "Th" can go in either position on the blending board. There are 2 "th" cards. Place one in the initial position (can be voiced or unvoiced), and place the other one in the final position (unvoiced only).
- Give the unvoiced "th" a visual hand gesture of a "thumbs-up" to indicate an unvoiced key word (i.e., *thumb*).
- In the Visual drill after unvoiced /th/ is taught, use one "th" card. When the "th" card comes up, students should state the voiced sound first and then the unvoiced sound. Teachers can give the visual cue of the hand on the throat and then thumbs-up.
- The unvoiced "th" is a fricative formed by sticking the tongue out between the teeth.

Phonological Awareness:

Materials Needed:
tokens, sound boxes, one-minute activities, or Zgonc PA book

Use the PAST assessment to determine a starting point for instruction. Incorporate daily phonological awareness activities by using Zgonc's tiered activities and/or Kilpatrick's One-Minute Activities in *Equipped for Reading Success*.

Phonemic awareness warm-up: Use tokens (or letter tiles once concepts have been taught) and sound boxes to do a quick phonemic awareness activity that ties in with the new concept, if appropriate.

Three-Part Drill

Materials Needed:
review cards, sand, blending board, vowel tents or sticks

Do this at least 3x per week. Use the Flip Chart for steps. Include the new concept after Day 1.

- Include the Vowel Intensive with "a," "e," "i," "o," and "u."

V	VC	CVC
a	ag, ap, ab	lat, cad, zan
e	et, en, eb	zeg, ren, med
i	ig, ib, im	lin, hib, fid
o	ob, ot, oz	rom, hob, cog
u	un, ud, ub	sup, pum, dut

- Below is a sample script now that students know more than one way to spell a sound. Remember to use all of the review concepts.

1. **Visual:**
   (T) Tell me the sounds you know for these letters.
   (S) /m/, /l/, etc.
   Alternative:
   (T) Tell me the names and sounds you know for these letters.
   (S) m says /m/, l says /l/, etc.
2. **Auditory/Kinesthetic:**
   (T) You know two ways to spell this. (S) split trays. (T) Eyes on me.
   Spell /k/. Repeat.
   (S) /k/ c says /k/; k says /k/

© IMSE 2022

3. **Blending:**

(T) Tell me the sound for each letter as I point. Then blend the sounds together to read the word or syllable. Give me a thumbs up if it is a real word.

(S) /mmm/ /ŏŏŏ/ /mmm/ *mom* (thumbs up)

Alternative:

(T) Watch me first. /mmm/ /ŏŏŏ/ /mmm/ *mom*

(T) Do it with me. (T&S) /mmm/ /ŏŏŏ/ /mmm/ *mom*

(T) Your turn. (S) /mmm/ /ŏŏŏ/ /mmm/ *mom* (thumbs up)

*Vowel Intensive: Model the visual cue while calling out the sound. Students will do the visual cue as they repeat the sound. Students will then hold up the vowel tent while stating the letter name and sound.

- (T): Eyes on me. The sound is /ă/. Repeat.
- (S): /ă/ a says /ă/

 ## Teaching a New Concept

Materials Needed:
concept card, screen, green crayon, object, sand, decodable readers, literature, P/G chart

Introduce on Monday, and practice daily.

1. (T) Reads alliteration sentences. (S) Identify the target sound.
   a. Thelma threw thirty thimbles.
   b. Thea thanked thirteen thirsty things.

2. (T) Shows the new concept card.
   a. (T) Tells students that "th" is a digraph. A digraph is two letters that work together to make one sound. "Th" says /th/ (unvoiced). Have students repeat, 3 times.
   b. (T) Tells students that it is an unvoiced sound. Teach the visual gesture of a "thumbs-up" to think of the word "thumb."
   c. (T) Uses mirrors to discuss the mouth, tongue, and teeth placement.

3. (T) Shows an object.
   a. (T) Allows students to manipulate the object and discuss prior knowledge. Reminds (S) that the object has the target sound spelled with the target letters.

4. (S) Brainstorm.
   a. Brainstorm words that have the target sound. (Accept all answers, but place incorrect answers in a "thought bubble" to discuss.) The brainstorming can be a teacher-directed activity if students need extra support.

5. (T) Teaches Letter Formation, *if needed*. Students could begin to learn cursive.
   a. Use the steps for teaching letter formation on the Flip Chart.
   b. Use house paper to teach lowercase letters.
   c. Teach capital letters throughout the week. Capital letters go outside the house.

6. (T) Dictates target sound. (S) Practice in the sand or other medium.
   a. Practice writing the letters using a different medium, such as sand, shaving cream, finger paint, gel board, iPad app, air writing, etc.
   b. Do this while stating: th says /th/ (unvoiced), 3 times.

7. (T) Connects with literature.
   a. Have students signal when they hear the target sound for the first page or two.
   b. Read again for language comprehension.
   c. Continue to work on language comprehension with rich literature throughout the week.

8. (S) Use decodable readers to practice the concepts learned.
   a. (S) Highlight words with the new concept. Read those words.
   b. (S) Highlight Red Words. Read those words.
   c. (S) Start reading the decodable reader.
   d. (S) Continue reading throughout the week.
   e. (S) Read a clean copy on Friday.

9. (T&S) Mark the Phoneme/Grapheme (P/G) chart by highlighting the target sound.

 ## Word Dictation

Materials Needed:
fingertapping hand, dictation paper, pencil

Create any syllables using the new concept and previously taught concepts. Practice daily. Use the Flip Chart to follow the steps for word dictation.

Day 1:	1. bath	2. moth	3. pith	4. thud	5. them
Day 2:	1. with	2. math	3. kith	4. fish	5. Seth
Day 3:	1. path	2. Beth	3. shut	4. thin	5. with
Days 4-5:	Review prior words.				

Below is a sample script:

1. (T) States word: *mom*. Uses it in a sentence: My *mom* is a wonderful lady. (Pounds) *mom*. (T) Models fingertapping if needed: /m/ /ŏ/ /m/. (Pounds) *mom*.
2. (S) State while pounding: *mom*. (Fingertap) /m/ /ŏ/ /m/. (Pound) *mom*. Write the letters known for the sounds.
3. (T) When yours looks like mine, rewrite the word.
4. (S) Rewrite.
5. Repeat the process for each word.
6. (S) Read the list of words multiple times to build automaticity.

Sentence Dictation

Red Words are underlined. Students can fingertap the green words. Use the Flip Chart to follow the steps for sentence dictation.

1. Beth can jog with the dog.
2. Seth had a big thud from the log.
3. Math is not that bad with a chum.
4. Jim and Beth will run on the green path.
5. The math sum is six.
6. The path is at the top.
7. Did the ax hit the box with a thud?
8. Beth and Seth are thin.
9. Josh can run up the path to get to the red shed.
10. Come get the pith off the mat.
11. The log was cut and did thud.
12. A white moth got in the bath.

- Below is a sample script for sentence dictation.

> 1. (T): Listen to the sentence. *Tad had a cat.*
> 2. (T): Listen while I pound the syllables. *Tad had a cat.*
> 3. (T): Pound it with me. (T&S): *Tad had a cat.*
> 4. (T): You pound the sentence. (S): *Tad had a cat.*
> 5. (T): Watch me as I point to the lines while stating the sentence. *Tad had a cat.*
> 6. (T): You point to the lines while stating the sentence.
> 7. (S): *Tad had a cat.*
> 8. (T): Now write the sentence. Fingertap if needed.

- Below is a sample script to check CUPS*.

> 1. (T): C stands for capitalization. Did you remember a capital letter at the beginning of your sentence? It's also a name. *Tad* would always be capitalized. If you forgot, fix it. If you remembered, put a tally mark above the capital letter. Add a mark in the box for C.
> 2. (T): U stands for understanding. Is your sentence neat? Reread it to yourself. Does it make sense? Could someone else understand it? If not, fix it. Add a mark in the box for U.
> 3. (T): P stands for punctuation. Did you remember a period at the end? If not, fix it. If you remembered, put a tally mark above the period. Add a mark in the box for P.

4. (T): S stands for spelling. Did you spell your words correctly? Check them. Now, check yours with mine (show the teacher's copy). Fix any words you spelled incorrectly. Put a tally mark above the words you spelled correctly. Add a mark in the box for S.

5. (T): Rewrite your sentence with all of the corrections.

6. (T): Check for CUPS again. Put another mark in the boxes.

7. (T): Let's read the sentences.

8. (S) Read the sentences for fluency and automaticity.

*__Please note:__ Once students understand how to use CUPS, transition to letting them check their sentence independently before showing the teacher's copy.

Weekly Red Words

| **Materials Needed:**
screen, red crayon, red word paper

Introduce on Tuesday, and practice daily. Use the Flip Chart for steps.

New:	Review:	New Read-Only:	Review Read-Only:
come	the, was, is, a, and, to, for, like, of, will, want, said, you, put, see, stop, from, off, has, have, his, as, my, into, now, new, give, or, by, went, do, are, they, any, black, blue, brown, gray, green, orange, pink, purple, white, yellow, one, two	her	stop, eek, ouch, look, good, help, three, four, five, seven, eight, nine

Steps for Teaching a New Red Word:

1. (T) States the word. (*come*)

2. (T&S) Use tokens to determine how many sounds are in the word. (/c/ /ŭ/ /m/; 3)

3. (T&S) Discuss how we would expect to spell each sound as the teacher writes the grapheme(s) correctly. Identify what is unexpected or irregular about the spelling of the word. It could also be expected, but the concept hasn't been taught yet.

4. (T&S) Discuss the etymology of the word, if appropriate (lexical words). Visit www.etymonline.com for more information on the word.

5. (T) Defines the word, and writes a sentence using the word.

6. (T) Writes the word on Red Word paper with the screen underneath, using red crayon.

7. (S) Write the word on Red Word paper with the screen underneath, using red crayon. (S) Show the word to the teacher.
(**NOTE:** The teacher should have students chunk the word if it has more than four letters.)

8. (T&S) Stand up, holding the Red Word in the nondominant hand. Armtap word while naming each letter. Then "underline" the word by sweeping left to right while stating the word, 3x. (**NOTE:** Left-handed students will place their left hand on their right wrist. They tap to their right shoulder. Underline from wrist to shoulder. Right-handed students place their right hand on their left shoulder. They tap to their left wrist. Underline shoulder to wrist.)

9. (T&S) Trace crayon bumps with the pointer finger while naming the letters, 3x.

10. (T&S) Place the screen over the paper and trace the word with the pointer finger while naming the letters, 3x.

11. (S) Turn paper over. With red crayon, write the word without the screen one time, and hold up the word for the teacher to check. (S) Write the word two more times.

12. (S) Write an original sentence in pencil and underline the Red Word with a red crayon.
(**NOTE:** The sentence can also be dictated by the teacher while the student writes or dictated by the student while the teacher writes it.)

Review Ideas for Red Words:

- Sculpt the word using red Play-Doh or clay. Have students spell the word as they smash each letter.
- Print flashcards from IOG, and practice reading.
- Armtap the word to review.
- Cross-clap the word to review.
- Do Spelling Aerobics.

Fluency, Vocabulary, and Comprehension

- Incorporate fluency into your literacy lessons daily/weekly (minimum 30 min/week) by using Rapid Word Charts, IMSE Decodable Readers, words and sentences, Acadience Reading K-6 or DIBELS 8th Edition, repeated reading, and other activities.

- Incorporate vocabulary into your literacy lessons daily/weekly (minimum 50 min/week) by choosing 3-5 appropriate tier two words (can pull from rich literature or decodable readers). Teach the words through explicit, direct instruction using student-friendly definitions, word webs, vocabulary charts, illustrations, and other activities.

- Incorporate oral language comprehension into your literacy lessons daily/weekly (approximately 100 min/week). Comprehension instruction should be explicit, direct instruction that includes teacher modeling, guided practice, and independent practice. Plan ahead to build on students' background knowledge, language structures, verbal reasoning, and literacy knowledge.

Extension Activity Ideas

- Continue to add to the multi-sensory ABC book. Have students glue thimbles (or another object) in the shape of the target grapheme.
- Make a paper thumb. Have students glue pictures of words that begin with the unvoiced /th/ sound on the thumb.
- Have students go on a "sound hunt" around the room or outside to find objects that begin with the target sound.
- Coding activity: Have students underline and label the letters in words or syllables with a "v" for vowels and a "c" for consonants. For example, when using the word *mom*, each letter should be underlined with the labels "cvc" underneath the word. This activity will help prepare students for decoding multisyllabic words later in the sequence.
- Visit IMSE's Orton-Gillingham's Pinterest page for more ideas.

Weekly Lesson Reminders

- Any of the above extension activities
- Practice writing the target grapheme (capital and lowercase) using a screen, green crayon, and house paper.
- Practice writing the target grapheme using another medium (sand, paint, shaving cream, pudding, iPad app, etc.).
- Practice writing the target grapheme using age-appropriate paper and pencil.
- Daily practice with writing the weekly Red Word(s)
- Kilpatrick's "One-Minute Activities" for daily phonological awareness practice
- Zgonc's phonological awareness activities
- Listen to rich literature to work on oral language comprehension.
- Target grapheme practice sheets from IMSE's practice books and handwriting books
- Practice test on Thursday and test on Friday

wh as in whistle

Card Pack #30	Decodable Reader #24; optional Decodable Reader #25 (m-wh and multisyllabic words)
Object Ideas:	**Literature Ideas:**
whip, whale, whistle, whipped cream, wheel, wheat	<ul><li>*Whistle for Willie* by Ezra Jack Keats</li><li>*Humphrey the Lost Whale: A True Story* by Wendy Tokuda and Richard Hall</li><li>*Baby Beluga* by Raffi</li><li>*Where the Sidewalk Ends* by Shel Silverstein</li><li>*Where the Wild Things Are* by Maurice Sendak</li><li>"Wheels on the Bus" song</li><li>*Who Says Women Can't Be Doctors?: The Story of Elizabeth Blackwell* by Tanya Lee Stone</li><li>*Whoosh!: Lonnie Johnson's Super-Soaking Stream of Inventions* by Chris Barton</li></ul>

 Notes

- Use the Comprehensive Flip Chart for the steps on how to teach each part of IMSE's Lesson Plan.
- Di means two; graph means letters. A digraph is two letters that make one sound.
- In the P/G chart, the digraphs listed in the Consonant Digraphs column are only the consonant digraphs that make a *new* sound.
- Digraphs get an extra visual cue under the grapheme line. This is a wavy line that informs the student to be careful, as there are two letters that make this sound.
- The wavy grapheme line only goes with the word dictation, not sentence dictation.

- "Wh" must go in the initial pile on the blending board.
- "Wh" can be taught as /w/ or /hw/. If the spelling is taught as /w/, it will be highlighted next to /w/ in the Consonants column on the P/G chart. Students would then know two ways to spell the /w/ sound when doing the Auditory/Kinesthetic drill. If "wh" is taught as /hw/, it will be highlighted in the Consonant Digraphs column and dictated as a new sound. (The visual cue of a wavy line for word dictation can be used regardless of whether the sound is taught as /w/ or /hw/.)

- **NOTE:** The unvoiced /hw/ sound is losing its distinctiveness. Most Americans pronounce these sounds the same way. Some teachers still use it to distinguish between spellings for the /w/ sound (Moats & Tolman, 2019).
- Because "wh" is not a common concept for one-syllable words with short vowels, you can also choose to remove this from the card deck. You can wait and teach it after Bossy R (er, ir, ur) has been taught, as it occurs more often in words with more complex vowel sounds or multiple syllables (e.g., *while, whisper, whistle, whether*).
- Regardless of which sound is taught for "wh" (i.e., /w/ or /hw/), word dictation is optional this week because there aren't many CVC words containing "wh" that are applicable to children of this age. Instead, an option can be to focus on teaching "wh" question words (e.g., *who, what*) as Red Words.
- "Wh" is a glide formed by puckering the lips together.

Phonological Awareness:

Materials Needed:
tokens, sound boxes, one-minute activities, or Zgonc PA book

Use the PAST assessment to determine a starting point for instruction. Incorporate daily phonological awareness activities by using Zgonc's tiered activities and/or Kilpatrick's One-Minute Activities in *Equipped for Reading Success*.

Phonemic awareness warm-up: Use tokens (or letter tiles once concepts have been taught) and sound boxes to do a quick phonemic awareness activity that ties in with the new concept, if appropriate.

Three-Part Drill

Materials Needed:
review cards, sand, blending board, vowel tents or sticks

Do this at least 3x per week. Use the Flip Chart for steps. Include the new concept after Day 1.

- Include the Vowel Intensive with "a," "e," "i," "o," and "u."

V	VC	CVC
a	ag, ap, ab	lat, cad, zan
e	et, en, eb	zeg, ren, med
i	ig, ib, im	lin, hib, fid
o	ob, ot, oz	rom, hob, cog
u	un, ud, ub	sup, pum, dut

- Below is a sample script now that students know more than one way to spell a sound. Remember to use all of the review concepts.

> 1. **Visual:**
> (T) Tell me the sounds you know for these letters.
> (S) /m/, /l/, etc.
> *Alternative:*
> (T) Tell me the names and sounds you know for these letters.
> (S) m says /m/, l says /l/, etc.
>
> 2. **Auditory/Kinesthetic:**
> (T) You know two ways to spell this. (S) split trays. (T) Eyes on me.
> Spell /k/. Repeat.
> (S) /k/ c says /k/; k says /k/
>
> 3. **Blending:**
> (T) Tell me the sound for each letter as I point. Then blend the sounds together to read the word or syllable. Give me a thumbs up if it is a real word.
> (S) /mmm/ /ŏŏŏ/ /mmm/ *mom* (thumbs up)
> *Alternative:*
> (T) Watch me first. /mmm/ /ŏŏŏ/ /mmm/ *mom*
> (T) Do it with me. (T&S) /mmm/ /ŏŏŏ/ /mmm/ *mom*
> (T) Your turn. (S) /mmm/ /ŏŏŏ/ /mmm/ *mom* (thumbs up)
>
> ***Vowel Intensive:** Model the visual cue while calling out the sound. Students will do the visual cue as they repeat the sound. Students will then hold up the vowel tent while stating the letter name and sound.
> - (T): Eyes on me. The sound is /ă/. Repeat.
> - (S): /ă/ a says /ă/

Teaching a New Concept

Materials Needed:
concept card, screen, green crayon, object, sand, decodable readers, literature, P/G chart

Introduce on Monday, and practice daily.

1. (T) Reads alliteration sentences. (S) Identify the target sound.
   a. Whitney's white whistle was whirling.
   b. Why would Will wait until Wednesday?
2. (T) Shows the new concept card.
   a. (T) Tells students that "wh" is a digraph. A digraph is two letters that work together to make one sound. "Wh" says /w/. Have students repeat, 3 times.
   b. (T) Tells students that it is a voiced sound.
   c. (T) Uses mirrors to discuss the mouth, tongue, and teeth placement.
3. (T) Shows an object.
   a. (T) Allows students to manipulate the object and discuss prior knowledge. Reminds (S) that the object has the target sound spelled with the target letters.

4. (S) Brainstorm.

   a. Brainstorm words that have the target sound. (Accept all answers, but place incorrect answers in a "thought bubble" to discuss.) The brainstorming can be a teacher-directed activity if students need extra support.

5. Teaches Letter Formation, *if needed*. Students could begin to learn cursive.

   a. Use the steps for teaching letter formation on the Flip Chart.

   b. Use house paper to teach lowercase letters.

   c. Teach capital letters throughout the week. Capital letters go outside the house.

6. (T) Dictates target sound. (S) Practice in the sand or other medium.

   a. Practice writing the letters using a different medium, such as sand, shaving cream, finger paint, gel board, iPad app, air writing, etc.

   b. Do this while stating: w says /w/; wh says /w/ (3 times). (Because this is the second spelling learned for /w/, students should write all known spellings for the sound [i.e., w, wh]).

      Please note: If the /hw/ sound is taught for "wh," there would only be one known spelling for that sound. Students would write while stating: wh says /hw/, 3 times.

7. (T) Connects with literature.

   a. Have students signal when they hear the target sound for the first page or two.

   b. Read again for language comprehension.

   c. Continue to work on language comprehension with rich literature throughout the week.

8. (S) Use decodable readers to practice the concepts learned.

   a. (S) Highlight words with the new concept. Read those words.

   b. (S) Highlight Red Words. Read those words.

   c. (S) Start reading the decodable reader.

   d. (S) Continue reading throughout the week.

   e. (S) Read a clean copy on Friday.

9. (T&S) Mark the Phoneme/Grapheme (P/G) chart by highlighting the target sound.

 ## Word Dictation

Materials Needed:
fingertapping hand, dictation paper, pencil

Create any syllables using the new concept and previously taught concepts. Practice daily. Use the Flip Chart to follow the steps for word dictation.

Day 1:	1. whim	2. whop	3. moth	4. when	5. rash
Day 2:	1. when	2. path	3. whip	4. whit	5. thud
Day 3:	1. wham	2. whiz	3. thud	4. whet	5. then
Days 4-5:	Review prior words.				

Below is a sample script:

1. (T) States word: *mom*. Uses it in a sentence: My *mom* is a wonderful lady. (Pounds) *mom*. (T) Models fingertapping if needed: /m/ /ŏ/ /m/. (Pounds) *mom*.

2. (S) State while pounding: *mom.* (Fingertap) /m/ /ŏ/ /m/. (Pound) *mom.* Write the letters known for the sounds.

3. (T) When yours looks like mine, rewrite the word.

4. (S) Rewrite.

5. Repeat the process for each word.

6. (S) Read the list of words multiple times to build automaticity.

Sentence Dictation

Red Words are underlined. Students can fingertap the green words. Use the Flip Chart to follow the steps for sentence dictation.

1. When did Beth chug that?
2. On a whim, Val did run.
3. Whop the big bug!
4. When will the pet cat get fed?
5. Why did Tad do it on a whim?
6. When was the ham on the dish?
7. Where did Tim chop the log?
8. When did Ben put the hog in the sun?
9. Let Bob whip up the dish for Beth.
10. Who hid the whip in the shed?
11. What did Josh wish?
12. When did Dash the dog run the path?

▪ Below is a sample script for sentence dictation.

1. (T): Listen to the sentence. *Tad had a cat.*
2. (T): Listen while I pound the syllables. *Tad had a cat.*
3. (T): Pound it with me. (T&S): *Tad had a cat.*
4. (T): You pound the sentence. (S): *Tad had a cat.*
5. (T): Watch me as I point to the lines while stating the sentence. *Tad had a cat.*
6. (T): You point to the lines while stating the sentence.
7. (S): *Tad had a cat.*
8. (T): Now write the sentence. Fingertap if needed.

▪ Below is a sample script to check CUPS*.

1. (T): C stands for capitalization. Did you remember a capital letter at the beginning of your sentence? It's also a name. *Tad* would always be capitalized. If you forgot, fix it. If you remembered, put a tally mark above the capital letter. Add a mark in the box for C.

2. (T): U stands for understanding. Is your sentence neat? Reread it to yourself. Does it make sense? Could someone else understand it? If not, fix it. Add a mark in the box for U.

3. (T): P stands for punctuation. Did you remember a period at the end? If not, fix it. If you remembered, put a tally mark above the period. Add a mark in the box for P.

4. (T): S stands for spelling. Did you spell your words correctly? Check them. Now, check yours with mine (show the teacher's copy). Fix any words you spelled incorrectly. Put a tally mark above the words you spelled correctly. Add a mark in the box for S.

5. (T): Rewrite your sentence with all of the corrections.

6. (T): Check for CUPS again. Put another mark in the boxes.

7. (T): Let's read the sentences.

8. (S) Read the sentences for fluency and automaticity.

***Please note:** Once students understand how to use CUPS, transition to letting them check their sentence independently before showing the teacher's copy.

Weekly Red Words

Materials Needed:
screen, red crayon, red word paper

Introduce on Tuesday, and practice daily. Use the Flip Chart for steps.

New:	Review:	New Read-Only:	Review Read-Only:
who, what, where, why	the, was, is, a, and, to, for, like, of, will, want, said, you, put, see, stop, from, off, has, have, his, as, my, into, now, new, give, or, by, went, do, are, they, any, black, blue, brown, gray, green, orange, pink, purple, white, yellow, one, two, come		stop, eek, ouch, look, good, help, three, four, five, seven, eight, nine, her

Steps for Teaching a New Red Word:

1. (T) States the word. (*who*)

2. (T&S) Use tokens to determine how many sounds are in the word. (/h/ / $\overline{oo}$ /; 2)

3. (T&S) Discuss how we would expect to spell each sound as the teacher writes the grapheme(s) correctly. Identify what is unexpected or irregular about the spelling of the word. It could also be expected, but the concept hasn't been taught yet.

© IMSE 2022

4. (T&S) Discuss the etymology of the word, if appropriate (lexical words). Visit www. etymonline.com for more information on the word.

5. (T) Defines the word, and writes a sentence using the word.

6. (T) Writes the word on Red Word paper with the screen underneath, using red crayon.

7. (S) Write the word on Red Word paper with the screen underneath, using red crayon. (S) Show the word to the teacher.
(**NOTE:** The teacher should have students chunk the word if it has more than four letters.)

8. (T&S) Stand up, holding the Red Word in the nondominant hand. Armtap word while naming each letter. Then "underline" the word by sweeping left to right while stating the word, 3x. (**NOTE:** Left-handed students will place their left hand on their right wrist. They tap to their right shoulder. Underline from wrist to shoulder. Right-handed students place their right hand on their left shoulder. They tap to their left wrist. Underline shoulder to wrist.)

9. (T&S) Trace crayon bumps with the pointer finger while naming the letters, 3x.

10. (T&S) Place the screen over the paper and trace the word with the pointer finger while naming the letters, 3x.

11. (S) Turn paper over. With red crayon, write the word without the screen one time, and hold up the word for the teacher to check. (S) Write the word two more times.

12. (S) Write an original sentence in pencil and underline the Red Word with a red crayon. (**NOTE:** The sentence can also be dictated by the teacher while the student writes or dictated by the student while the teacher writes it.)

13. Repeat the steps for what (/w/ /ŭ/ /t/; 3), where (/w/ /ā/ /er/; 3), why (/w/ /ī/; 2).

Review Ideas for Red Words:

- Sculpt the word using red Play-Doh or clay. Have students spell the word as they smash each letter.
- Print flashcards from IOG, and practice reading.
- Armtap the word to review.
- Cross-clap the word to review.
- Do Spelling Aerobics.

Fluency, Vocabulary, and Comprehension

- Incorporate fluency into your literacy lessons daily/weekly (minimum 30 min/week) by using Rapid Word Charts, IMSE Decodable Readers, words and sentences, Acadience Reading K-6 or DIBELS 8th Edition, repeated reading, and other activities.
- Incorporate vocabulary into your literacy lessons daily/weekly (minimum 50 min/week) by choosing 3-5 appropriate tier two words (can pull from rich literature or decodable readers). Teach the words through explicit, direct instruction using student-friendly definitions, word webs, vocabulary charts, illustrations, and other activities.
- Incorporate oral language comprehension into your literacy lessons daily/weekly (approximately 100 min/week). Comprehension instruction should be explicit, direct

instruction that includes teacher modeling, guided practice, and independent practice. Plan ahead to build on students' background knowledge, language structures, verbal reasoning, and literacy knowledge.

Extension Activity Ideas

- Continue to add to the multi-sensory ABC book. Have students glue wheat (or another object) in the shape of the target grapheme.
- Make a paper whale. Have students glue pictures of words that begin with the /hw/ or /w/ sound on the whale.
- Have students go on a "sound hunt" around the room or outside to find objects that begin with the target sound.
- Coding activity: Have students underline and label the letters in words or syllables with a "v" for vowels and a "c" for consonants. For example, when using the word *mom*, each letter should be underlined with the labels "cvc" underneath the word. This activity will help prepare students for decoding multisyllabic words later in the sequence.
- Visit IMSE's Orton-Gillingham's Pinterest page for more ideas.

Weekly Lesson Reminders

- Any of the above extension activities
- Practice writing the target grapheme (capital and lowercase) using a screen, green crayon, and house paper.
- Practice writing the target grapheme using another medium (sand, paint, shaving cream, pudding, iPad app, etc.).
- Practice writing the target grapheme using age-appropriate paper and pencil.
- Daily practice with writing the weekly Red Word(s)
- Kilpatrick's "One-Minute Activities" for daily phonological awareness practice
- Zgonc's phonological awareness activities
- Listen to rich literature to work on oral language comprehension.
- Target grapheme practice sheets from IMSE's practice books and handwriting books
- Practice test on Thursday and test on Friday

© IMSE 2022

Review for Concepts m-wh

After teaching the first 32 concepts, the following words and sentences may be utilized for review. Teachers can dictate a different list (A, B, C, or D) and three sentences each day of the review. Teachers can spend up to a week on review *if needed*. If a review is not needed, this page can be skipped or partially utilized. Students can use IMSE workbooks or age-appropriate paper for recording their answers.

List A	List B	List C	List D
1. when	1. moth	1. Josh	1. Seth
2. mash	2. chum	2. whiz	2. this
3. thud	3. cash	3. chug	3. shag
4. chip	4. them	4. thus	4. path
5. that	5. whop	5. math	5. chop
6. shop	6. chin	6. she	6. shut
7. bath	7. dish	7. with	7. them
8. wish	8. them	8. chap	8. fish
9. chat	9. rash	9. than	9. Chad
10. this	10. Beth	10. mesh	10. whim

Sentences:

1. Beth and Seth are thin.
2. Jim will chop the hot log.
3. Is the cash in the shop?
4. When did Ben put the hog in the sun?
5. Is that them on the ship?
6. Sal hit his shin on the log.
7. Did Pam cash this?
8. Did the ax hit the box with a thud?
9. Tim and Chad had a chip.
10. The rash on his leg is red.
11. Did the chap chop the log?
12. When will the pet cat get fed?

Notes:

_____

_____

_____

_____

_____

_____

_____

_____

_____

_____

_____

_____

_____

_____

_____

_____

_____

_____

_____

_____

_____

_____

_____

Appendix

Page Intentionally Blank

Table of Contents
Appendix

THREE-PART DRILL

1. VISUAL

(T) Display cards one at a time in random order.

(S) Say sound(s) - if letter(s) represents more than one sound (or unit of sounds), **(S)** state first sound (or unit of sounds) learned, then next sound (or unit of sounds). (Can also name letter[s] and sound[s].)

2. AUDITORY

(T) Use phoneme/grapheme chart to dictate known sounds in random order. (Eyes on me. Spell /b/. Repeat.)
Remind students if there is more than one way to spell a sound.
(You know two ways to spell this. Spell /k/.)

(S) Repeat (/b/).

(S) Using sand tray or other medium, **(S)** write the letter(s) while naming it and underlining L to R saying the sound(s). (Ex. /b/ b says /b/.)

3. BLENDING

(T) Separate cards into three piles: C/V/C.

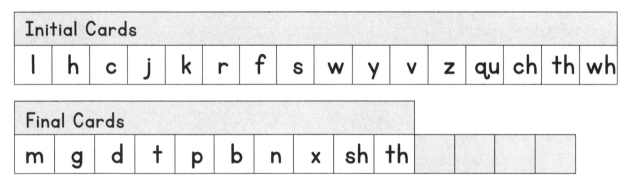

| Initial Cards | | | | | | | | | | | | | | | |
| l | h | c | j | k | r | f | s | w | y | v | z | qu | ch | th | wh |

| Final Cards | | | | | | | | | | | | | |
| m | g | d | t | p | b | n | x | sh | th | | | | |

*Never use Magic E or hard and soft c & g cards on the blending board.

(S) Say sound for each letter and blend into syllable. Give thumbs up for real words. If the syllable is not a word, students can think of a multisyllabic word that has that syllable.
Ex: fam is a syllable for family.

VOWEL INTENSIVE

V The sound is ...	VC The syllable is ...	CVC The syllable is ...
a	ag, ap, ab	lat, cad, zan
e	et, en, ep	zeg, ren, med
i	ig, ib, im	lin, hib, fid
o	ob, ot, oz	rom, hob, cog
u	un, ug, ub	sup, pum, dut

(S) Place vowel sticks or tents in ABC order – use only those vowels previously taught.

(T) State vowel sound. (Eyes on me. The sound is /a/. Repeat.)

(S) Repeat vowel sound while doing the visual cue.

(S) Hold up appropriate vowel, naming the vowel and saying its sound.

(T) Progress into VC syllables and then into CVC syllables. (Eyes on me.
The syllable is /ag/. Repeat.)

(S) Continue to listen for the correct vowel sound, naming the vowel and its sound.

**The chart represents some examples. (T) can create additional VC and CVC syllables.

/ă/: Place hand under the chin and drop your jaw.

/ĕ/: Pull corners of the mouth back with thumb and pointer finger.

/ĭ/: Scrunch nose and point to it.

/ŏ/: Circle your mouth with your finger.

/ŭ/: Push in on stomach.

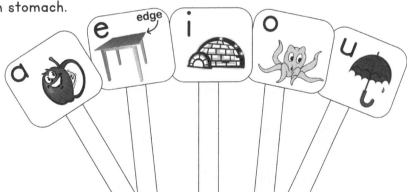

I. Review Using Three-Part Drill and Vowel Intensive (AFTER m-a-l-o HAVE BEEN TAUGHT)

II. TEACHING A NEW CONCEPT (m-wh)
A. MULTI-SENSORY EXPERIENCE
1. **(T)** Read **alliteration** sentences.
   (S) Identify target sound.
2. **(T)** Show new **card** and inform **(S)** of letter name(s) and sound(s).
   (S) Repeat (ex: "m says /m/") using a mirror to see and feel position of lips, teeth, and tongue. Discuss whether sound is voiced or unvoiced.
   (T) Show **position** of letter in the alphabet. Discuss whether the letter is a consonant or vowel.
3. **(T)** Show **object** (ex: marshmallow) to be used in an activity.
4. **(S)** **Brainstorm** words beginning with the letter and sound.
   (T) Write the brainstorm words on chart paper.
      *For short vowels, have students brainstorm word families or rhyming words containing the vowel sound.
5. **(T)** Teach **letter formation** - Use large house paper with directional arrows and starting points.
      *Use screen and green crayon.
      *You may progress to small house paper.
      *Teach capitals with lowercase if capitals are not yet learned.
6. **(T)** **Dictate** target sound(s).
   (S) **Practice** all known spellings in sand (or other medium) 3 times.
7. **(T)** **Read** book - ex: *Mixed Me* by Taye Diggs - Have **(S)** listen for words containing the new sound. Work on oral language comprehension skills.
8. **(S)** **Read** IMSE decodable reader.
9. **(T&S)** **Mark** Phoneme/Grapheme chart and **place** card in review deck.

Extension Activities
1. Drawing
2. Collage
3. Alphabet Book
4. Multi-Sensory Activities
5. Supplemental workbook pages

B. APPLICATION OF NEW CONCEPT
One-Syllable Word Dictation
1. **(T)** State word: ex: "mom."
   (T) Use word in a sentence.
   (T) State word while pounding (ex: "mom"), model fingertapping (if appropriate), then pound word.
2. **(S)** State word while pounding (ex: "mom").
   (S) Fingertap word with off hand (/m/ /o/ /m/) and pound word.
   (S) Write word on appropriate paper.
3. **(S)** Check word and rewrite.
4. **(S)** Read all words to practice fluency.

Sentence Dictation: (Can also have **(S)** create their own sentences.)
1. **(T)** State the sentence: ex: "The lid is hot."
2. **(T)** Pound syllables in the sentence with off hand.
3. **(T&S)** Pound syllables in the sentence.
4. **(S)** Pound syllables without help from Teacher.
5. **(T)** Model pointing to word lines while saying sentence.
6. **(S)** Point to word lines while saying sentence. Write sentence, fingertap words (if necessary), check using **CUPS**. Rewrite sentence.
7. **(S)** Read all sentences to practice fluency.

TEACHING LETTER FORMATION
Steps for Letter Formation with House Paper

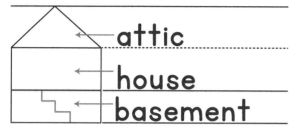

attic
house
basement

Write lowercase letters inside the house.

Write larger capital letters outside of the house.

Place screen under paper.

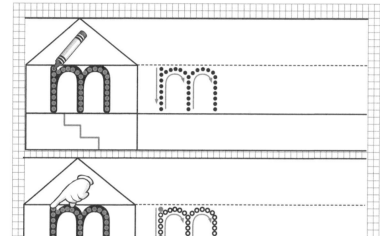

← Step 1:
(T) models "how to" with solid; (T&S) trace solid with crayon and screen 3x to create bumps-verbalizing while tracing (m says /m/).

← Step 2:
(T&S) trace crayon bumps 3x with finger-verbalizing while tracing (m says /m/).

← Step 3:
(S) trace dotted letter with crayon 1x.

← Step 4:
(S) create letter 1x independently.

Step 5: (not shown)
(S) move to smaller house, trace solid with screen and green crayon, and continue creating letter. (S) circle best example.

DECODABLE READER

MONDAY

1. (S) Highlight or underline words with the new concept in green. Read those words.
2. (S) Highlight or underline Red Words in red. Read those words.
3. If time allows, (S) start reading the decodable reader.

TUESDAY - THURSDAY

(S) Read the decodable reader.

NOTE: If a student makes an error on a phonetic word, have the student look at the letters, sound out the word, and read the word. If the student can't read the word or if the word is a Red Word, the teacher will state the word. Then the student should reread the sentence with automaticity.

FRIDAY

(S) Read a clean copy without pictures.

NOTES

- Comprehension questions are included with each decodable reader and can be incorporated throughout the week.
- A writing prompt is included with each decodable reader. The writing prompt can be incorporated at any time during the week.
- Decodable readers provide critical opportunities for students to apply the phonics skills that have been taught. They also help increase students' reading fluency. Decodable readers should be utilized *every week*.

I. **Review With Three-Part Drill Before Teaching New Concept**

II. **TEACHING A NEW CONCEPT (ADVANCED)**

   A. **MULTI-SENSORY EXPERIENCE**

   1. **(T)** Show new **card(s)**, inform **(S)** of letter name(s) and sound(s). Discuss spelling rule when applicable.
      (S) Repeat (ex: "ck says /k/").

   2. **(T)** Show **object** (ex: backpack, clock) to be used later in follow-up activities.

   3. **(S)** **Brainstorm** words when appropriate to establish spelling rules.
      (T) Write brainstorm words on chart paper.
         *Students can brainstorm word families or rhyming words, sort words, etc.

   4. **(S)** **Handwriting practice**, if needed.

   5. **(T)** **Dictate** sound(s).
      (S) **Practice** all known spellings in sand or on paper. (ex: "We know three ways to spell this. Spell /k/.")

   6. **(T)** **Connect** concept with literature. Work on oral language comprehension skills.

   7. **(S)** **Read** IMSE decodable reader.

   8. **(T&S)** **Mark** Phoneme/Grapheme chart and **place** card(s) in review deck.

   B. **APPLICATION OF NEW CONCEPT**

   One-Syllable Word Dictation

   1. **(T)** State word: ex: "mom."
      (T) Use word in a sentence.
      (T) State word while pounding (ex: "mom"), model fingertapping (if appropriate), then pound word.

   2. **(S)** State word while pounding (ex: "mom").
      (S) Fingertap word with off hand (/m/ /o/ /m/) and pound word.
      (S) Write word on appropriate paper.

   3. **(S)** Check word and rewrite.

   4. **(S)** Read all words to practice fluency.

   Multisyllabic Word Dictation

   1. **(T)** State word: "sunset."
      (T) Use word in a sentence.
      (T) Repeat word while pounding each syllable: "sun," "set."

   2. **(S)** State while pounding each syllable.

   3. **(T&S)** Pound first syllable: "sun." Fingertap, pound, and write first syllable.

   4. **(T&S)** Pound second syllable: "set." Fingertap, pound, and write second syllable.

   5. **(S)** Check word and rewrite.

   6. **(S)** Read all words to practice fluency.

   Sentence Dictation (Can also have **(S)** create their own sentences.)

   1. **(T)** State the sentence: ex: "The lid is hot."

   2. **(T)** Pound syllables in the sentence with off hand.

   3. **(T&S)** Pound syllables in the sentence.

   4. **(S)** Pound syllables without help from Teacher.

   5. **(T)** Model pointing to word lines while saying sentence.

   6. **(S)** Point to word lines while saying sentence. Write sentence, fingertap words (if necessary), check using **CUPS**. Rewrite sentence.

   7. **(S)** Read all sentences to practice fluency.

LEARNING A RED WORD

1. **(T)** State the word.
2. **(T&S)** Use tokens to determine how many sounds are in the word.
3. **(T&S)** Discuss how we would expect to spell each sound as the teacher writes the grapheme(s) correctly. Identify what is unexpected or irregular about the spelling of the word.
4. **(T&S)** Discuss the etymology of the word, if appropriate (lexical words).
5. **(T)** Define the word, and write a sentence using the word.
6. **(T)** Write word on Red Word paper with screen underneath, using red crayon.
7. **(S)** Write word on Red Word paper with screen underneath, using red crayon.
   (S) Show word to teacher.

> **For longer words, chunk groups of letters to facilitate memory.**
> **(T)** Scoop parts of word with red crayon.
> **(S)** Copy scooped word parts on their paper.

8. **(T&S)** Stand up, holding Red Word in nondominant hand. Armtap word while naming each letter. Then "underline" word by sweeping left to right while stating the word, 3 times.
   Left-Handed: Place left hand on right wrist, tap to right shoulder, underline from wrist to shoulder.
   Right-Handed: Place right hand on left shoulder, tap to left wrist, underline shoulder to wrist.
9. **(T&S)** Trace crayon bumps with finger while naming the letters, three times.
10. **(T&S)** Place screen over paper and trace word with the pointer finger while naming the letters, three times.
11. **(S)** Turn paper over. With red crayon, write word without screen one time, and hold up word for teacher to check.
    (S) Write word two more times.
12. **(S)** Write an original sentence in pencil and underline Red Word with red crayon.
    Once comfortable with the standard process, creative adaptations are encouraged.

> **Reviewing Red Words**
> Throughout the week, review Red Words by armtapping each Red Word once. Students may look at words while reviewing but should progress to spelling from memory. Red Word Activity Centers or extensions should be incorporated regularly for review.

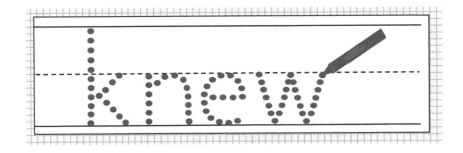

SYLLABICATION GUIDE

1. Use *The Syllable Division Word Book* to choose appropriate words.
2. Inform **(S)** that this is a strategy that will help them with vocabulary and word attack skills when they encounter an unfamiliar word.

How to Divide Two-Syllable Words:

1. Find the first two vowels (vowel sounds), underline them and label each with a V.
2. Draw a line (bridge) connecting the bottom of the two Vs, ex.: V__V.
3. Underline and label the letter(s) above the bridge with a C, ex.: <u>VCCV</u>.
4. Have **(S)** find pattern and divide word into syllables.
5. Have **(S)** label each syllable type (Cl, O, ME, VT, BR, C-le).
6. Have **(S)** read each syllable, then blend together into a word.
7. Check for comprehension or refer to dictionary for meaning.

How to Divide Words with Three or More Syllables:

1. Find the first two vowels (vowel sounds), underline them, and label with a V.
2. Draw a line (bridge) connecting the bottom of the two Vs, ex. V__V.
3. Underline and label each consonant with a C above the bridge. If there are three or more consonants, some consonants go together as one consonant unit (digraphs or blends).
   Example: b <u>a</u> <u>th</u> <u>t</u> <u>u</u> b
          <u>V C C V</u>
4. Have **(S)** find pattern and divide word into syllables.
5. Check to see if there is another vowel that is not an *e* at the end of the word.
6. If so, cover up the letters before the second labeled vowel, find the next vowel, and label with a V.
7. With off hand still covering up to the second labeled vowel, draw a bridge connecting the bottom of the vowels.
8. Label the consonant(s) above the bridge with a C, ex. <u>VCCV</u>.
9. Have **(S)** find pattern and divide word into syllables. If there is an additional vowel that is not an *e* at the end of the word, then go back to steps 6-8. If there are no additional vowels, then continue to steps 10-12.
10. Have **(S)** label each syllable type (Cl, O, ME, VT, BR, C-le).
11. Have **(S)** read each syllable, then blend together into a word.
12. Check for comprehension or refer to dictionary for meaning. Be sure **(S)** can write or say a sentence using the new word.

Remember

If two consonants are in the middle of a word, split the word between the two consonants. (Exception: If the two consonants are a digraph [sh, ch, th], they cannot be split.) If there are three or more consonants, some letters go together as one consonant unit (look for known digraphs or blends).

VISUAL CUES FOR WORDS AND SENTENCES

Words

——————	grapheme(s) line
qu	qu
sh	digraphs (sh, th)
b r	initial and final 2-letter blends
n ch	final digraph blends (-nch)
s t r	3-letter blends
sh r	initial digraph blends (shr-, thr-)
s qu	squ-
smile ★★★	Magic E
+ed	suffix

Sentences*

——————	word line
══════	Red Word line
⛰	capital
☐	punctuation

*Remember not to use word visual cues for sentences.

Students should utilize CUPS to self-edit sentences.

Capitalization
Understanding
Punctuation
Spelling

Weekly Lesson Reminders (Comprehensive OG Plus)

Day	Components
Monday	☐ Phonological Awareness ☐ Three-Part Drill ☐ Teaching a New Concept: Multi-Sensory Experience ☐ Decodable Reader ☐ Language Comprehension with Rich Literature ☐ Teaching a New Concept: Application/Dictation of Words and Sentences
Tuesday	☐ PA Warm-Up or Activity ☐ Review Red Word(s) ☐ Introduce Weekly Red Word(s) ☐ Application/Dictation of Words and Sentences ☐ Decodable Reader ☐ Language Comprehension and Vocabulary ☐ Fluency (e.g., Rapid Word Chart) ☐ Written Expression
Wednesday	☐ PA Warm-Up or Activity ☐ Three-Part Drill (Include Monday's New Concept) ☐ Review Red Words ☐ Application/Dictation of Words and Sentences ☐ Decodable Readers ☐ Language Comprehension and Vocabulary ☐ Syllabication (after Concept 35)
Thursday	☐ PA Warm-Up or Activity ☐ Review Red Words ☐ Decodable Readers ☐ Syllabication (after Concept 35) ☐ Fluency (e.g., Rapid Word Chart) ☐ Language Comprehension and Vocabulary ☐ Written Expression ☐ Pretest or Additional Application/Dictation of Words and Sentences
Friday	☐ PA Warm-Up or Activity ☐ Three-Part Drill ☐ Review Red Words ☐ Decodable Readers (Clean One-Pager) ☐ Fluency Activity or Progress Monitoring ☐ Language Comprehension and Vocabulary ☐ Test with Green and Red Words

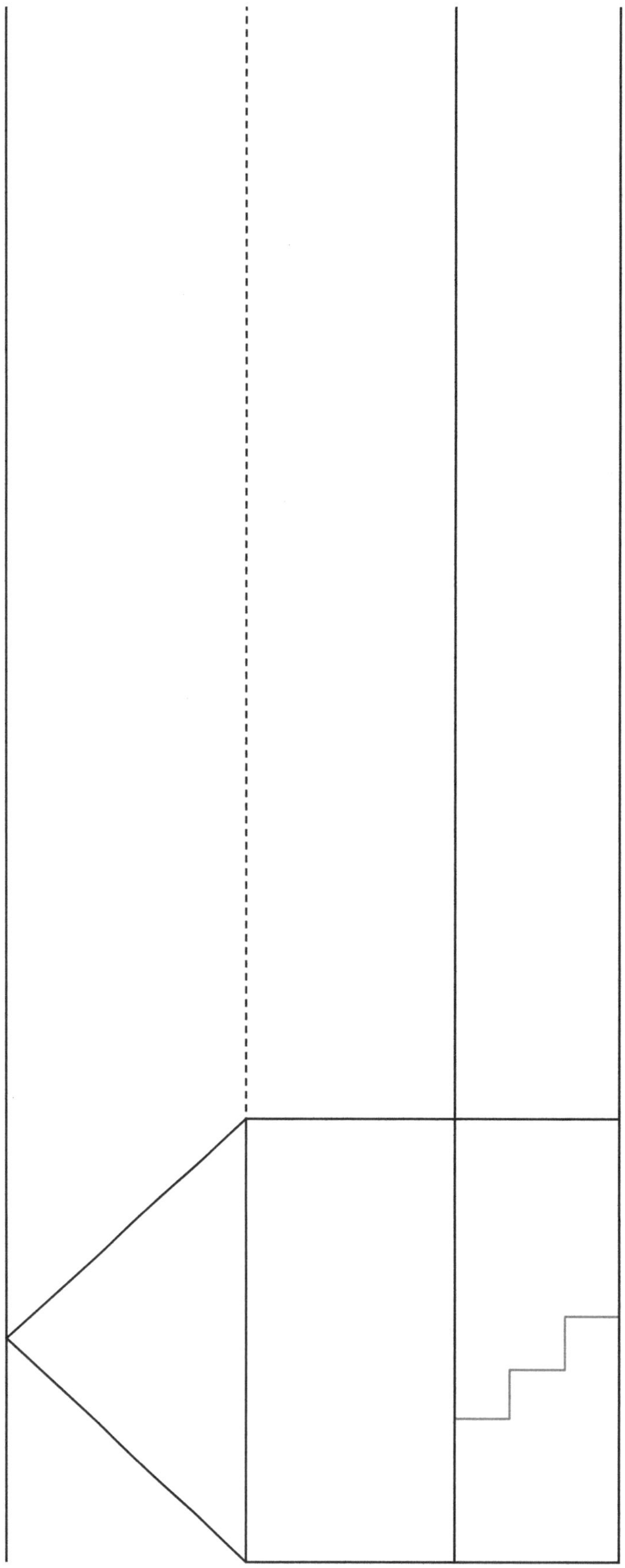

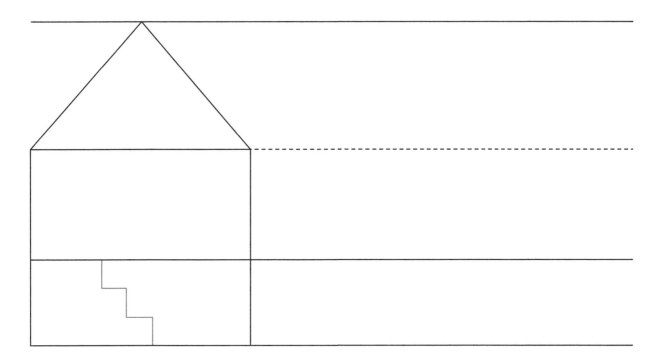

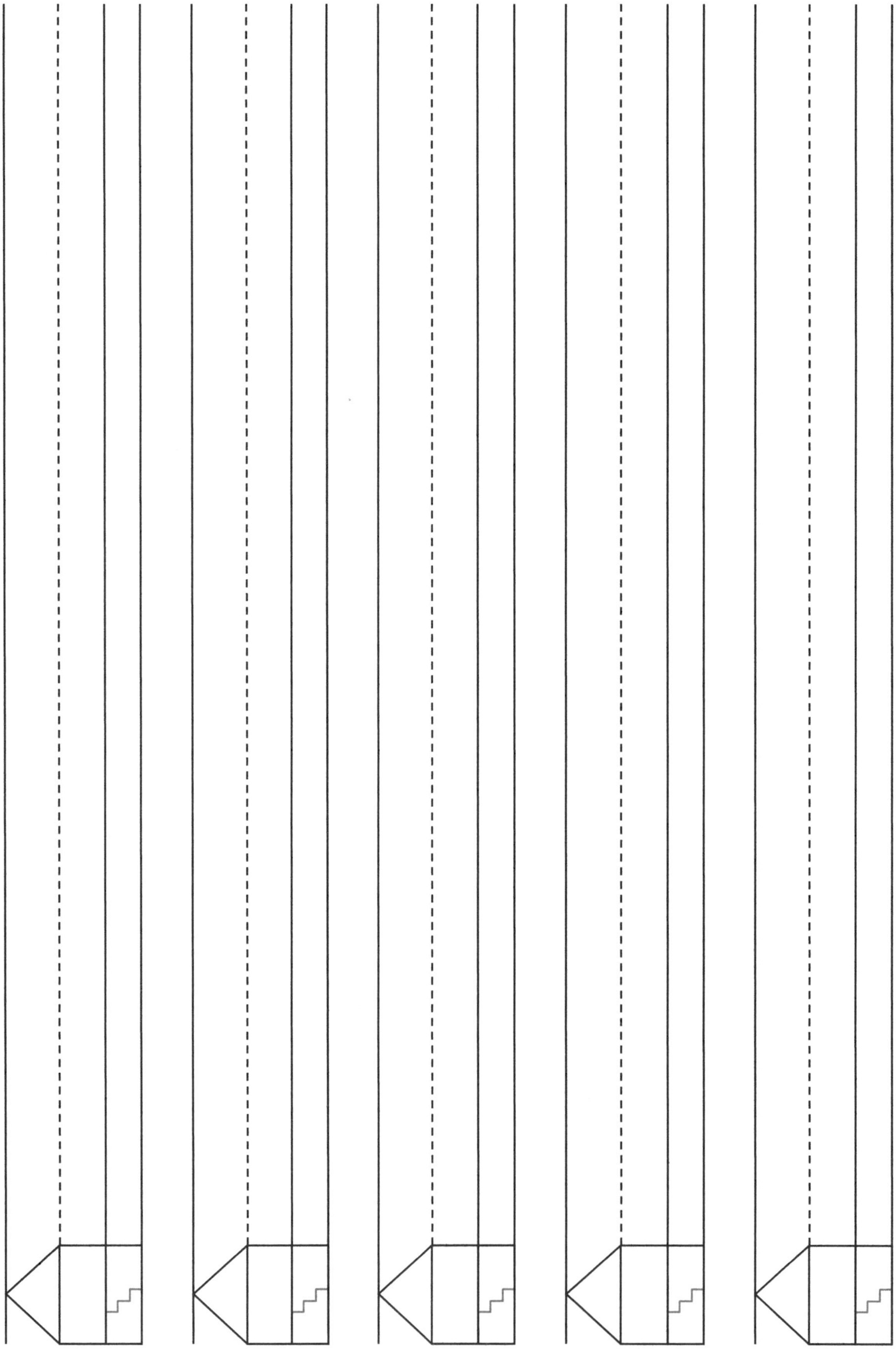

© IMSE 2022

PHONEME/GRAPHEME CHART

Usage:
- Progress Reports
- Auditory/Kinesthetic Component of Drill

Consonants

#	Phoneme	Graphemes
1.	/b/	b
2.	/k/	c, k, -ck, -que, ch
3.	/d/	d, -ed
4.	/f/	f, -ff, -gh, ph, gh
5.	/g/	g, gh
6.	/h/	h
7.	/j/	j, -dge
8.	/l/	l, -ll
9.	/m/	m, -mb, -mn
10.	/n/	n, kn, gn, mn
11.	/p/	p, pt
12.	/kw/	qu
13.	/r/	r, wr, rh
14.	/s/	s, -ss, c, -se, sc, ps
15.	/t/	t, -ed, -bt, pt
16.	/v/	v, -ve
17.	/w/	w, wh
18.	/ks/	x
19.	/y/	y
20.	/z/	z, -zz, -se, -s

Consonant Digraphs

#	Phoneme	Graphemes
1.	/ch/	ch in chop, -tch e.g., latch
2.	/sh/	sh in shop, ch in chef, s in sure
3.	/TH/	th (voiced) e.g., this
4.	/th/	th (unvoiced) e.g., thimble
5.	/hw/	wh in whisper
6.	/zh/	s in treasure or in exclusion

Short Vowels

#	Phoneme	Graphemes
1.	/ă/	a
2.	/ĕ/	e, ea
3.	/ĭ/	i, y
4.	/ŏ/	o
5.	/ŭ/	u
6.	/aw/	au, aw, e.g., August
7.	/o͞o/	oo, u, e.g., look

Velar Nasal Units

#	Phoneme	Graphemes
1.	/ŋ/	-ang, -ing, -ong, -ung, -ank, -ink, -onk, -unk

Long Vowels

#	Phoneme	Graphemes
1.	/ā/	a, a-e, ai, ay, eigh, ei
2.	/ē/	e, e-e, y, ea, ee, ie, ei, ey
3.	/ī/	i, y, i-e, y-e, igh, ie
4.	/ō/	o, o-e, oa, oe, ow
5.	/yo͞o/	u, u-e, ew, eu, ue, e.g., cute, feud
6.	/o͞o/	u, u-e, oo, ew, ou, ue, ui, e.g., scoop

Kind Old Words

#	Phoneme	Graphemes
1.	/ī/	ild, ind
	/ō/	old, olt, ost

Diphthongs

#	Phoneme	Graphemes
1.	/oi/	oi, oy, e.g., coin
2.	/ou/	ou, ow, e.g., clown

R-Controlled Bossy-R

#	Phoneme	Graphemes
1.	/ar/	ar, ear, e.g., start, heart
2.	/er/	er, ir, ur, or, ar, ear, our, e.g., her, heard, onward, worthy
3.	/or/	ore, oar, or, ar, our, e.g., torn, war, quart

Other Combinations

#	Phoneme	Graphemes
1.	/air/	are, air, ar, ear, er, e.g., stair, arrow
2.	/eer/	ere, ear, eer, e.g., hear, steer
3.	/ire/	ire, e.g., tire
4.	/ure/	ure, e.g., cure

Consonant -le

#	Grapheme
1.	-ble
2.	-cle
3.	-dle
4.	-fle
5.	-gle
6.	-kle
7.	-ple
8.	-tle
9.	-zle

Blends

Beginning
1. br, cr, dr, fr, gr, tr, pr
2. bl, cl, fl, gl, pl, sl
3. sc, sk, sm, sn, sp, st
4. dw, sw, tw
5. scr, shr, spl, squ, str, thr

Ending
1. -ct, -ft, -lt, -nt, -pt, -st, -xt
2. -ld, -lf, -lp, -lk
3. -mp, -nch, -nd, -sk, -sp

Higher Level Concepts:

Suffixes:
1. /d/: suffix -ed
2. /s/ and /z/: suffix -s
3. /ĭz/: suffix -es
4. /ĭŋ/ suffix -ing

NOTE: Do not use these for the Aud/Kin part of the Three-Part Drill:
1. Contractions: am, is, are, has, not, have, would, will
2. Schwa /ə/
3. Three Great Rules: Double, Drop, Change
4. Homophones: to, too, two, there, their, they're

Other:

PHONEME/GRAPHEME CHART

Usage:
• Kindergarten

Consonant

1. /b/: b
2. /k/: c, k
3. /d/: d
4. /f/: f
5. /g/: g
6. /h/: h
7. /j/: j
8. /l/: l
9. /m/: m
10. /n/: n
11. /p/: p
12. /kw/: qu
13. /r/: r
14. /s/: s
15. /t/: t
16. /v/: v
17. /w/: w, wh
18. /ks/: x
19. /y/: y
20. /z/: z

Consonant Digraphs

1. /ch/: ch in chop
2. /sh/: sh in shop
3. /th/: th in this (voiced)
4. /th/: th in thimble (unvoiced)
5. /hw/: wh in whisper

Vowels

Short – closed syllables

1. /ă/: a
2. /ĕ/: e
3. /ĭ/: i
4. /ŏ/: o
5. /ŭ/: u

Long – open syllables

1. /ā/: a
2. /ē/: e
3. /ī/: i
4. /ō/: o
5. /yōō/: u

© IMSE 2022

1.

2.

3.

SENTENCE:

_____

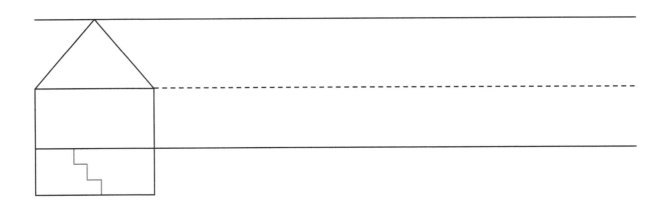

1.

2.

3.

SENTENCE:

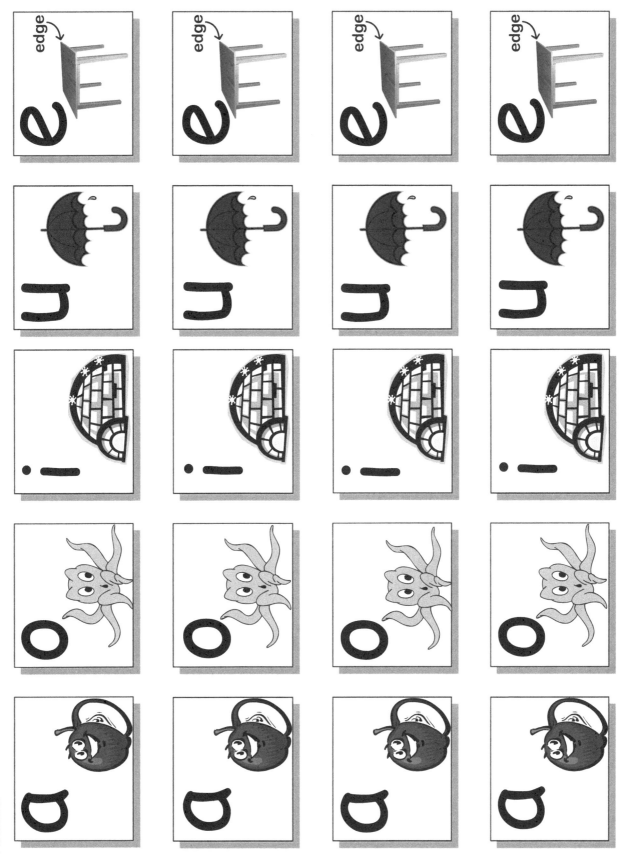

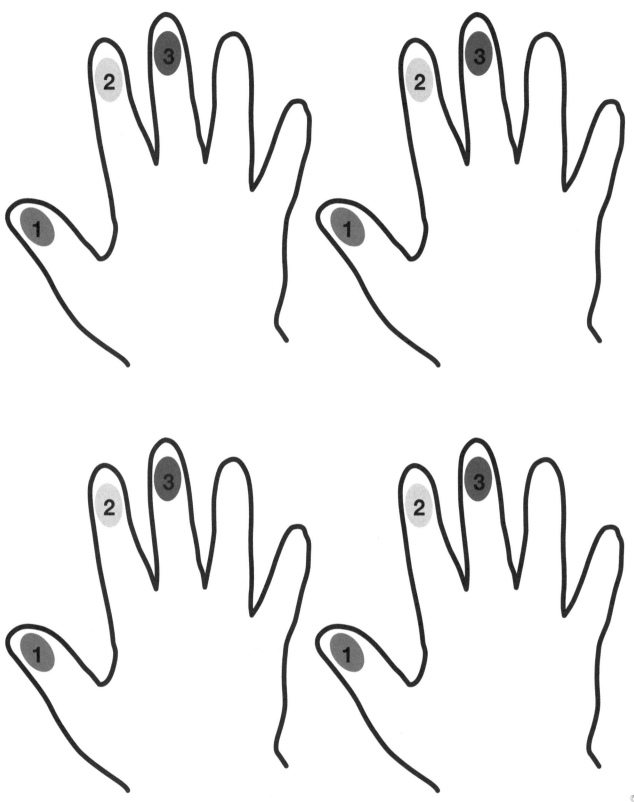

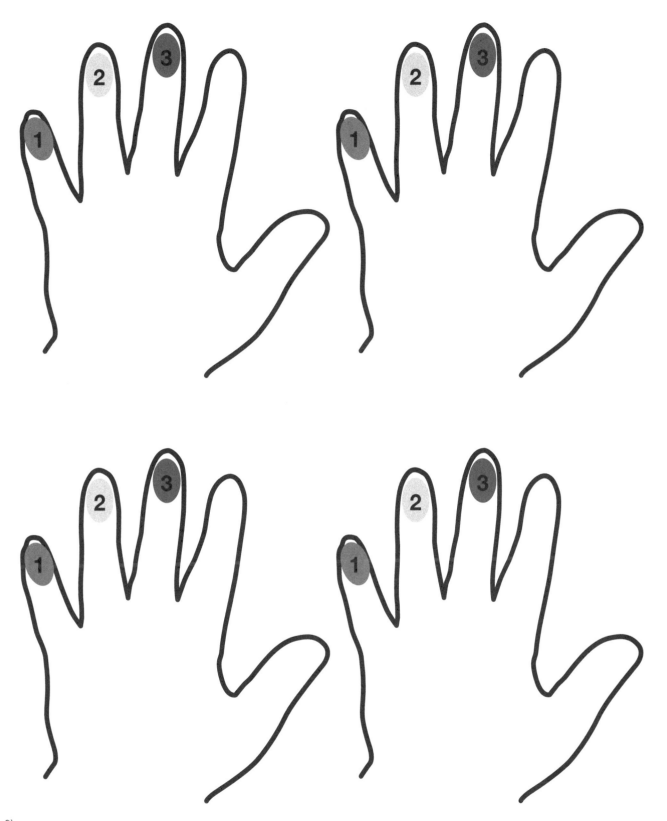

Phoneme Activities Worksheet (Blending Strip)

3

2

1

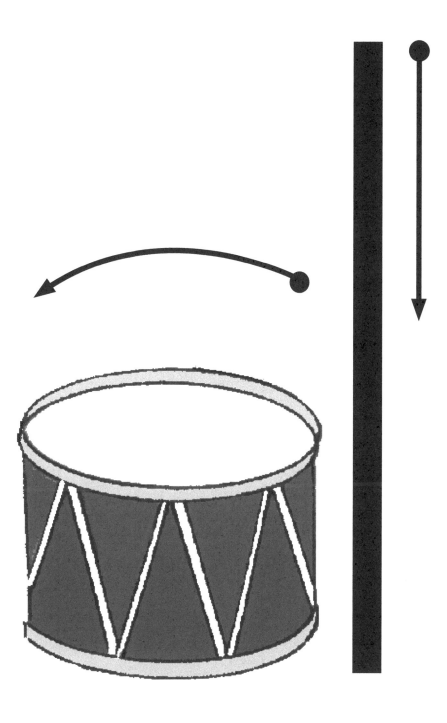

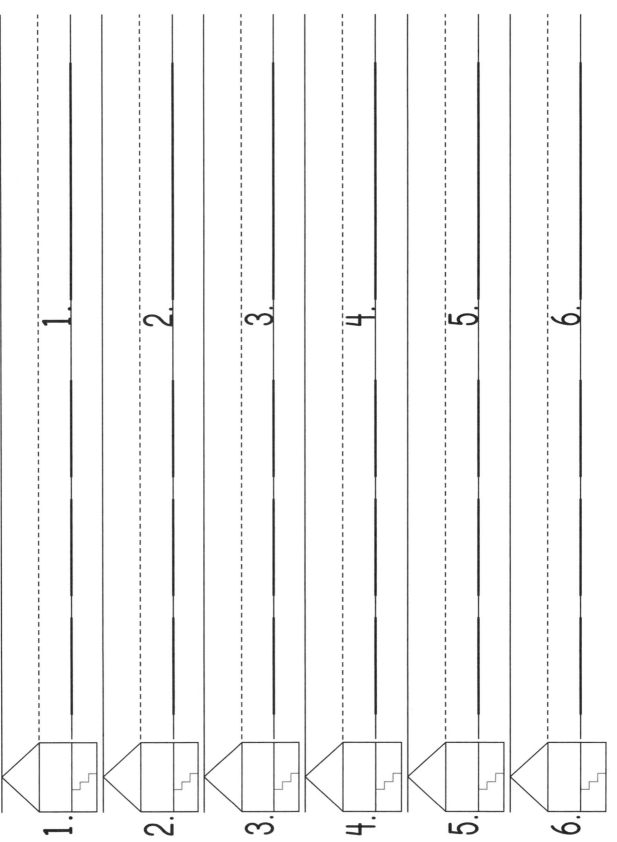

Sentence Dictation

Name: _____

Date: _____

C	☐
U	☐
P	☐
S	☐

Capitalization

Understanding

Punctuation

Spelling

k /k/

kit, kept, smoke

c /k/

a a o u

consonant

cat, cot, cut, clap

LESSON DICTATION (_____)

— WORDS —	— REWRITE —
1.	1. _____
2.	2. _____
3.	3. _____
4.	4. _____
5.	5. _____

SENTENCES

1.

1. _____

☐ C
☐ U
☐ P
☐ S

2.

2. _____

☐ C
☐ U
☐ P
☐ S

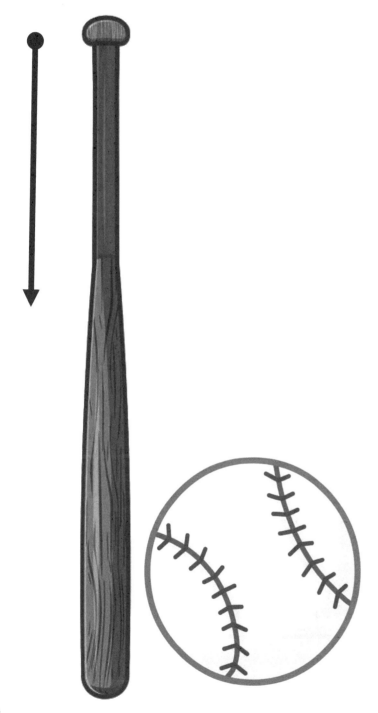

Door Examples

web, wed, bed, bet, beg, Ben, hem, hen, Meg, men, met, wet, hit, hip, hid, him, gob, got, sob, sod, nod, not

Remember, a knob goes on the door with the consonant!

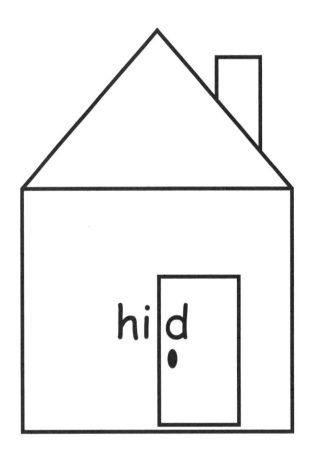

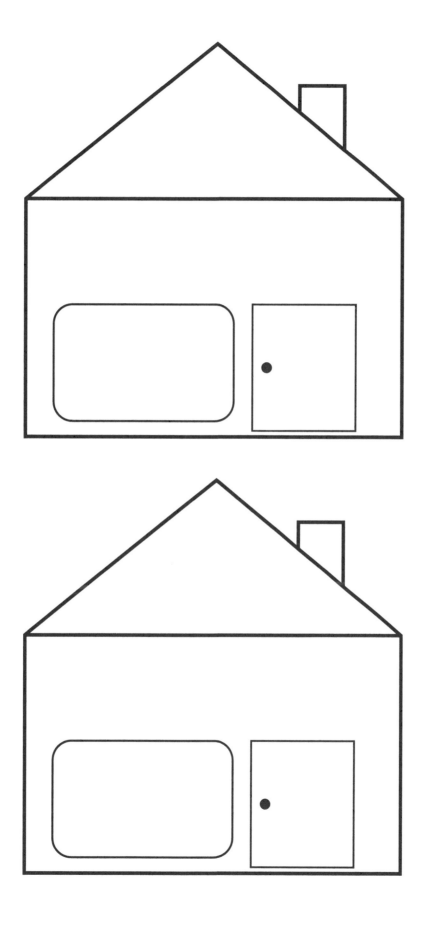

/yō̄o/ vs. /ō̄o/ spelled with the letter 'u'

When the following letter precedes the long u sound, it is pronounced:

/yō̄o/	/ō̄o/
b: bugle	d: dude
c: cute	j: juvenile
f: fume	l: luminate
g: argue	n: numeral
h: huge	r: prune
m: mule	s: sue
p: putrid	t: tube
	y: yule
	th: enthused

Note: Usually, when long u begins a syllable, it is pronounced /yō̄o/ regardless of any preceding letter. For example: unicorn, volume, value, evaluate, menu, January, monument.

When a t is next to a long u, the t makes a /ch/ or /sh/ sound as in habitual or actual. When a d is next to a long u, the d will make a /j/ sound, as in graduate.

Weekly Lesson Plan Template (Comprehensive OG Plus)

Day	Component	Checklist	Materials	Time:
Daily	**Phonological Awareness** *PA by Zgonc* p. ——————— *Equipped* by Kilpatrick Level ——————— p. ———————————	❑ Direct Teaching ❑ Training/Reinforcing	❑ Tokens ❑ Sound Boxes ❑ One-Minute Activities ❑ Zgonc PA Book Materials:	1-10 min.
Minimum M, W, F	**Three-Part Drill** Concepts: ———————	❑ Visual ❑ Auditory/Kinesthetic ❑ Blending ❑ Vowel Intensive	❑ Cards (review) ❑ P/G Chart ❑ Sand (or another medium) ❑ Blending Board ❑ Sticks or Tents	10-15 min.
Monday	**New Concept(s):** ——————————— **Multi-Sensory Experience** *Comprehensive OG Plus Teacher's Guide* p. ———————	**Multi-Sensory Experience** ❑ Alliteration (m-wh) ❑ Card ❑ Object/Picture Connection ❑ Letter Formation if Needed ❑ Practice Sound/Letter ❑ Connect with Literature ❑ Decodable Reader ❑ Mark P/G chart	❑ Screen ❑ Green Crayon ❑ Handwriting Paper ❑ Sand	20-30 min.
M-F	**New Concept(s): Application/Dictation** *Comprehensive OG Plus Teacher's Guide* p. ———————	❑ Words: Visual Cues ❑ Sentences: Visual Cues, CUPS	❑ Fingertapping Hand ❑ Dictation Paper ❑ Differentiation Needed ❑ CUPS Poster	5-15 min.
T-F	**Red Word(s)** *Comprehensive OG Plus Teacher's Guide* p. ———————	❑ Spell & Read ❑ Read Only ❑ Etymology needed	❑ Tokens ❑ Red Crayon ❑ Screen ❑ Red Word Paper ❑ Other:	10-30 min.
W-TH	**Syllabication** *Comprehensive OG Plus Teacher's Guide* p. ——————— *SDWB* p. ———————	❑ Choose 6+ Words	❑ Strips of Paper ❑ Written Words ❑ Highlighter ❑ Syllable Division Posters	10 min.

Day	Component	Checklist	Materials	Time:
Daily	**Fluency**	❏ Read Green Words ❏ Read Red Words ❏ Read Clean Copy	❏ Decodable Readers ❏ Rapid Word Chart ❏ Other:	10-20 min.
Weekly	**Vocabulary**	❏ Specific Word Instruction ❏ Word Learning Strategies ❏ Word Consciousness ❏ Tier II Words: _____ _____ _____ _____	❏ Vocabulary Maps ❏ Decodable Readers ❏ Other:	Minimum 50 min.
Weekly	**Comprehension**	❏ Comprehension Planning Checklist	❏ Decodable Reader ❏ Rich Literature ❏ Other:	Approx. 100 min.
Weekly	**Writing and Grammar**	❏ Incorporated Grammar with Writing ❏ Writing Activity	❏ Decodable Reader ❏ Journal Entry ❏ Other:	10-30 min.
TH: Pretest F: Test	**Weekly Assessment**	❏ Green Words ❏ Red Words	❏ Paper ❏ Pencil	10-20 min.

References

Archer, A. L., & Hughes, C. A. (2011). *Explicit instruction: Effective and efficient teaching.* The Guilford Press.

Chall, J. S. (1967). *Learning to read: The great debate.* McGraw-Hill.

Chall, J. S. (1996). *Stages of reading development* (2nd ed.). Cengage Learning.

Core Knowledge. (2013). *Core knowledge sequence: Content and skill guidelines for grades K-8.* Core Knowledge Foundation. https://www.coreknowledge.org/free-resource/core-knowledge-sequence/

Ehri, L. C., Cardoso-Martins, C., & Carroll, J. M. (2014). Developmental variation in reading words. In C. A. Stone, E. R. Silliman, B. J. Ehren, & G. P. Wallach (Eds.), *Handbook of language and literacy: Development and disorders* (2nd ed., pp. 285-407). Guilford Press.

Gough, P. B., & Tunmer, W. E. (1986). Decoding, reading, and reading disability. *Remedial and Special Education, 7*(1), 6-10. https://doi.org/10.1177/074193258600700104

Hirsch, E. D. (2020). *How to educate a citizen: The power of shared knowledge to unify a nation.* HarperCollins.

International Dyslexia Association. (2018, March). *Knowledge and practice standards for teachers of reading.* https://dyslexiaida.org/knowledge-and-practices/

Joshi, R. M., Dahlgren, M., & Boulware-Gooden, R. (2002). Teaching reading in an inner-city school through a multisensory teaching approach. *Annals of Dyslexia, 52*(1), 229-242. https://doi.org/10.1007/s11881-002-0014-9

Kilpatrick, D. A. (2016). *Equipped for reading success.* Casey & Kirsch Publishers.

Kohler-Curtis, J. (2022). *The IMSE Comprehensive Orton-Gillingham Plus teacher training manual.* The Institute for Multi-Sensory Education.

Moats, L. C., & Tolman, C. A. (2019). *LETRS* (3rd ed., Vol. 1). Voyager Sopris Learning.

The Reading League. (2021, Feb. 3). The Reading League Winter Symposium.

Scarborough, H. S. (2001). Connecting early language and literacy to later reading (dis)abilities: Evidence, theory, and practice. In S. Neuman & D. Dickinson (Eds.), *Handbook for research in early literacy* (Vol. 1, pp. 97-110). Guilford Press.

Seidenberg, M. S., & McClelland, J. L. (1989). A distributed, developmental model of word recognition and naming. *Psychological Review, 96*(4), 523–568. https://doi.apa.org/doiLanding?doi= 10.1037%2F0033-295X.96.4.523

Spear-Swerling, L. (2018). Structured literacy and typical literacy practices: Understanding differences to create instructional opportunities. *Teaching Exceptional Children, 51(3),* 201-211.

Zgonc, Y. (2010). *Interventions for all: Phonological awareness.* Crystal Springs Books.